Anatomy Of A Federal Drug Agent
The true story of the St. Louis 1980s
DEA Drug Task Force.

2017 Timothy C. Richards, Author.

ISBN-13: 978-1541131002

Xznark Press LLC

Anatomy of a Federal Drug Agent

The true story of the St. Louis 1980s
DEA Drug Task Force.

Published by xznark Press LLC
St. Louis, Missouri 63129
$19.95

INTRODUCTION

In 1968, the Department of Justice realized there was a chronic drug problem in the United States of America. The Bureau of Narcotics and Dangerous Drugs was established.

There were 1500 Special Agents hired for the bureau, not nearly enough to combat the drug problem. Local big-city police departments were asked to assign local cops to the federal entity to assist the federal agents in drug investigations. The hook for the local departments was asset forfeiture. The cities involved were awarded part of drug assets seized and legally forfeited.

In 1973 the Bureau of Narcotics and Dangerous Drugs was reformed and called the Drug Enforcement Administration.

The St. Louis Metropolitan Police Department is quasi-military and more than quasi-political. Who you know or are related to plays big in where the individual cop will be assigned.

The cops assigned to the DEA Task Force were paid more than average cops, they had undercover cars to drive and they got to wear soft clothing. The investigations were intense and interesting. Cops lobbied for the assignment.

The Task Force assignment is a young cops dream and in most cases cop's offspring were assigned there.

It was almost a standing joke within the police department as to how the assigned cop would fare with the assignment. The scuttlebutt was that anyone who went to DEA was never the same when they returned, if they returned.

I went at age 42. The scuttlebutt was, and is, the gospel.

I.

CATFISH AND CROCODILES

International and national fads and mores tend to hit the little big city of St. Louis, Missouri last. In the mid to late 1960s, the hippie revolution was strong on the west coast.

The California dreaming kids were wearing tie-dyed clothing, didn't shave, partook of free love and free rent, free everything. They didn't even have to get jobs.

Scores of impressionable St. Louis hippie wannabes headed for the West Coast, after all, St. Louis was, and is the gateway to the West. Only the sick, the lame and the lazy hesitated here, got stuck in the mediocrity of the region and stayed.

I mean, the system for survival was easy to read here: get a menial low-paying job, go into debt for a small house, raise your children to do the same thing, and die. Where's the adventure in that?

In that same time period of the 1960s, marijuana usage grew tremendously in the United States. Alcohol and weed were the drugs of choice for most Americans.

In the St. Louis region, weed was hard to come by: it had to be imported, but it still made its way into the region in limited quantities. Organized criminals recognized the desire for this illegal substance and began devising ways to profit in the smuggling and distribution of it.

To the masses of weed smokers, these organized criminals weren't thought of as crooks; it was deemed a cool way to get rich quick in America. Being a smuggler was respected. The rock band, The Eagles, even wrote and performed a tribute to the adventurous smugglers, "Smugglers Blues."

North St. Louis was the home of blue collar white folks back in the early 1960s. It was made up of German and Polish immigrants, factory workers, shop owners and small businesses.

The entire city was drab and dreary and old fashioned. The architecture was 1700 Russia, ugly brick buildings and homes, huge Catholic cemeteries with humongous tomb stones could and can be seen from the streets and roads of the city. Death is big business in St. Louis.

The smog in St. Louis was unbelievable. It hung over the city like a pall of death, but hardly anyone complained. The sun didn't hit the soil very often. With its archaic architecture and dingy air, St. Louis had the look of 1800s London when Jack the Ripper was getting his evens with unattractive hookers.

The parochial school kids of the north side, many of whom were super intelligent because of the tutelage bestowed upon them by priests and nuns who taught common sense, were forced to make decisions on how they were going to live their lives in St. Louis. There was wealth within their reach; west St. Louis County was where the elite lived, but to gain stature in any region takes cash flow and wealth.

If mediocrity teaches anything, it alerts the victims of this disease that who you know, and who you befriend has a bearing on the outcome of a mediocre St. Louisan's plan to gain wealth.

The demographics changed in St. Louis. Old north St. Louis went completely black. The white German and Polish Catholics fled to north St. Louis County.

The federal government had a plan to revitalize downtown St. Louis. They paid for and built the Poplar Street Bridge, connecting Missouri with Illinois via the interstate highway system.

On the eastside, gangster Frank (Buster) Wortman, who controlled the labor and trade unions, welcomed scores of hardened gangsters from Chicago to be ghost workers on the bridge, which was referred to as, The Tunnel Project, by the feds.

The ghost workers were paid enormous amounts of overtime and never once went to the work site. Chicago gangsters migrated to the west side of the Mississippi River and infiltrated our labor and trade unions.

The Gateway to the West (Arch) was built and the riverfront was modernized. Classy high rise apartment buildings with views of the Mississippi and East St. Louis were built in the downtown corridor Air pollution laws were enacted and the little big City of St. Louis looked like it might make a comeback.

One of the ghost worker gangsters was Paul Robinson, an eastside pimp and tough guy. He killed people for Buster Wortman. When Wortman died in 1968, Art Bernie, a country hick gangster, took control of the unions and rackets on the eastside. Paul Robinson killed people for Bernie, also.

If these gangsters doing work for the Outfit in Chicago wanted someone intimidated, or beaten instead of killed, Paul Robinson was their man. He was big and thick with bulging biceps. He had dark hair and eyes, and brown skin. He resembled an eastern European Gypsy, the ones who live in caravans and pimp and steal from city to city.

There were five Robinson brothers: Rich (who is a federal fugitive at this writing) Ervin, Dan, and Paul. The fifth brother isn't a criminal. They all looked alike.

They grew up in the projects in East St. Louis, Illinois. The working class people on the eastside hear the stories of the gangsters and they don't forget them. It's a part of life over there. It is survival of the fittest and smartest in the jungle of the eastside.

I'm an eastside guy. I had heard of Paul Robinson but had never seen him.

Paul's bad ass reputation flourished in the eastside communities. A marijuana smuggler in St. Clair County, Illinois, Cadillac Bill, originally from East St. Louis, was smuggling large quantities of weed from Jamaica. He was in a partnership with other eastside smugglers: Robert Romeo, Eddie Vaughn, and Dirk Stokes. They were stealing from Cadillac Bill.

Cadillac asked Rich and Paul Robinson to provide protection for him and to monitor his smuggling operation. Paul and Rich headed for Miami and eventually took over the enterprise.

Paul advised Cadillac that the operation was now his. Cadillac got nothing for his toil. Cadillac was himself a tough guy, but he wouldn't go against Paul Robinson. Paul and Rich made huge amounts of money. Rich Robinson left the partnership with Paul and struck out on his own.

Rich married a beautiful blonde Miami girl, started a coin laundry business, bought a big house and lived the Florida lifestyle. His avocation was setting up prospective smugglers with Colombian weed growers. This worked well for him for decades until the IRS started investigating him.

He fled the country and is possibly hiding in Central America. He left his wife, his business and his life in Miami. IRS investigators watch his wife constantly. Every birthday, every holiday, every special occasion, the IRS has Rich Robinson's wife, house and family under surveillance.

Paul Robinson rented a huge house in Hollywood, Florida. He rented houses for an ex-wife and three of his current girlfriends, and bought each of them a new car. He spent $20,000 a month to keep these four women.

Rich Latchkey, a north side parochial school graduate, was hooked on marijuana. He loved weed more than almost anything, except money.

Rich asked one of his parochial school buddies, Terril Huelsman, who had been supplying Rich with weed for several years, if there was a way he could start smuggling weed into the St. Louis area.

The house in Hollywood, Florida that Paul Robinson had rented and lived in was St. Louis dope smoker folklore in sleepy old St. Louis. From a Missouri perspective, it was almost paradise. It was huge, had a pool, all the dope you wished to smoke, snort, or inject for nothing and the dreamer had the protection of super pimp, Paul Robinson.

All walks of life from St. Louis flocked there. There were West St. Louis County girls, street girls, bad-ass union organizers, entrepreneurs wanting to get rich quick in the drug trade and the north side doper with a future, Rich Latchkey.

Paul welcomed them all in to his domicile, but not without a price. The beautiful young girls were required to service him in any way he imagined and some of them were forced into prostitution. Everyone there was a servant to Paul Robinson.

Rich Latchkey wanted to be a guest in the house in paradise, and he yearned to be a part of the get rich quick gamble of the dope game.

Rich Latchkey, through his friend Terril Huelsman, got a job driving loads of marijuana from the Miami area to St. Louis. He was introduced to Paul Robinson and he met the rest of the organization: Rich DeClue, Larry Miton, Allen Rogers, Bob Young, William Henderson, Ted Kotoff, Don Grosse, Bob Carswell, Ivan Lafaurie, Michael Horton, and

Dirk Stokes.

Most of the members of the organization were St. Louis residents staying in South Florida and getting rich from smuggling weed. Their connections were here in St. Louis, as well as south Florida and they seldom ventured into their home state. They left that task to couriers, like Rich Latchkey.

Rich Latchkey was schooled by Paul Robinson in the survival tactics of the smugglers game. "If you get arrested, don't make a statement," Paul began. "We have the best criminal attorney money can buy, Norm London. We will bail you out and pay for Norm London. Just sit in jail and relax until we come for you. Understand?"

"Yes sir," Rich replied.

1970 rolled around quickly. After my Marine Corps duty, I joined the St. Louis Metropolitan Police Department. My most vivid memory of St. Louis cops was that they were all broke.

Having spent more than four years on active military duty, I was eligible for veteran benefits. One of those benefits was On the Job Training, if I attended college. The Veterans Administration paid me $300.00 a month to take classes at the University of Missouri, St. Louis, so I did.

I had money, a new car and my wife and I took big vacations while the other mediocre cops pinched pennies. By 1975 I had a bachelor's degree and was settled in as a St. Louis cop.

1978 came even quicker: Some police administrator saw promise in me and I was asked where I wanted to go within the police department. I responded, "Intelligence Unit", and was almost instantaneously transformed into a detective in the prestigious Intelligence Unit of the police department. We spied on the Mafia and other organized criminal groups.

It was a dream job.

Our investigative unit knew about Paul Robinson's house in Florida. We were in touch weekly with a detective in Hollywood, Florida who kept us abreast of the comings and goings there.

But we were a snooty bunch of guys and gals. We didn't care about drugs. Drug investigations were for the losers of law enforcement we surmised.

We didn't trust drug cops. We felt, as a group, that they were thieves and ne'er-do-wells taking advantage of the system and reaping the benefits of loose cash.

So most of the cops in the Intelligence Unit turned a blind eye to the tons of weed that were coming into the city.

In our brainwashed minds, we were the elite of the cops and crooks game and our job was not really a job, it was an art form.

We did have an interest in Paul Robinson's younger brother, Dan Robinson, though. He was married to a beautiful Italian gal who had an uncle who was a "made" guy in the Mafia. We had Dan under surveillance often.

Dan Robinson's surveillance led to Rich Latchkey, George Fletcher, Lenny Miton and Terril Huelsman. The snobby Mafia investigators were now working drugs in old St. Louis and not liking it.

Cops easily fall into a comfort zone. They know where to score a free meal, a free six-pack, a place to get their personal car worked on, and they never pass up an opportunity to leave work a little early. There is nothing more unassuming and bungling than a big-city cop out of his element.

Our groovy, elite, spy unit was a shambles. There was little direction from the cop supervisors. Each team of detectives, consisting of two men, and Detective Patty Rice, an expert on downtown organized criminals, the only female assigned with us, was basically on its own in any investigation.

The unit bosses, assigned to Intelligence for years, baited us with talk of the "old days" of illegal wire taps. They were trying to motivate us to scare up cases for the unit to investigate.

More cases of organized crooks meant more loose cash floating across the supervisor's desks. In the 1950s and 60s the budget for the Intelligence Unit was large. It was, and is the chief's personal investigative group of guys and gals.

The budget was abused by the chiefs and the commanders. They were using the allotted money for their own personal ventures.

I knew there was a problem in the unit when a unit cop recovered a large number of 35 mm cameras from a stolen shipment. The chief of police high tailed it down to the unit office asking for his camera. He was given one.

One of the guys in the unit (lead dog) had executed a search warrant and confiscated items that had been shop lifted from exclusive shops in west St. Louis County.

The items were on display in a large locked room, and there were hundreds of them. I came into the office on a Saturday to retrieve a tape recorder from my desk and bumped into the commander, the deputy commander, and several of the higher ranking cops in the ivory tower. Our commander was allowing the cop royalty to shop, gratis, in the locked room where the lead dog's prized seizure was stored.

We as a unit no longer had the cash to rent apartments or hotel rooms and to set up elaborate surveillance on the Ku Klux Klan and small time organized crime groups. It's what intelligence meant back then.

But even in the 50s and 60s the unit bosses didn't wiretap

the St. Louis Mafia; that would have been too dangerous.
The Mafia was closely aligned with the St. Louis political
scene as organized criminals were an accepted segment of
St. Louis culture.

Local organized crooks were related to the mayor, the
board of alderman and high ranking city employees. St.
Louis was a "safe city" for them.

An illegal wire-tap on local crooks would have led to jail
time for the commander of the unit involved. Without
electronic surveillance we were "intelligence" in title only.

The powers that be in the region were actively searching
for that right person to lead the Intelligence Unit back to the
"good old days" of electronic surveillance even though such
spying was a violation of federal law. The feds are the only
ones who can wire-tap, legally.

My partner, Detective Tom Rangel, and I were always
scrambling for something to do. The chore of starting an
investigation on someone, whom scores of other agencies
and cops had already targeted, was almost a joke to us.

At this stage of our not so illustrious careers, which
consisted of misguided surveillance of organized crooks, car
stops of black drug dealers, and dignitary protection details,
we were now lost and roaming around a camp ground in
Lincoln County, approximately fifty miles west of the fine
City of St. Louis. Just up the road on highway seventy nine
(aka Little Dixie Highway) was the little berg of Old
Monroe, Missouri.

The Mississippi River and a tributary, the Cuivre River,
were to the north of the road. To the south the terrain shot
straight up under dense forest. Farm land was minimal, and
while Tom and I roamed the countryside, I tried to figure
out why anyone would want to live here. There was little or
nothing in good old Lincoln County, except maybe

seclusion.

The name of the camp ground was Cherokee Lakes and there were some small fishing lakes scattered around the grounds near the Cuivre.

We had been detached (unofficially) to the Drug Enforcement Administration to surveil the owner of a frozen onion ring company. His legitimate business was just down the road from the camp ground. He was allegedly taking delivery of huge amounts of marijuana via onion trucks coming from the south.

Tom and I were given an old motor home to snooze in and a lunch-box style military radio (this was before cell phones) to stay in contact with another surveillance motor home perched on a hilltop above the onion ring factory. A police explorer scout could have spotted the surveillance motor home perched high above the factory. I was embarrassed by its unprofessional placement.

Dope dealers are like migrating wildebeest running wildly through the African Plain. Crocodiles (DEA agents) lay in wait for the crazed animals to run through their streams. Hundreds of thousands of these migrating animals plunge into the crock-infested waters. Only a few get killed and eaten.

The lucky survivors are the ones who step over the crocks, or jump on their comrades backs as they go down to a terrible death. The smart wildebeest watch for the crocks and wildly jump over them and land in the middle of the stream. The migration continues and the animals never look back. They survive until their luck runs out. Smart wildebeest and smart dope dealers never get caught.

The government's theory on surveillance was (and is) that the drug dealers are so busy making cash that they tend to overlook the obvious. The catch phrase for DEA agents is, "Dope dealer today, dope dealer tomorrow." If we miss you today, we'll get you later.

The new trend for get-rich-quick drug conspirators is: move your operation to the boonies, pay off the locals, give the inhabitants jobs, buy a big-house and live the good life raking in the cash from the cash crop.

Lincoln County was rural to say the least. There was hardly anything there, except this camp ground and adjoining fishing lakes.

There were other cop jurisdictions assisting Tom and me on the boondoggle. Missouri Highway Patrol was there, and the St. Louis County Police Intelligence Unit. In the region, the county police force is separate from the city.

Our cover tale was that we were with the Corps of Engineers. But there was a problem with that cover. Tom and I would be there occasionally during the afternoon hours and another crew would take our place for the night watch and then another crew would show up for the day watch.

Finally we were placed on straight afternoons at the motor home with nothing to do and no one to talk to except our neighbors in a camper next to ours. The radios supplied by the government were inoperable.

We were there for approximately a week and didn't receive any radio assignments. We were supposed to be following the eighteen wheelers and any other suspicious vehicles coming and going from the onion ring plant. Since that plan never came to fruition, we fished and drank beer. One thing I remembered about the Marine Corps was to improvise when given the opportunity.

The government sent an expert from Chicago to solve the problem with the lunch box radios. He worked for a couple of hours, told us they were repaired and then high tailed it back to Chicago. The radios worked part of the time.

This fiasco of a plan materialized and was dreamt up by a

DEA Agent named Walt Miller. Walt, a little man with a full head of white hair and a cigarette in his hand or mouth, was a good guy, and he hung around the area police departments adopting drug cases for the DEA St. Louis Field Office.

If and when a city cop would get a substantial amount of weed or cocaine, maybe even heroin, Walt would show up and take the case federal, that way the local cop would testify in federal court instead of state court, the feds would get the statistics of a good arrest and a fair amount of drugs seized, and everybody would be happy with the outcome.

But there was new hitch in the cop/agent/drug dealer war. Asset forfeiture! The agency that gets the arrest will get a fair portion of the drug dealer assets; houses, cars, jewelry, and cash.

The St. Louis Metropolitan Police Department was still in the dark ages. Cops still paid state legislators $3500.00 for a promotion to sergeant. Higher ranks cost more. The state ran and controlled the police department by state statute. If a cop had a friend or relative who had the sitting governor's ear, he was miraculously promoted over and over again. The trench cops just sat back and watched the carnage as the royalty cops tried to lead them into battle. It was a joke!

The guys in charge (political cops) were accustomed to a quid pro quo system of policing. "Take care of yourself." was the catch phrase of many commanders in the headquarters building, commonly referred to as the ivory tower.

Agent Walt was nearing retirement. He wanted to go out with a bang. He had heard of the onion ring conspiracy, and he sold his idea to the cop commanders with the promise of drug dealer assets.

The commander of the Intelligence Unit worshipped money. He was political allies with the chief, who likewise had a weakness for cash. To the other politically aligned, crooked commanders (some would steal the nickels off of a dead man's eyes) this was an offer too sweet to resist. I watched our commander, Captain Bud, as Walt pitched him on the joint operation.

Captain Bud leaned back in his chair and nonchalantly listened to Walt's spiel. When Walt came to the part in the program where asset forfeiture came into play and when Walt said, "cash" Captain Bud nearly jumped out of his chair. "We'll put the whole unit on the case," Captain Bud replied.

Agent Walt must have gotten the same response from the Highway Patrol, and St. Louis County Intelligence, because we were all there, riding around in the boonies with radios that didn't work, urban cops in a jungle without street signs.

For Tom and me, on the afternoon watch, things were going fairly smoothly. We had caught some nice fish and drank some cold beer and there was no pressure on us to do anything but wait for the non-functioning government phone to ring.

But there is always a hitch in the cop and crook game. I was fishing at dusk and had gone to the Cuivre River side of the lake. I stood on a levee with swamp behind me, watching out for snakes. There was a severe drought in the region and ground mammals would come to the fishing lake for water in the evening.

Snakes, being predators, would lie in the grass behind the levee and ambush anything they could get their fangs into. I had almost stepped on a huge snake as I was walking along the levee. I almost dropped my beer as I struck out at the snake with my rod and reel. As the snake slithered toward the swamp I stopped and started casting out into the muddy lake water.

I was using a plastic minnow with a weight on it and I could cast it far out into the lake. I was fishing but I didn't expect to catch anything. It was just something to do to get out of the nasty little motorhome we were working out of.

When Tom and I first got to the motorhome, we walked in to a death like stench. Tom and I stayed outside, camped at a picnic table.

Agent Walt Miller finally showed up. "The motorhome smells like someone died in it. What's up?" I asked him. We came to the conclusion that the human waste holding tank was full. Walt and Tom didn't know how to empty it. Walt left, leaving us to solve the problem.

We figured out how to empty the tank, but the stench was still there, just not as bad. We figured it was going to be a long detail. Fishing saved us from having to sit in the stinking motorhome.

Before I knew it, it was pitch dark. My beer can was empty and I figured I'd better make my way back on the levee toward the campground, hopefully without getting snake bit. I reeled in and something hit my bait. My rod bent big-time, and I figured I'd inadvertently caught a huge snake.

I quickly fought with the thing on the end of my line and got it to the edge of the levee. I couldn't see what it was but I knew it was heavy.

I grabbed the lure by the lead weight, held the thing out so it couldn't bite me and headed back toward the motorhome. I was running and jumping over shadows of huge snakes. I yelled for Tom who came running with the lunch box radio and his gun drawn.

"I caught something big," I yelled at him. There was a

street light configuration on a pole between our motorhome and a trailer next to us. We'd seen the folks living in the trailer. He was a guy who looked like he was in his late seventies. The gal looked like she was in her late forties. There was a sign on the door which read, "Don't come a knockin if this trailer is a rockin." Whenever we saw one another we'd say, "Hello" but that was the extent of our communication.

The gal had a hard body as if she had worked on a farm or in a factory for most of her life. She smoked and coughed and had a raspy voice.

Cops tend to visualize themselves in other people's lives. I wondered if I would someday be living in a camper with a hard bodied smoker. Cops didn't get paid much and the cop pension is meager. I figured my wife would someday leave me for a younger man with a better paying job. I had seen it happen to cop friends.

The problem with the cop job is that it can sometimes be fun and rewarding. Deep down inside most cops know that they are wasting their lives doing such a ridiculous thing for a living. But we push on with stupid cases that no one cares about, lying on affidavits and in court, hoping that someday we will meet that important person with state clout who will get us promoted.

We walked under the street light and examined my catch. It was a large catfish, grunting and flapping around still on the little minnow lure. "I've been fishing all of my life and I've never caught a catfish that big," Tom exclaimed.

"I thought it was a damned snake," I replied. "What the hell are we going to do with it?"

Our neighbors came out of their trailer, aroused by the commotion. "Damn, that's a nice catfish," the man said. "Let's weigh it." The old codger went into his trailer and came back with a scale. He unhooked the fish and attached it to the scale, "Eleven pounds," he said. He shook my hand.

"Thanks," I responded.

"What are you boys going to do with this fish?" he asked.

"I don't have any idea," I replied. "We don't have anything to cook it with. Would you like to have it?"

"I'll cook it tomorrow afternoon," the codger's girlfriend said. "We'll have a feast."

"How many people will this fish feed?" I asked.

The gal studied the fish, "ten, at least. I'll make fried potatoes and have a garden salad. Are there anymore guests you can invite.?"

"Maybe," I replied. I looked at Tom, "You think the other guys would come down here for a feast?"

"We'll ask them," Tom said.

"Let's skin it," the old codger said. He removed it from the scale, got a hammer and a ten penny nail from his trailer and nailed the head of the catfish to the street light pole. He carefully cut the skin in a circular fashion and used a pair of pliers to pull the skin away from the flesh. He gutted it and let the guts fall onto the ground, removed the fish from the nail and cut off the head. He gave the cleaned fish to his girlfriend and she quickly took it inside to the refrigerator. There's more than one way to skin a cat!

"Tomorrow at five in the afternoon?" the old codger asked.

"Yeah," Tom and I said simultaneously. We stashed our fishing gear in the trunk of our undercover car and went inside the stinking little motorhome.

Tom got on the lunchbox government radio and tried to make contact with any of the other undercover cops. It was to no avail. It was a reality check for us. We were on our own in this covert federal drug probe. Finally a pair of Missouri State Police undercover cops drove up to our motorhome. We observed their car and walked outside to see who they were.

They identified themselves and introductions were made. I asked them to join us for a catfish fest on the following day. They accepted the invitation.

Our relief was due at 1100 hours, but they usually didn't arrive until 0100. Tom and I made certain the motorhome was free of any fishing gear or evidence of fishing or beer drinking. Cops in specialized units are snitches.

There are guys and gals in every organization who gravitate toward being favored in the eyes of the bosses. It's no different in the cop/crook game.

When our relief arrived, to our dismay two of the crooked captain's snitch puppies, the lead dog and his influential friend, the little pedigree dog, knocked on the motorhome door. The crooked captain no doubt sent them to relieve us and to find out exactly what was occurring on the alleged surveillance. He hadn't seen any cash cross his desk and it had been a couple of weeks. He was no doubt anxious.

Tom and I were cordial to the crony cops, but in fact we were leery of them. They would lie on a cop just as fast as they would lie on a crook. They were both great cops, that fact was indisputable, but they were intent on gaining rank and that made them unconscionable.

The smaller of the two cops came from Pipefitters Local 562. His brother was a high ranking officer in the union. The local had union card carrying state representatives. The local contributed heavily to the sitting governor, Democrat or Republican.

The little guy could have been promoted without paying the $3500.00 surcharge if he would have just stayed out of trouble, but he didn't. His trouble came from allegations of being corrupt as a district detective. He had been accused of everything from taking bribes to murder for hire. There were federal agencies and the Internal Affairs Division of the police department with open investigations on him. But he was never indicted or formally charged. His nickname was The Teflon Detective.

He was actually a friendly guy. He was an asthmatic, and I got the impression from him that he had to work to be rotten. It didn't come natural to him, but he was good at it.

He bragged about being a body guard for union gangster Tommy Callanan, the son of the founder of Pipefitters Local 562. Tommy got blown up, twice, by car bombs. He eventually succumbed to his injuries, but it took years.

Joey (Doves) Aiuppa got Tommy Callanan. But the Chicago mobster didn't get the little pedigree's older brother. He gained power and stature in the local. He had friends in high places in Jefferson City, the capitol of the State of Missouri.

That was long before the little pedigree dog decided to become a St. Louis cop. He had a reputation of being a sucker puncher as he tried to build his reputation as a bad ass.

He wasn't a bad ass, but he was a back shooter and ruthless as a cop detective. The chief of police liked him because of his political influence and his moxie. Being a crook/cop in the 1970s wasn't a bad thing to have on your resume.

He was in the Intelligence Unit to let his reputation cool down so that he could be promoted and get on with his program of becoming the chief of police.

When the little fellow was in the police academy he advised a training officer while on a routine ride along with a district cop that he came to the police department to become the chief. "Oh," replied the old cop, "How do you know that?"

"Because my brother told me I would be the chief," he replied.

There were several keys to the promotion lock box. One was obsession with promotion. Obsession went hand-in-hand with statistics. If a cop was statistically correct, then he was politically correct. Corruptness could and would be overlooked if a cop was a hard charger.

When the governor's cronies made the suggestion that a certain police officer should be promoted, the chief and the deputy chiefs would call a meeting to go over the individuals who they, as a group, had to okay for promotion. These guys lived in glass houses; they weren't about to cast the first stone.

"He makes a lot of arrests," was the pass phrase to promotion. Both of my relief cops made a lot of arrests. They just had to dance for the crooked captain to satisfy their obsession.

Tom and I were driving back to civilization at about the same time the old codger and the youngish girlfriend tapped on the door of the stinking government motorhome asking the captain's cronies where Tim and Tom were.

The catfish story followed and the two cronies of the crooked captain were given enough ammunition to blow Tom and me off of the promotion list (as if we desired promotion) and quite possibly out of the prestigious spy unit, which would have been disastrous. We both loved the freedom the unit provided and we got to act important even though we knew we were just lucky instead of good.

The next day I was summoned to the crooked captain's office in the afternoon before going to the boonies to sit in the motorhome. He didn't summon Tom, just me. It's the way cop supervisors conduct interviews. They divide and try to conquer.

He sat back in his big reclining chair, sucked on a nasty cigar and blew smoke at my face. He knew I didn't smoke and that tobacco smoke infuriated me.

"What's this shit about you fishing while on surveillance?" he began.

I was trying to make contact with some people who might possibly work at the onion plant," I replied. "It was all a part of being undercover. If I would have just sat in the motorhome waiting for the nonfunctioning radio to ring, people would have wondered why. We were told to use the Corps of Engineers as our cover. Those guys would have fished."

He stared at me with hatred because he wasn't able to force me to rat on Tom. He wanted me to say, "Tom was fishing, too, why isn't he in here?" but I didn't.

"Get the fuck out of my office," he finally said.

I picked Tom up and drove like a madman to get to the campground. Tom and I arrived at the motorhome in the boonies a little late. The guys we relieved were upset, but rationalization is a wonderful thing which cops use frequently.

The old codger observed us arrive and he was at the door with a smile and two cold beers for us. "Girlfriend will be back real soon, she'll start cookin then." He was studying us the way an old man studies a young person.

He had been around long enough to know that our cover story about the Corps of Engineers didn't hold water. "Is there some other guys coming to dinner?" he asked.

"Yeah, I think so," I replied, "Maybe two, hopefully more."

"Are they with the Corps of Engineers, too?"

"Oh yeah," I lied as he studied me.

The old codger regrouped and got serious…..."You know,

there's two rivers beyond that swamp, the Missouri and the Cuivre. When this drought ends, and the rains begin again, there's going to be some bad flooding here. This campground will be under water. Me and my girlfriend will have to move our trailer. She'll have to leave her job."

"Flood?" I replied, and then flushed with embarrassment. Corps of Engineers guys would know about the rivers and their floods.

"Job?" Tom and I said simultaneously.

"Yeah, she works down the road at the onion ring factory. She runs one of those machines that slices the onions into rings, makes pretty good money, too."

Tom and I stared dumbfounded. "I'll see you boys about five," he said as he turned and walked away.

Tom and I wandered into the stinking motorhome. "If the captain finds out we're making friends with the enemy we'll be back in the blue, answering radio calls in some dark and dank police district." Tom said. "We won't be important anymore. Our peers won't respect us and we won't have an undercover police car to drive around and drink beer in."

"He won't find out," I assured Tom.

"The unit snitches might find out. If they do then he will know. He knows we were fishing," Tom moaned.

"Don't worry about it," I said with confidence, "Let's just do our thing and see what happens. What do you want to do, cancel the catfish fest? The highway patrol cops are coming. It's too late to back out," I countered.

Tom sat and stewed in a barrel chair looking out of the window as he nursed his beer. The lady friend from the next trailer must have come home. We could smell the aroma of fried potatoes and breaded catfish.

The old codger was setting the picnic table and shooting glances at our stinking motorhome. The highway patrol undercover guys slowly pulled up to our motorhome. We walked outside and greeted them. They were nice guys, but everybody, including cops, hate highway cops. We tried to be cordial to them. They had a cooler of cold beer and we instantly accepted them as comrades in arms.

The food was good, the conversation was limited, and the beer flowed like water. We sat around until darkness fell on the campground and the country mosquitoes started attacking us. The old codger and the onion plant woman cleared the table and headed for their trailer.

"Where are you guys stationed?" I asked the highway patrol guys.

"We're mobile," the older one said. "We have rolling surveillance on the plant, the target's residence, and a tavern they own in O'Fallon. It's called "Daddy's Money." It's a classy drug lord bar. You guys want to go along with us? We're going to the bar after we leave here."

"I'll go," I replied.

"I'm staying here," Tom replied.

I crawled into the backseat of the Chevy Impala two door, scrunched down and nursed a beer. The highway patrolman climbed into the front and the older guy, who was a sergeant, drove us out to route seventy nine. He turned right and we cruised by the onion ring factory. The cop was speeding in the darkness of the country road.

I mused in the backseat on how strange it was for me to be in the presence of these guys, relaxed, being paid to drink beer and ride around in the boonies without a care in the world.

Suddenly a cop car was behind us with its roof lights lighting up my karma. I instinctively scrunched deeper into the seat placing my beer between my legs.

I figured the cop pulling us over knew the highway cops and was stopping them to shoot the breeze. A chunky

unattractive young woman approached the highway patrol
driver. He lowered his window.

"Give me your license," she said. "You were doing
eighty in a fifty." She perused his driver's license.
"Everything current here?"

"Yes," he said. She walked back to her car, and in about
five minutes returned to his window. "Sign this," she
ordered. He signed it. "Your court date is in the lower right
hand corner of the summons." She turned and walked away.

The highway cop drove away and there was silence in the
car. The irony of the event struck me and I started giggling.
I'd been given tickets all over the country by irate and
unfriendly highway cops. Most people who have ever
travelled the interstate highways in their lives have had
similar experiences.

My giggle turned into a large laugh and the highway
guys joined me in the comedy of the event. "You know
what's really comical about this?" the highway cop driver
asked.

"No," I replied.

"I used my undercover "funny" driver's license. It has a
fictitious name and address on it. Lincoln County, Missouri
will never get anything from me." We all laughed until I
thought I was going to cry.

Daddy's Money was a classy bar. Everything was new
and chrome and leather. The place was packed with guys
and gals, but I studied every face and I didn't see anyone
who I knew or had seen on any surveillance or in any crime
memorandums.

"Are there any drug dealers in here?" I covertly asked the
older highway cop.

"Probably," he replied.

We sat at the bar and drank beer. We got loosened up and
the true personalities of the highway cops came out. They

were super friendly, country and slow to trust anyone, but they acted like they truly liked me. Problem was there was a culture gap present. I was born in East St. Louis, Illinois. I was an urban guy who was raised around gangsters. We were as different as night and day.

Finally one of the country highway cops said, "Do you work any secondary employment?"

I shunned secondary although it would, in my future, become a reality for me. We had just had our first child and in order to survive in the cop/crook game the cop has to have two jobs.

"No," I replied, "but I wouldn't turn down a good offer."

"We drive used cars to California for local dealers," the younger of the two advised. "If you're looking for employment driving, give me a call and I'll get you on."

"Cool," I said.

The night dragged on with country music and cold beer. The highway cops conveyed me back to the motorhome and Tom and I talked over the events of the evening.

"They offered me a second job," I advised him, "driving used cars to California."

"They're probably stolen," Tom said.

"You think they'd do that?"

"Yep!"

The onion ring caper died a slow death. Nothing ever came from the surveillance. It was two months of wasted time. The onion ring factory owner was a "smart dope dealer". The corrupt captain was incensed, he didn't get any cash to pilfer.

Tom and I figured the operation was compromised. The onion ring guy was a wealthy and well liked member of St. Louis society. He had friends in high places. Information leaks out of police headquarters.

Good guy, Special Agent Walt Miller retired from DEA. The unit attended his retirement party, except for the captain.

I thought a lot about the old codger and his youngish girlfriend in the camper beside us. It was the end of life for him, the middle of the affray for her. I figured she'd leech onto some other old guy for survival when the time came.

The two highway cops were indicted but not prosecuted for driving stolen automobiles across state lines. The sergeant was demoted and sent to a remote area of southeast Missouri. His friend was sent even farther into obscurity. But they didn't lose their jobs.

Tom and I figured that if we had been involved with them, just trying to make an honest dollar, we would have been prosecuted and sent to prison. Cop survival is a bitch!

The onion ring caper was my first experience with the Drug Enforcement Administration but it would not be my last.

II.

PUMMELLED INTO REALITY

Tom and I returned to our life of being undercover big-city-detectives, investigating the Mafia. It was heady and we strutted and posed and did everything celebrities were supposed to do. We would have signed autographs if asked.

But there was another fly in the ointment of the Mafia/St. Louis cop game. The FBI had flipped a hired killer for the mob and he was informing on everyone associated with St.Louis organized crime.

The guy (Jesse Stoneking) was a certified tough guy and killer. He had a resume that impressed everyone in or outside of the criminal world. If Jesse walked into a room, people would come up to him and brag about their criminal escapades, everything from murder to disposing of a car for the insurance money, commonly referred to as "wire fraud".

And to add insult to injury, organized crooks, Mafia types met with him to hire him to put pressure on people, or murder them.

All of these happenings were on tape, thanks to good old Jesse. He cleaned up organized crime in good old St. Louis, and in neighboring East St. Louis, Illinois.

With these crooks gone there was a void in the Intelligence Unit. Our job description was to investigate organized criminal groups. The groups were now gone.

The unit was dwindling. Tom got transferred back to uniform. A new Captain came in and he was honest, which didn't fare well for him. He didn't last long.

After Tom left the unit I was so devastated that I stopped drinking beer. Good partners are hard to come by.

The lead dog was promoted and left for a short time, then returned. He was a cop supervisor now, and he was given the responsibility to save the unit from being disbanded.

New organized criminal groups were being formed; drugs were now the product for crooks to deal in. It was more lucrative than anything else the old Mafia types had made money from; union corruption, gambling and prostitution.

In ancient times the Mafia dealt in white heroin, got the black race hooked on it and watched as they self-destructed because of it.

Young, brave, ambitious St. Louis entrepreneurs, like Rich Latchkey and Paul Robinson, or crooks with access to cash, would drive to Florida, hook-up with someone in a bar and purchase large amounts of weed. The weed would be shipped back to St. Louis or neighboring Illinois in the trunks of cars, or in small trucks. It was a cash crop business.

The young entrepreneurs could easily rationalize their criminal enterprises by saying that there was nothing wrong with weed and people desired it. But there was a marketing strategy initiated by the drug sources: you want weed? We'll sell it to you but you must also buy cocaine and Quaaludes, or 714, which was the number stamped onto the pills, a narcotic downer.

Quaaludes was a prescription/hypnotic drug invented to treat anxiety and insomnia. It was deemed a dangerous drug and taken off of the market. It then became a black market drug sought after by the weed smokers of the era.

So the young lions of crime purchased what they could get and brought it to St. Louis and sold it to anyone who would buy it. They got rich, quick.

Many of these enterprising young drug dealers lived in blue collar north St. Louis County. It's where the 562

Pipefitters headquarters was, and is still located, although the St. Louis Zoo purchased all of the 562 land and are in the process of turning it into an animal refuge.

562 is relocating to St. Charles County. Many of the young dope smugglers were card carrying members of the local. This author also lived there, as did the lead dog and the little pedigree. The community was targeted by the feds. Poor city blacks were being given down payments for the purchase of homes in Spanish Lake, an unincorporated community in north St. Louis County.

It was a neat place to live before the influx of city blacks. Housing was cheap, the houses were palatial ranch homes with pools and giant oak trees, two car garages with large driveways.

Blacks were steered toward it. Plush apartment complexes were becoming section-eight housing. Most of the whites moved on to better neighborhoods. All were incensed at the loss of their homes.

The Intelligence Unit was slowly turning into a narcotics unit, although the police department already had one. But we, as a semi-secret unit, could do almost anything we wished.

The entire police department was working drugs, uniform guys, district detective bureaus, even homicide due to the killings of consignment drug deals gone awry.

The lead dog was stocking the unit with his cronies, most of which had worked drugs at some time in their careers. The unit turned into a kennel for wayward cop/dogs.

They were all hound dogs seeking promotion. As I casually observed the daily events unfold, I likened their behavior to that of an Alaskan sled dog team pulling a sled in the Iditarod.

The lead dog morphed into the lead sled dog. The other

dogs would become excited when he was placed in the front of the line to lead them. The new captain was the driver of the sled and the chief was the passenger, both covered with blankets and coddled, waiting for asset forfeiture funds to drift their way.

The powers that be, the Honorable Board of Police Commissioners, authorized the Intelligence Unit to act in secrecy. The semi-intelligent leaders of the unit initiated that power to pursue revenge on their enemies and the enemies of the members of the board and the deputy chiefs, in and outside of the police department. The power snowballed into a lust for deceit and hatred. The lead dog had lust for power.

But it wasn't completely his fault that he became this cop/fellow with power lust. He observed and learned quickly that the justice system was there to be played.

Local, state, federal, the justice system is a business where the smart and aggressive players get the power. Prosecutors know it, judges and criminal defense lawyers are aware of the playing of the system. Few cops are, but the lead dog was. I give him accolades for this.

His lust was reinforced by the political power of the little pedigree puppy, his politically connected best friend. They plotted their course to greatness and the little pedigree eventually got promoted and left the unit, never to return. He had bigger fish to fry; eventually became the Chief, the crooked cop who never had any official charges sticking on him.

The lead dog was seeking a target, a dope dealer, preferably black and operating out of the north St. Louis County corridor.

There were scores of white dope dealers there, one of the largest weed and coke dealers in the state lived across the street from the little pedigree. The little pedigree, and the lead dog were well acquainted with him, and they left him alone. He was a card carrying member of the Pipe Fitters union, 562.

Criminals talk, especially after they have been arrested. There is no honor among thieves, or dope dealers. The word got back to the lead dog that there was an out of town, wealthy black man who was bringing large amounts of cocaine into the St. Louis area.

The cocaine was being distributed by a group of blacks living in north county. The lead dog initiated a surveillance on this group. There is only so much that can be learned through surveillance.

The identities of the players was established; their addresses, places of employment and telephone numbers. It wasn't enough for the lead dog was on a fast track to super stardom. He desired instant gratification.

He borrowed a pin register machine (a device that documents who telephones whom) from an agent friend at Alcohol Tobacco and Firearms. This particular machine had a switch on it that allowed the user to listen to phone conversations.

There is a saying in the cop/crook business: "Anything a cop or federal agent does to catch a bad guy is legal and okay. We are cops to catch crooks, all is fair." The statement is a factoid and if repeated over and over again it eventually becomes fact.

The machine was set-up in a secret office closet, one that had been used in ancient times when the Intelligence Unit was actually a spy unit. The office was a maze of locked doors and clandestine rooms.

Whenever information became scarce, the lead dog would retreat into the closet and return with fresh and accurate information.

The cop dope dogs would genuflect at his presence, he

was their cop God. They begged him to lead them, and he did.

When the feds decided to adopt the case there was surveillance at Lambert Field International Airport. One of the smugglers, an attractive woman, was hand carrying kilos of cocaine in carry-on baggage.

She had been doing it for months, smuggling hundreds of kilos of cocaine from Los Angeles to St. Louis. Security was so lax in the eighties that she even smuggled it in checked luggage.

The feds wanted to verify that cocaine was actually being smuggled in. They desired to inspect her checked baggage, but she was slick, she was booked on one flight but switched to another flight. The feds waited for her baggage but did not see it. Someone called the lead dog and advised him of the confusion.

Within five minutes, the feds were advised that the smuggler gal had changed flights at the last minute. "How does he know when she's coming in?" A fed exclaimed. "Where is he getting this information?"

Enough probable cause was gathered for a legal wiretap. A federal judge has to give the okay for such an infringement of constitutional rights and a federal law enforcement agency must be involved.

The feds were so enthralled with the case that both the FBI and DEA were jointly working it. The case was moving along nicely.

The lead dog made it evident that he did not want me to work on his drug case. I was transferred to the Drug Enforcement Administration Task Force, federally sworn and given an undercover fed car. I was also making more money.

But I didn't want to go there. I felt I was slumming. I was an organized crime spy, a warrior against the American

Mafia. I knew them from coast to coast and some of them knew me. But I left the unit and walked into DEA with a negative attitude. I was forced to hit the ground running.

As fate would have it, the entire DEA task force was assigned to a wire-tap at FBI Headquarters in downtown St. Louis working on the Intelligence Unit's cases.

We sat in an office with headphones on and listened to telephone calls between the black north county dope smugglers.

These guys were out of their league. They had never had money before but now they were rich. They insisted on reinforcing one another with telephone calls about their new found wealth and their lucrative careers in the dope game.

The conversations would always start out with one of them saying, "No business talk!"

The reply would be, "Right on brother, no business talk." The conversation would continue for approximately three minutes, then they would start talking about their lucrative dope business. Crooks never let you down.

But cops never let you down either, especially St. Louis cops. Within federal circles St. Louis cops had a reputation of "anything goes" in reference to police work.

Federal agents working with the local cops turned their heads during joint investigations. In the federal crime and punishment game their playing of the system meant gleaning information and statistics from the entitlement cops.

Federal agents padded their resumes with work done by the cops. Commenting about cop actions, whether it be illegal wiretaps or lying on affidavits, would be the "kiss of death" for many federal agents. If the cops didn't lie, there wouldn't be any cases to share.

The DEA job could have been a neat way to make a living. Our offices were in the Chrome Alloy Building in classy Clayton, Missouri, a high rise with views.

Clayton is the financial center of the region, It's where companies, lawyers and big-business desires to have their zip code.

Our office was on a floor with a restaurant and bar just seconds away. "The Club" was the focal point of the high rise. Most of the building patrons ate and drank there, including DEA agents and cops.

But there was another fly in the ointment in the cop/drug dealer game. The cops I was working with were young, in their twenties. I was in my forties and most everybody was cold to me, even the secretaries.

The special agents were particularly cold to me, even unfriendly. There were three groups; two were special agents only, and the task force, which is where I was assigned, was made up of agents and cops.

One of the agent groups acted like they wanted to do me bodily harm. I had never met any of them, but when I would pass them in the hallways I would be called "dope dealer" and "asshole."

A group of city cops were standing at my desk and lowly talking about one of the secretaries in another group. She was a looker and the single dog cops wanted to ravish her. The group supervisor, Steve Palance, came out of his office and approached my desk. "Stay away from her," he advised the cur dogs. "She's spoken for."

I had come from an intelligence environment. Every telephone in my old unit was bugged. It was obviously the same here. The feds put bugs in the telephone itself, not just in the receiver. That way every conversation heard inside of a room is recorded. My workplace was bugged and I wondered why.

One evening I had the duty, which meant I had to stay late and answer the telephones. I wandered into the group's office where I was obviously hated. A deranged special agent pulled out a nine millimeter Glock, pulled the slide back chambering a round, and pointed it at my face. I backed out.

I attributed this treatment to the lead dog, one of the snitch puppies from the Intelligence Unit. I figured that he had laid the ground work for my character assassination before I ever walked through the doors of the DEA field office. My theory on law enforcement was different than his. I didn't lie to make myself look better than I actually was.

I took the abuse, mainly because I had nowhere else to go except back to uniform in some dingy police district. In my mind that would have been accepting failure. I had worked too hard to lie down and let the cop machine play God with me, so I kept my mouth shut and tried to go with the flow.

I was sent to DEA School in Kansas City, came back and continued to roll with the punches.

On a drug deal in downtown St. Louis, I got beat up in a hotel room while my comrades in arms allowed it to happen. In fact they initiated the beating.

I had the guy handcuffed, after wrestling with him. He was a large and dangerous man. I had had dealings with him before, in Intelligence. He was a leg breaker for Teamsters Local 600. I didn't remember him, but he remembered me.

Little Stevie Wonder (S/A Steve Stoddard) removed the cuffs, and a St. Louis County cop pushed him toward me.

His first punch knocked me down. He jumped on top of me and continued to beat me in the face.

A city cop, Steve (Johnny) Reszler was the first cop or agent to assist me. He pulled the monster off of me and I jumped up. I was seeing double, so I continued to shake my head to try and clear my vision. I grabbed the house phone and bashed it across the teamster's face and head. After three or four hits, the phone had disintegrated.

Other TFD's jumped in and we got him to the floor. He was on all fours, taking a beating by four cops, being pistol whipped and gurgling blood. I finally got my cuffs back on his wrists. The crazed cops were still beating him.

I could tell that they were going to beat the teamster to death. No human can take a beating from four cops and survive. But he refused to go down to his stomach. He stayed on all fours and took the savage beating. Rodney King was at a picnic compared to this beating.

"Stop," I shouted. "He's re-cuffed, stop beating him." The teamster went to his stomach and was on his way to death. He was a wounded wild animal, blood gurgling from his mouth and oozing from his face and head. He was semi-conscious. Somebody called an ambulance.

My nose was bent sideways and bleeding. I went into the bathroom, blew my nose into a towel and snapped it back into place. The bleeding stopped.

I packed another towel with ice and applied it to my swelling face and eyes. I was confused and dismayed but this incident was a wakeup call. As usual, I was on my own at DEA, just like I was in the police department.

I felt stupid for thinking I could trust anyone in law enforcement. I had been a Marine for four years. It was every man for himself in the Corps; it's the same everywhere.

The camaraderie in the unit was limited and shallow. When we were all drunk together we were the best of friends. Beyond intoxication we were all just competitors searching for promotion. Unlike the agent who pulled the Glock on me in one of the other groups, I felt I had some trust in a few of the TFD's.

After a quick emergency room visit I drove myself home. Paul Wayne King, the guy who beat me up, wasn't as lucky. He was eventually taken to the Springfield, Missouri federal prison hospital where he almost died.

He lost one of his fingers in the melee. He survived the beating, but he was subsequently sentenced to several years in a federal prison. The irony of the cop job. I saw him frequently after he was released from prison. We both lived in the north county corridor. He would look at me, and I would return the look but we never acknowledged each other.

After I got healed, the group supervisor, Special Agent Steve Palance, summoned me to his office. I had done some soul searching while I was healing from the beating.

I had always been a person who resisted following the herd. In fact, I despised herd mentality. It didn't take long for any supervisor I ever had to recognize this trait in me.

I was certain my reputation had preceded me and that the beating I received was due to my past. I stood in front of Palance's desk. He was a federal agent on the fast tract. He only cared about statistics and promotions.

If my questionable attitude stood between him and a promotion, then I was disposable. Palance had the young TFD's (our title, Task Force Detectives) sewed up and on his side. He was a friend to them, drank with them, partied with them and he was a womanizer, even though he was married with children. His wife was a registered nurse and made good money.

There was a picture of Palance's wife and kids behind his desk next to a picture of his girlfriend, who conveniently worked at the United States Attorney's office.

Palance began his speech: "The problem we have here is that you are an individual. There are no individuals here at

DEA. We are a team here. Do you think you can reform your attitude and work with those guys out there in that office? Do you think you can be one of the boys?"

I knew I was at the end of my rope with the police department. Going back there meant going back to a district in uniform, at the time, failure, a fate worse than death.

"Yes sir, I can do it," I replied. But I really wanted to say, "Was that team spirit when a special agent pulled a cocked Glock on me and stuck it in my face? Why am I being called a dope dealer, and an asshole? Why is my work space bugged?" But I didn't say it.

"Dismissed," Palance said. I exited his office and walked to my desk in the big open office on the fourth floor, in fashionable Clayton, Missouri.

All eyes were on me. Cops and agents were writing reports about the previous evening's dope deals. There were deals nightly, most of them "buy busts" which meant a young undercover cop detached to DEA would buy dope from someone and then the task force would arrest him.

The master plan was for the guy arrested to snitch on his supplier, set him up and DEA would work its way up the ladder until they get the main supplier. It hardly ever worked that way.

The dope dealer giving his dope on consignment had contingency plans. If the consignee didn't telephone the consignment guy in a certain amount of time, that meant he was probably taken off by DEA. That also meant that the guy giving the dope on consignment would not communicate with the seller. The United States Attorney's case was usually against the original seller of the dope.

The young guys on the Task Force were the group supervisor's favorites. Being young, they were the best undercover dope buyers. Palance spoiled them, gave them carte blanche in the unit, the newest and best undercover cars, and the most leeway in every way imaginable.

I desired to establish myself in the Task Force. I could have ridden shotgun to the young guys, but I wanted more. There were experiences here and I wanted to partake of them.

I had a black business friend who knew lots of people, black and white. I called him on my DEA bugged telephone and we talked about my new assignment. I asked him for an informant and he gave me a name. I called her, met up with her, gave her some DEA cash and she agreed to set something up for me. I had nothing to lose.

A week or so went by and the informant contacted me. She knew a guy named "Main" who was selling pounds of cocaine for a guy from the Island of Belize. The guy from Belize was careful not to get involved with the drug deals, but if the money got screwed up he would kill his salesman, "Main."

I told her to set up a deal with Main for the sale of a pound of cocaine. She did and I went to Group Supervisor Palance to inform him and get flash money from him.

After advising him of the deal, Palance recommended having Reszler as the undercover agent instead of me. Obviously, I was perceived as ancient and clean cut and no self-respecting black dope dealer would trust me enough to sell me dope.

The deal was set up in north city and Reszler purchased the pound of cocaine. We took Main off, conveyed him to our offices and he sat on the hot seat wondering how long he would live. He feared the guy from Belize.

We only had an hour or so and Main was supposed to meetup with the Belize dope dealer and give him the dope cash, then Main would get his cut and get along waiting for the next deal.

After given the facts of dope dealer life concerning DEA and the federal government, Main agreed to give up the Belize fellow, testify against him a court of law, and make a controlled delivery of the cash the doper was owed. But he wanted protection from the federal government.

I conveyed Main's desires to Palance. "Tell him we will protect him," Palance said. I conveyed Palance's protection answer to Main and the case continued on.

We wired Main and he delivered the cash. We waited for a couple of weeks before doing anything else with Main and the Belize guy. Palance wanted to make some more buys from him, using Main.

I was in contact with Main frequently. He called me advising that he was in fear of his life. The guy from Belize was into Voodoo and he told Main that he thought Main was setting him up for an arrest. He told Main the spirits had told him that Main could not be trusted.

The Belize guy did some Voodoo chants at Main, killed a chicken and some frogs and basically terrified Main. Main was a big guy, he could have squashed the guy from Belize, but the guy had the Voodoo ups on Main. He controlled him through black magic.

"I need the black magic to survive," Main said. "I need the Voodoo cocaine to survive; I need the cash the Voodoo drug gives me to support my family. If the Voodoo man goes away, I will have no way to survive."

Main told me he wasn't going to do anything more for DEA and that he wanted the protection we had promised him. He knew life was going to be short for him.

I advised Palance of my conversation with Main. "Tell him to do a buy-bust and we'll give him protection," Palance replied.

I advised Main and he refused. The Voodoo guy had several groups of people working for him selling cocaine in pound quantities. Like Main, they were all terrified of the guy from Belize. I decided to let it rest for a while and see how it played out.

Main telephoned me frequently. I got to know him. I knew I was supposed to hate him because he was a cocaine dealer, but Main had a good side to him. He was actually a kind and considerate guy. He had a family and a job, but he needed cash, just like everyone else.

But Main's primary problem was that he actually believed in black magic, Voodoo, and creepy things like that. He was obsessed with the dark side.

He advised me he knew that the Belize Voodoo priest was going to kill him. He was begging me for DEA help in hiding him and his family.

I went to Palance with Main's request and Palance ignored me. He waved me off. I told him that the Belize guy had several people working for him selling pound quantities of cocaine.

"Arrest the Voodoo guy and bring him in here," Palance finally said.

Mad Dog Larry Wheeler and I arrested the Belize dope dealer. We conveyed him to our offices and processed him. It was during working hours and the doper Voodoo priest quickly took stock of his surroundings. This wasn't a jail; it was an office environment with lots of people around. He started acting like a Voodoo priest.

I began taking his fingerprints and he resisted me as much as possible without actually fighting with me. Mad Dog intervened and together we muscled him to the floor and handcuffed him. We photographed him and stuck him in a holding cage.

I now knew why most of our deals were done at night. The building is deserted at night. The dopers don't really know where they are or what's going to happen to them. They don't realize they are just in an office building.

If the Voodoo priest from Belize had acted in an uncooperative way at night he would have been beaten unconscious.

The Voodoo priest was conveyed to the United States Marshall's Service, arraigned and given the opportunity to make bond. Bond was high, but he had the ten percent needed for a professional bondsman and he was set free. It was a weenie charge, Conspiracy to Distribute Cocaine, a catch all federal charge that is usually thrown out of court by the request of any reputable defense attorney.

Main was shot dead as he sat in a car in north St. Louis. The Voodoo priest fled to Belize and to this day is free, probably living on a beach in paradise, spending his dope money from his adventure in St. Louis.

I kind of liked Main! Actually he wasn't a bad guy. He was a St. Louis street guy trying to make a quick dollar. I felt badly that he got killed and was not given the protection he was promised.

I quickly learned that street dealing black folks are not the recipients of federal protection. They are expendable. I was thinking to myself; to DEA the TFD's were also expendable, but not the special agents.

There was different lingo at DEA......blacks were referred to as Canadians, cute girls were called snakes and behind the backs of the special agents they were referred to as fucking assholes. The TFD's hated most of the agents, and the feeling was mutual.

TFD Joe Ringer was a rising star and Steve (Johnny) Reszler was on the same plane. They looked like they were in their late teens. Dope dealers trusted them. They were lethal.

Ringer, being a St. Louis County cop and a sports fan, desired to gain free admittance to sporting events like the city cops did. City cops flashed their city police badge and were waved in to every event.

At DEA we were given federal credentials and hardly anyone carried their badge. It would be the kiss of death if someone felt a badge or observed one in our wallet.

Ringer asked me if he could borrow my badge and I said yes. I didn't need it. I didn't go to ball games, and if I did I had my wife with me and I wouldn't want anyone to know I was a cop. As soon as a drunk gets in a fight they start looking for the "mooching" cops. Ringer carried my badge for two years.

In law enforcement in St. Louis, in those days (1980s) it helped if you had a family pedigree if you wished to further your career in the police department, City or County.

Most people had "aces" (influential friends) who helped them along in their careers with outside influence. I had more than one and so did most ambitious cops. The holy-grail was promotion and cops fought for it. I wasn't seeking promotion. I just enjoyed investigation. I was foolish enough to think that I could breeze through a long career in the St. Louis Metropolitan Police Department as an investigator.

Ringer had his influential high ranking city cop dad and other aces. Reszler's dad was a city cop without rank and he was still able to help Johnny through the maze of hypocrisy and get him into a specialized and glorified unit like the DEA Task Force. Being here was better than a promotion. It was amazing to me that I was just fifteen years younger than Reszler's dad.

Ringer was admired by other cops. He was cocky, but a good cop. He had ambition and confidence. County police department cops working drugs would make buys for their unit and then set the guy up with Ringer for a DEA buy.

Ringer kept the unit busy and Group Supervisor Palance happy. He provided a lot of stats for Palance's promotion.

Reszler was introduced to the department surgeon, Doctor James F. Cooper shortly after becoming a cadet in the police department. He was just a kid, right out of high school.

There was a cadet program wherein kids could do menial jobs within the police department, go to college on their off duty hours and eventually become police officers. Reszler, with the help of his non-ranking semi-influential dad mapped out this route to stardom.

Doctor Cooper, whose brother-in-law was the governor of Missouri, Warren Hearnes, held clout within the police department. He requested that Reszler be assigned to his medical division as a cadet. Doctor Cooper always got what he wanted.

Reszler earned an associate degree from the junior college and was accepted into the police academy. He was assigned to the rough and tumble third district as a police officer and when he had three years there he was eligible for a transfer to a specialized unit.

"Go to the DEA Task Force," Doctor Cooper advised him. Doctor Cooper called his friend, the chief, and Reszler was transferred.

As is usual, there is always a fly in the ointment in the cop/crook game. Reszler was a big drinker. He would drink until he would pass out. And he was using anabolic steroids supplied by Doctor Cooper.

He would get huge and his face would swell from the booze and drugs and then he would cycle out of the steroids and be normal. He never cycled out of the alcohol abuse.

Alcohol was a part of the Task Force job. We even gave

beer to our suspects after we beat them. It was kind of like an apology for mistreatment. Even though they hated us, they never turned down the cold beer. Most of them applied the cold can to their faces to reduce the swelling.

Group Supervisor Palance recognized future DEA talent, and he actively worked at recruiting the young guys in the unit to apply for permanent DEA employment.

The "buzz question" for errant TFD's was "Where can I get assigned when DEA hires me?"

Palance seized the opportunity to brainwash the young cops. "I'll be promoted by then and be in DEA headquarters. I'll make certain you guys go where you want. Phoenix? San Diego? Miami? You guys get me stats and I'll repay you with a good duty assignment."

The naïve little cops beamed with enthusiasm. They weren't worldly guys, they were spoiled brat cops kids who had always had everything given to them. No one had ever said "No!" to them.

Palance baited them with the trendy and sunny locales of the world. "There are DEA offices in Europe, South America, anywhere you guys want to go, I'll take care of it," he advised them.

The problem most of them had was that they didn't have bachelor degrees. Most had associate degrees. But there was a way to work around that problem.

There were colleges in the area that would take all of the classes from the junior college and also give credit for police academy training. Some would even give credit for just being a cop. All the colleges cared about was the tuition money. They were diploma mills.

After some investigation by Palance and Reszler, they decided that Reszler should attend Tarkio College in nearby Jefferson County, Missouri.

Reszler did what most city and county cops did upon attending their first class. He approached the instructor of every class, advised he or she that he was an undercover cop detached to DEA and that it would be rough for him to attend every class.

The instructors would usually recommend that the cop/student write term papers based on the text books used for the classes. There was always a secretary or some sort of civilian aide who would write a paper for a cop.

Some instructors would recommend that the cop/student attend some of the important lectures at the college. Reszler would tell the task force cops that after an hour or so to "beep" him (we all carried pagers) and that he would tell the teacher that he had an emergency DEA drug deal he had to attend to. He would be excused.

Tarkio College had a mascot slogan for their football team, "The Hoot Owls." Reszler would walk around the DEA offices singing about the "Hootie Owls". Tarkio was his ticket to greatness.

All of the long range plans pertaining to being hired by DEA revolved around relocation. The guys on the possible hire list spoke about their future duty assignments. It was like prisoners talking about what they were going to do when they got released from prison.

The young cops would talk about what kind of cars they would buy, where they would buy a house, or a boat. They were convinced that the DEA job would make them wealthy. City cops were living on peanuts at that time. DEA agents were living high on the hog.

We all knew that this DEA detachment thing was never going to last. It was a dream assignment. We were playing federal agent with temporary unimpressive DEA credentials.

We knew that we were being played by the federal system, doing ninety percent of the work so that the special agents could pad their resumes with our cases and get promoted and sent to Phoenix, San Diego, Los Angeles or Miami. We all dreamed of leaving St. Louis, getting a fat federal paycheck and never returning, except for me. I was too old for recruitment.

They were pipe dreams fueled by beer and task force Supervisor Palance. If he kept us interested and motivated, we would work like dogs for him and he would get his promotion. To all parties involved, it was righteous.

Manipulation is the key to drug enforcement. Federal cops quickly learn that they must control informants and low level drug dealers in order to catch bigger fish.

The problem with manipulation is that it can't be turned off and on. It's a trait, once learned, that stays with the manipulator for life.

In a federal agency like DEA, manipulation is referred to as "pimping" when it is used against cops and other federal underlings. It's a tongue in cheek process to get people to do what you want them to do. Palance was an expert in "pimping" the young task force cops.

There must be a "hook" to make the "pimping" process a success. New undercover cars, travel to warm climes during the winter, and a fast track to a DEA job were Palance's hooks. He held the attention of the young St. Louis cops.

If a DEA agent was asked a direct question by a TFD, one the agent chose not to answer, the agent would perform a "skit" for all to watch.

The "skit" was comprised of the agent standing and leaning against a wall, eyes closed and lightly snoring as if he was being lulled to sleep by the boring and dispensable TFD question asker. The TFD's quickly learned that they were not detached to DEA to ask questions, just to work and gather stats for the federal entity.

III.

YOU CAN CHOOSE YOUR FRIENDS

In the winter of 1986, I was sitting at my DEA (bugged) desk wondering where I had gone wrong in life. It was dark and dank and depressing and I didn't have any deals or any informants calling me with information.

My phone rang and I quickly answered it. It was a friend from City Intelligence, one of the new guys who were working drugs.

The guy was intense, but in a likable way and I enjoyed speaking to him occasionally. We would pick each other's brains trying to find something out or gain new information.

"You knew this guy Rich Latchkey, didn't you?" he casually asked me.

"Yeah, I knew him," I replied. "Owns a restaurant downtown, hooked up with Dan and Paul Robinson. Paul Robinson went to the Florida State Penitentiary. I'd heard that Rich Latchkey went straight. Not true?"

"Not exactly," my friend replied. "You know Paul is living at the Creve Coeur Stables. It's owned by Tommie Venezia?"

"I'd heard that," I lied. Tommie was a big-time gangster who eventually murdered his young girlfriend and then shot himself in the head.

"Word I got was that he summoned Rich Latchkey and Latchkey responded with a quick visit. Seems they are getting the business together again."

"Interesting," I replied. "Wish to share your informant?"

"No, want to share yours when you get into this

federally?"

"No!" The conversation ended with a laugh. I wondered what the bosses at DEA thought about the conversation between me and my friend. I figured they knew who Paul Robinson was, but not Rich Latchkey.

I kept my ear to the ground waiting for any Paul Robinson information being tossed around the office. Never heard any!

The St. Louis region is like a small town, everyone is connected to someone, either through friendship or relation. The region includes the eastside of the Mississippi River. East St. Louis, Illinois is the city directly east of the City of St. Louis, Missouri.

East St. Louis is in St. Clair County, Illinois and includes several sizeable cities further east. I was born in East St. Louis, Illinois and I had relatives living in St. Clair County.

Some of my relatives were in law enforcement. I had a cousin who worked for ATF (Alcohol, Tobacco and Firearms). Her husband was employed by the State of Illinois Police. He was an investigator.

Drugs were easily obtainable and drug dealers were running rampant on both sides of the Mississippi River. In St. Clair County, being a drug dealer was not looked down upon.

Judges' kids, doctors' kids, people of means, owners of successful restaurants, car dealerships, highly educated citizens and politicians dealt in drugs.

In the early 1970s, two entitlement kids from St. Clair county (their parents owned the two biggest and most successful restaurants in the county) who were fortunate enough to have pilot licenses and their own airplanes, periodically flew to South Florida and smuggled loads of marijuana into the area.

They hangered their airplanes at the Cahokia Airport, near Belleville, Illinois and offloaded the dope without fanfare.

They were warned that DEA was going to inspect their airplanes for marijuana residue, so they burned their airplanes. In doing so, they burned the entire airport to the ground. Every plane there was destroyed.

Their parents collected the insurance money for the burned airplanes, bought their children bigger and faster airplanes; the smuggling operation continued for decades.

The Belleville, Illinois area is where the German Catholic East St. Louis folks settled after fleeing the black invasion of East St. Louis in the 50s.

In their minds, they were taking a stand, digging in and they were not going to be run out of the City of Belleville like they were run out of East St. Louis.

The children of the governing class in Belleville, Illinois attended private schools, were trained in the art of studying and focusing on what the teacher was trying to relay to them, and were drilled by their parents that money was the way to happiness in America, no matter how you get it.

Many of these governing class families produced drug smugglers and dealers. They sold their product to their friends, people like them, educated, coddled and smart. The bottom line was cash.

The non-governing class, police officers being part of that ilk, watched as the chosen and educated ones flipped dope and got richer. There was a tongue in cheek attitude by the local cops. Without prima facie evidence, any case against a "chosen one" citizen from the upper class would have been thrown out of court by any of the local state judges. St. Clair County, Illinois is still a cesspool of juris prudence.

I had another cousin who was a St. Clair County deputy sheriff. He was not educated but had done a stint in the Army after high school and through his politically connected mother was hired by the sheriff's department.

I had heard through the family grapevine that my ATF cousin was beaten up by her state police husband. I figured my St. Clair County sheriff deputy cousin had gotten the same news. I was incensed by it and vocal. Men were not supposed to beat up women and get away with it.

A family gathering brought us all face to face and I was not friendly to the state cop investigator. Little did I know that the state cop investigator was working a drug case with DEA, group two, St. Louis Field Office, on my deputy sheriff cousin, who was allegedly a dope dealing deputy sheriff.

I had seen the state cop in the Intelligence Unit offices meeting with the lead dog. It isn't unusual for other agencies to come to our unit seeking information. I thought no more about it.

A DEA agent in the group where the gun was pulled on me was working the case. The state cop investigator convinced the DEA agent that I was part of a drug conspiracy involving my deputy sheriff cousin in St. Clair County, Illinois. I was in the presence of my Illinois cousins at funerals and weddings. I would go years without seeing or conversing with them.

I also had a cousin who worked in the United States Attorney's Office in Fairview Heights, Illinois. She was highly respected there and had clout within the office. My deputy sheriff cousin was dragged into the United States Attorney's office and questioned.

Apparently there was evidence implicating him in a drug conspiracy with some other deputies. The Illinois state cop

investigator and the DEA agent working the case had
listened to telephone conversations between my deputy
sheriff cousin and some other St. Clair County, Illinois drug
users and dealers.

In attendance at the meeting was the DEA agent, the
Illinois state cop investigator, the United States Attorney,
and an Assistant United States Attorney.

When the deputy was asked about his involvement in a
drug conspiracy he replied, "My cousin, Tim Richards,
works for DEA in the St. Louis field office."

The good old boy system kicked in and the deputy was
allowed to escape federal prosecution if he agreed to resign
from the St. Clair County sheriff's department, and to never
go back into law enforcement.

He agreed, quit his job and got a job as a security guard
at a factory in another eastside town. I wasn't aware of these
happenings, and several months went by and my family and
I were invited to the state cop's house in Troy, Illinois for
some sort of family celebration.

I loaded my wife and two kids into my brand new Chevy
DEA undercover car, with the DEA radio in the glove box,
and headed for Troy.

It was in June and the weather was warm and sunny. The
state cop had a pool and everybody was drinking beer and
getting along. My deputy sheriff cousin was even in
attendance.

My United States Attorney office cousin told me the drug
conspiracy story while we were going through the food line.
She didn't pull any punches and I was shocked that my
deputy cousin could have been so stupid.

I came to the realization that I was in the home of the
enemy, with my wife and kids, in a DEA car. I felt stupid
and betrayed. Everyone acted like nothing had ever
happened. You can choose your friends but you can't

choose your relatives.

I reflected on the police department; the chief must have known about my relative and the drug accusation. He must have been advised by the lead dog that I was a suspect.

The chief knew me well; he was the first supervisor I had when I came from the police academy. He knew I would never deal in drugs, or steal, or lie. He sent me to DEA to quell any claims against me.

It is the irony of law enforcement, trial by fire. DEA takes whomever the police department sends them. They're going to whore them off, anyway. The chief knows this fact.

The chief was telling DEA, "Okay you suspect him, now you've got him. He's your problem now."

We left early. It had all come together for me, the lead dog's hatred of me, the beating from Paul Wayne King, the coldness of the agents and cops, the cocked Glock stuck inches from my face.

I was back at work on Monday morning. Group Supervisor Palance called me into his office. "Do not use your "G" car as a family vehicle. Understand?"

"Yes, sir," I replied.

I later found out that my desk phone was definitely bugged and there was a good possibility that my home telephone was bugged. Little Stevie Wonder advised me during a beer drinking fest.

"It's how business is conducted here," Little Stevie told me. "You walked through the DEA door with a jacket. You will be investigated for the rest of your life. You are in NADDIS; it will never go away.

I eventually got a chance to speak to my goofy deputy sheriff cousin. He did not admit guilt, but he did admit that he dropped my name during an interview.

He also advised me that a month or so after the United

States Attorney's office interview, his house was
burglarized, nothing was stolen.

He advised me that the DEA agent who was seeking
prosecution of him stopped him in traffic and described to
him the interior of his home, in detail.

Apparently the DEA creed, "dope dealer today, dope
dealer tomorrow," did not fit the cousin connection criteria.
I had gained a clearer perspective of what the federal justice
system was about. It was close to the state judicial system,
but more streamlined. Cops are taught to worship the federal
system. It is the Rolls Royce of all judicial systems in the
entire world. I knew that was another factoid.

Reszler and his partner, T. Anderson were traveling drug
agents. They had received a tip that the Mayor of the little
town of Sikeston, Missouri, approximately 150 miles south
of St. Louis, was involved in a drug conspiracy.

Palance gave them permission to set up an undercover
investigation in Sikeston. They lived in motels, hit the bars
at night and eventually gained the confidence of someone
inside of the operation.

They purchased cocaine from the mayor. This operation
took months, but they eventually served a federal search
warrant on the mayor's house and his office and found drug
records and drugs. The mayor was prosecuted federally and
went away on a federal vacation.

This was a feather in the cap of Palance. Anytime the
feds can take down a politician, especially a Democrat,
they're more than pleased. The agents are mostly
conservative Republicans, but the civilian hierarchy of DEA
is liberal.

The fed is riddled with liberal civilian employees. Most
are stationed at headquarters in Washington D.C. These
liberal Democrats have power in the organization and when
they call, or visit, the agents in the field offices are forced to

cater to them. There is a mutual hatred.

In reality, the Federal Civil Service Commission is as close to socialism as anything in any other socialist country. These employees of the government shuffle paper, make decisions about how money will be spent and collect asset forfeiture funds from all of the federal law enforcement agencies. It's a money pit of liberal Democrats.

Palance got all of the credit for Reszler's and Anderson's labor. DEA probably didn't even know they existed.

The two undercover cops now had an open door to investigate drug dealers in the "Bootheel" area of southern Missouri, an area of reclaimed land from the Missouri swamps, where the citizens talk like Alabama farmers, and where rice paddies and cotton fields dot the landscape.

In the minds of Department of Justice bureaucrats, this was no man's land and dope dealer heaven. Reszler and Anderson were antsy to get back down south to Sikeston. Little Stevie Wonder (S/A Steve Stoddard) was the agent in charge of the investigation down there. Group Supervisor Palance advised me to pack a bag for a week because I was going with them.

I didn't wish to go to Southern Missouri and live in a motel. Palance's words of warning for me, "Be one of the boys" reverberated in my psyche.

I had never been one of the boys. Even in the Marine Corps I was always my own man. I had always gotten away with my independent attitude because I was never really concerned about the outcome.

But I had grown accustomed to freedom, and power, and I suffered from the curse of pride. I felt I was a special cop because I had been treated like a special cop for years. I was spoiled.

I had to be one of the boys in order to sustain my special

lifestyle. I was embarrassed that I had let the system trick me into thinking I was a chosen guy. I was "pimped!"

I was given a different "G" car for the Sikeston trip, an older Mazda RX7. It had been seized by Palance when he was working in Kansas City, Missouri.

He told me the story about the drug deal. He led me down the path of worship for him as he described the great things he did as a regular special agent for the government. I thought I was going to puke.

In my life as a Marine, or Mafia spy, I wouldn't have given him two minutes of my time. Now I was forced to act like I was impressed with his federal government antics.

I had been around government agents. I had been around government bureaucrats. I didn't like or was I impressed with either group. It was all about him, dope dealers, and the pimping process. I acted like I was impressed.

The Mazda smelled like a case of beer had been spilled in it and never cleaned up. But it was quick and fun to drive. It had a radar detector, a nice stereo, and a five speed stick. We headed off for Southern Missouri in a convoy of "G" cars, the Mazda in the front because of the radar detector. Everybody was drinking beer.

We spoke to each other via DEA closed circuit radio, cracked jokes, passed beers to guys in other cars who had run out, while tooling down the road at eighty. To the TFD's in their twenties this was heaven. It was hell for me, but I had no choice if I wanted to keep my special status.

We made a stop to urinate at a service station. The restrooms were out of order, so we all urinated on the lot. The owner of the establishment came out to confront us, upset with his hands on his hips and in fight mode. We jumped into our "G" cars and threw rocks on him with our spinning tires.

It is what almost everyone in America desires, besides

enormous wealth. Deep down in our souls, we desire freedom and immunity from prosecution. On the DEA Task Force we had what very few people ever experience.

We arrived at the motel in Sikeston. It was a nice motel, clean and quiet. Little Stevie Wonder cranked up a barbecue grill and prepared hamburgers and his specialty, stuffed baked onions. He loved cooking those damned onions on the grill.

We ate in one of the rooms and it was getting dark. I'm not a late night guy. Reszler and T. Anderson started drinking again, this time hard stuff.

The stereo was blaring and Reszler was standing on the king sized bed as if it was a stage, shooting down shots of vodka. The TFD's were egging him on, shouting and encouraging him.

"Gargle it," T. Anderson shouted over the din. Reszler took a shot and attempted to gargle it before he swallowed it. He started weaving on the bed and wobbling.

"Come on, Conan, (T.'s nickname for Reszler) you can do it," T. Anderson shouted. Reszler swallowed it down.

"I need my prescription," Reszler exclaimed. He jumped from the bed and retrieved a package of multiple vitamins, crammed them in his mouth and chased them with a beer. "I can drink healthy all night, now," he exclaimed.

"I love you man," T. Anderson said with a laugh. "Let's go bar hopping." T. was a thick built German with a ruddy red forehead that resembled rusted steel. The head butt was his favorite punch. I don't remember ever seeing him totally sober.

I looked at my watch and it was nine p.m. I was hoping to go to my room and get some sleep, but the majority of undercover work is done in bars late at night. We all headed out in our "G" cars, following TFD's Reszler and Anderson.

They stopped at a roadside bar not far from the motel. We all parked and T. Anderson came over to the Mazda as I climbed out. "Come in after us and sit at the end of the bar away from us, okay?"

"Yeah," I replied. I didn't look like a narc or a swamp rat. I kept my same appearance, probably out of protest. I wasn't going to grow a beard and long hair, wear dirty clothing and not bathe just to be accepted by some dope degenerate.

In my mind, I was out of place. I was an investigator of Mafia types, and other organized criminal groups. I knew them from coast to coast, because at some point in their crime seeking lives, they passed through the little city of St. Louis, Missouri and were documented by me, or someone like me.

I had connections on the west coast. I could make a telephone call and find out any kind of information on anyone in the United States. Another reason I figured I was special. I was having trouble letting go of the sophistication of my past in law enforcement.

Now I was hanging out with a group of kid cops, drinking with them and living in motel rooms. I had a wife and kids at home waiting for me. I was not a happy guy.

Reszler and T walked into the dingy bar. I waited five minutes and then I walked in, took a quick look around and walked to the end of the bar and plopped onto a bar stool.

The bar wasn't crowded but there were approximately twenty five people sitting or standing at the bar and at tables.

I ordered a beer and nursed it. Reszler was at the jukebox, cramming in dollar bills and choosing tunes. There was a booth of four young women near the rear of the bar. He sauntered toward them as the juke started playing country swing.

An unattractive southern belle danced with Reszler. He was so drunk that he was stumbling all over the dance floor.

T. , his big forehead looking like a rusted steel demolition ball due to the booze, was watching and laughing at his best friend Reszler.

When T. Anderson arrived at the task force fresh from a city police district, and the mean the streets of St. Louis, he was told to go on a deal back down in the city. There were a couple of special agents along for the ride to supervise the raid.

T. approached the shambles of a house and banged on the door. A guy, the drug dealer, answered the door with a rifle in his hands at the ready. T. backed off and began firing at the rifle toting bad guy.

The bad guy wasn't hit by T's barrage of bullets and was taken into custody without any further incident, but the Special Agents were incensed at him for his gun action. They berated him and forced him to meet with the then group supervisor, referred to as "Edmund the Terrible"

Edmund the Terrible chastised T. as if he was an errant juvenile delinquent. Edmund the Terrible was eventually transferred, and Palance took his place.

The incident put a foul taste in T's mouth. He would never communicate with the special agents who caused the shooting episode to escalate into a DEA allegation against him. His attitude was soured toward the agency.

A group of guys were seriously eyeballing T and Reszler. They were typical "Bootheel" weed smokers and probably dope dealers. I observed T talking in low tones to one of them, the biggest and meanest looking of the group. I figured he was making contact, asking him where he could score some dope.

The guy was not friendly to T and I could tell that he was agitated. T shrugged and turned away from the big swamp rat. Reszler was still talking to the group of ladies at the booth, and they were giggling at him.

In almost every undercover drug bar campaign there comes a time when the undercover cop has to go to the restroom and the guy who is the toughest of all of the bar patrons follows him in to the restroom, corners him, and says, "Who the fuck are you guys, anyway?"

It happened on this fine night in beautiful downtown Sikeston, Missouri. Usually the undercover cop has a scripted line to toss back at the inbred doper, but TFD T. Anderson was never one to back down from a fight.

T. felt this doper desired to do him bodily harm, so he nailed him with his steel forehead at the base of his nose and sent the cotton farmer down on one knee.

T. allowed him to gain his footing, and the fight was on. There was banging and grunting and things being destroyed, the sound of fists hitting flesh and heads being banged on walls, but neither fighter called for help from a comrade.

The bartender picked up the telephone and dialed the sheriff's dispatcher. The sheriff deputy answering the call must have been in the parking lot because he walked in shortly after the telephone receiver was placed back in the carriage.

T. walked out of the restroom alone. The cotton farmer was out on the floor. All eyes were on T. and Reszler. I turned my bar stool around so I could watch and assist if needed.

The bartender, who was the owner, walked into the restroom and then walked out with the dazed and confused swamp rat. "I want him arrested," the bartender told the deputy as he pointed at T. Anderson.

"What charge?" the deputy asked.

"Destruction of property. He did $1000 damage to my restroom. He knocked down a wall and broke a sink and a mirror."

The deputy handcuffed T. behind his back and walked him out to his patrol car. Reszler and I followed them.

The sheriff took off with T. in the lock-up backseat. "What's the protocol for this?" I asked.

"We'll give it an hour or so and maybe he'll let T. go on a summons or something. If not, we'll go and bond him out," Reszler replied.

Will T. advise the sheriff that he's a DEA cop?" I asked.

"No, the sheriff's probably related to the dope dealers, this is like St. Louis, everybody's connected in some way. If they book him they'll be booking him on his phony drivers' license name."

We drove back to the motel and advised Little Stevie Wonder of the arrest. "Palance shouldn't be advised of this," Little Stevie said. "You guys go to the county jail and try to find out what's going on with the case. If you can, bond him out."

It was eleven p.m. when we got to the jail. T. was being released on a summons, with a court date for destruction of private property.

He walked out smiling, he was still drunk. We climbed into Reszler's Pontiac Trans Am "G" car and headed back to the motel.

The next morning we all met for breakfast. T. was on the pay phone seriously talking to someone. He hung up and joined the group.

"It's all taken care of," T. began. "We've got to take a grand to this lawyer friend of Reszler's and me, and he's going to give it to the bar owner, and then he will represent me in court on my court date and it will be expunged.

The conversation turned toward the braggadocio. T. and Reszler bragged about destroying a motel room In Poplar Bluff in a drunken steroid rage. "That cost us more than a thousand," Reszler said.

"I think we should cut our losses and head back to St. Louis," Little Stevie Wonder said. "There's nothing happening here. I think the populace is paranoid about any strangers since the mayor got taken off. I'll square it with Palance when we get back."

By the time we ate breakfast, packed, took saunas, showered, packed our ""G" cars, and waited for T. and Reszler to drive to Cape Girardeau to talk with their lawyer friend, and to give him cash, it was drawing toward dinner time.

We had dinner at the motel restaurant and started heading back to St. Louis in the government convoy. There wasn't any radio chatter, just four cars filled with hunters returning from the hunt, empty handed. Dope dealer today, dope dealer tomorrow.

As we drew closer to home, Detective Horowitz broke radio silence: "Let's go to a strip bar in Brooklyn, on the eastside" he suggested.

Little Stevie Wonder said, "No, I'm going home."

The other young undercover cops said, "Yeah, let's do it."

I had never been to a strip bar in the United States of America, and I didn't want to go now. The bars were situated in the East St. Louis, Illinois area. People who go there at night are gambling with fate. Many visitors never return alive. Many cops have been in late night gun fights in the neighborhoods surrounding the strip bars.

I had investigated the strip bars and massage parlors ownership when I worked organized crime. They were owned by regional gangsters, and some lawyers in Denver, Colorado. They were scummy and creepy, and the patrons were the same.

I was the only cop in the group who had responsibilities: wife, kids, car payment and a mortgage, and I didn't have any extra cash to waste in a strip bar. "I'm broke," I said over the air.

"Well take care of you," Reszler replied.

"Be one of the boys," Palance was saying in my ear. We arrived at the bar, locked our guns in our trunks and paid the entrance fee. Reszler paid mine.

The group of wayward young cops fought the crowd to get at the front of the stage. An unattractive stripper with the moniker "Pussy Lips" was tying and untying her pussy lips and the crowd was going nuts and throwing dollar bills at her.

I walked to the crowded bar and ordered a beer. I nursed it and watched the young cops make fools of themselves. I wondered if I was ever that stupid, and remembered my youth in the Marine Corps, going to the bars in Tijuana.

But there was a difference. I was seventeen years old. These guys are in their mid-twenties. By the time I was their age, I was a married guy, going to college and being a district cop.

These young cops had been coddled for their entire lives. Being a cop's son meant that you could speed, drive intoxicated, get into fights and intimidate your teachers at school.

Cops' sons don't get bullied, the coaches at the sport they aspire to give them special training. They drive nice cars, wear nice clothing, and are always well groomed. They expect to be treated differently, and they are.

It occurred to me that DEA was fashioned after the

Marine Corps. I observed some of the agents wearing Marine Corps cammies in the offices. Their hats even had the globe and anchor on them.

The Marine Corps was a brain washing machine. It changes people; the government owns your ass when you are a Marine. DEA owns my ass, now. I'm in the brain washing process. The young TFD's are already too far gone to save. I've got to be able to save myself.

Detective Horowitz sauntered up to the bar, ordered a beer and stood next to me. I had never worked with him but I knew of him. He was a likeable guy but he was a guy who pursued the bosses, at the police department and now at DEA.

He would send the bosses' wives flowers, expensive bouquets, and he would give them tickets to the Cardinals games, or the Blues Hockey games. It gave him leverage in the game of cop and crook. He was also treated specially.

Horrowitz had this thing for money. He worshipped it. He bragged that he could smell cash and if it was hidden he could sniff it out.

Some of the guys vouched for Horowitz and told stories about him finding cash hidden in dope dealers' homes. "Interesting," I muttered to myself.

But I wanted to keep Detective Horowitz at arm's length. I'd heard he was a thief, besides being a gigantic snitch and kiss ass. He wasn't my kind of a guy.

"I'm leaving," I told him. "See you guys in the office tomorrow."

I walked out and hoped I could make it to my trunk to retrieve my gun before I was approached by some neighborhood crooks intent on killing me. I drove home and went to bed with my head reeling.

IV.

LITTLE STEVIE WONDER'S LETTER

Our offices in fashionable Clayton were small and our desks were stacked against each other. Every telephone conversation was heard by the entire group.

Thanks to Little Stevie, I now understood the bugging of my desk area and desk phone, but the philosophy behind the bugging was offensive and humiliating.

DEA obviously had me classified as a stupid crook/drug dealer/cop. The amount of time needed to listen to my conversations equated to a non-productive waste of government money.

There were always stories filtering around the offices concerning agents, their friends and lovers, wives and girlfriends, and drug dealers who had been used as informants and became friendly with the agents.

Agent Steve Stoddard, AKA Little Stevie Wonder, told me the story about an agent assigned to the Intelligence Unit of the DEA field office in St. Louis.

Little Stevie and the agent flew to Miami to interview the ex-wife of a big time drug smuggler. They were to meet at a restaurant on Collins Avenue.

The two agents sat in the restaurant and watched the parking lot for the possible informant to arrive. The gal pulls up in a Mercedes convertible and climbs out. She was a Miami Beach beauty, white linen dress, blonde hair flowing in the ocean breeze, perfect body and tan.

The agent with Little Stevie was smitten immediately. The gal entered the restaurant, spied them and approached their table. The agent with Little Stevie could hardly talk, he so was mesmerized by her.

The meeting went well, but she advised them that she knew nothing about her husband's dope business (they all say that) and that she wished she could help them because they look and act like nice guys.

After about an hour the trio split. She jumped back into her Mercedes and the agent and Little Stevie headed for the airport.

But the agent with Little Stevie continued to contact the Miami gal. He called her daily; then started flying to Miami on long weekends to be with her. He was a married guy who told his wife that he was going to Miami on official DEA business.

The agent divorced his wife and convinced the Miami gal to come to St. Louis to live with him; she did. They eventually got married. DEA transferred the guy to Intelligence.

I wondered if DEA also wasted time and money listening to the conversations of him and his wife. They may have even had their home bugged. I often wondered if my home was bugged.

My point was, and is, DEA overreacted to some cop rumor about me and my stupid crooked cop cousin, a guy I hardly ever saw and barely even knew. The agent married a big time drug smugglers wife. Field office agents didn't refer to him as a dope dealer and asshole while he walked around the offices. He was their drinking buddy at The Club.

The guys started filtering in. Reszler was singing "Deck the halls with balls of Hootie Owls" still drunk from the night before. It wasn't the Christmas season, it was late fall with the dreary days of winter looming, but every day was Christmas for the young TFD's.

He glanced at me, red faced and bloated, "Hootie Owls

are gonna get me Phoenix," he mumbled. "You guys will still be here where the sun never shines."

I thought about what he said and I agreed with him, the sun hardly ever shines in good old St. Louis in the winter. But St. Louis is moderate, great fall weather and spring isn't bad. Arizona is stifling in the summer without any change of the seasons.

I sat and observed as they wandered in: Special Agent Mike Schweig, an agent who was not a self-starter and relied completely on the stats of the TFD's, dragged in, hung over to the max. His desk was across the office from me. The office folk watched him as he went through his ritual, smoking and gagging.

Schweig was just along for the DEA ride to retirement. He was drunk most of the time and another bad influence on the young cops. His mission was to keep the TFD's intoxicated and frazzled so they would work tirelessly for the group supervisor (Palance's) promotion.

He wore clothing that had come from garage sales, including old stinking shoes. On this morning he was wearing a plaid wool sport coat that I wouldn't have allowed my dog (Rebel) to lie on, jeans and an off color collared shirt. His brown shoes were turned up at the toe due to wear.

He sat, then stood and walked to The Club, just seconds away, and returned with a large black coffee. He fired up a Marlboro, smoked, drank coffee and gagged, as if he was going to vomit, but he never did.

After a long and deep draw and a gurgle of coffee, he started the gagging process, mouth wide open head down, veins straining, perspiration forming on his brow, but he never actually puked.

TFD Larry Wheeler, a St. Louis County cop, strolled in. He was the token black cop assigned to the task force. The city didn't have any black cops assigned to the task force. The black city cops with influence didn't wish to be heroic at the federal level. They desired promotion and they got it. Wheeler was a good guy, but every black guy associate is your friend when he is in the minority. I considered Larry a friend. But I had been friends with black guys in the Marine Corps. We all lived in the same barracks, slept on the same hard ground and ate crummy food out of cans in the jungle.

During drinking bouts at the enlisted man's club I had a black guy advise me to never trust a black man. "We aren't your friend," he continued. "We as a group hate you as a group of whites. Don't trust a black man."

His comments raised my observations about race in the Marine Corps. I noted that if a white guy was drinking with one black guy everything was all right. If there were two black guys and one white guy, there was tension. If there were three black guys and one white guy, the white guy was probably going to get sucker punched from behind and his so called black friend would join in on the beating of him.

But I still trusted and liked Larry Wheeler. I actually trusted him more than most of my white counterparts. I never felt safe when the white KKK cops were behind me with their big guns drawn while I sledge hammered a druggies door.

I imagined what it must feel like to have a high velocity bullet tear through your body. Not by a drug dealer; by a crazed drunk cop.

Larry's wife was an R/N and he had money to burn. He drove nice cars, lived in a nice house and didn't have the financial burdens most cops have. He was a good cop, which is why he was brought to the Task Force.

Wheeler loved his guns and he loved the fact that when detached to DEA he could stick them in suspect's faces at will. It's what DEA is noted for: pistol paralyzing and beating suspects. The bigger and more impressive the gun, the more intimidating it is to the person having it stuck in their face.

But when Wheeler had the chance to stick his big gun in a white man's face he morphed into a crazed animal. His face would distort and his eyes would almost close as he made guttural sounds and stared at his adversary. He was nicknamed "Mad Dog".

Wheeler (Mad Dog) had phobias; he feared elevators, the dark, snakes, spiders, bodies of water, forests and large white people. If he walked into a dark room, he would automatically pull his large Glock semi-automatic pistol. As soon as the door closed on an elevator, he would start breathing hard, sweat and have his hand on his Glock. He was always the first person out, even if he was at the back of the elevator car.

Palance assigned Mad Dog Larry Wheeler and me to follow up on another case initiated by St. Louis Intelligence. A goofy chiropractor was supplementing his income by dealing in cocaine. He would do the usual, drive to Miami, buy kilos and bring them back to St. Louis.

This guy was as stupid as most dope dealers; he spoke on the telephone. He told his sons that he hid the kilos under his porch, right on a busy street (1310 McCausland near I-64.)

City Intelligence ate him up, seized his dope, his money and his assets. It was a big laugh around cop circles on how stupid this guy was.

One of the chiropractor's sons lived in a house in the 4300 block of West Pine in the Central West End. It was alleged that there was cocaine hidden in the house. Mad Dog and I went to the house and waited for the son to arrive.

The scenario was for us to observe him, after surveillance, and to then advise Group Supervisor Palance.

The young guy showed up, parked his car on the street and proceeded to his front porch. Before I could get on the air and advise Palance, Mad Dog jumped out of the car and ran toward the guy with his big automatic at arms-length.

It was broad daylight and we were standing in the middle of West Pine, a neat tree-lined street with rehabbed turn of the century homes; it was where the up and coming lived. It was close to restaurants, bars and shopping.

But it was also close to the black ghetto, just four or five blocks away. It's the way it is in St. Louis, affluent neighborhoods surrounded by poor blacks. It was not uncommon for the poor blacks to wander into the better neighborhoods and rob and kill pedestrians.

The chiropractor's kid was certain he was going to be killed by Mad Dog. Mad Dog had his insane facial expression working for him and he was enjoying the moment.

"Please don't kill me," the chiropractor's kid pleaded. Mad Dog didn't identify himself as a cop or DEA agent, he just stood in the street and terrorized this little white guy.

"We're DEA," I advised the little guy. "We're doing a search warrant on your house, let's go inside and wait for the warrant to get here."

The three of us walked into the house and Mad Dog started searching while I guarded the little white guy. Mad Dog was upstairs and we could hear him pulling drawers out, tossing the mattress on the floor and emptying the closet.

"Sir," the little guy said to me. "Can I tell you something?"

"Yes," I replied.

"I have a pet python and he's escaped from his cage. He might be hiding in my bedroom. I don't want that cop to shoot him. He usually hides behind the dresser. Can I go upstairs and put him back in his cage?"

"Hey, Mad Dog," I yelled up to him. "There's a pet snake up there in that room. Don't shoot it. The guy down here says it's harmless."

"Snake?...... Snake!" Mad Dog screamed as he accidentally came across the creature. "There's a big fucking snake up here. I'm going to kill it."

"Sir, can I go up there and get my snake?" the little fellow asked.

"Don't shoot it, Mad Dog," I yelled to him, "We're coming up to get it."

"You better come up here fast," Mad Dog replied. "I'm gonna kill this motherfucker."

We ran upstairs and the kid corralled his python and placed it back in its cage. Mad Dog was unnerved. "Stupid fucking white people," he mumbled. "What the fuck kind of motherfucker would have a snake as a pet?"

TFD Jimmy Bob Vollmar, country and confident, actually the only cop on the Task Force who was a bona-fide hero, more than once. Palance loved him, but Jimmy was a likeable guy, always vocal and cracking jokes. Jimmy was usually accompanied by Ringer who was a St. Louis County cop, like Jimmy.

Palance liked these guys because they were County instead of city cops. County cops helped their comrades while they were in the Task Force, which meant they brought them cases. City cops did not support their cop friends. Palance liked the stats from the County cops.

For some strange reason, the county cops didn't feel as if they were in competition with each other for promotion. The city cops were always seeking recognition, searching for a pat on the head from the chief's office which hardly ever came. In the city it was "dog eat dog."

The group was sitting in the office doing reports and gossiping. Little Stevie Wonder was in attendance, talking loudly on the phone and acting important. I could sense an emittance of joy or happiness from Little Stevie. I dismissed it and started going over a report that I was doing.

Palance walked in and headed for his office situated at the front of the main office. He was in a cloudy mood, all of the agents and TFD's noticed it.

We were all trained attack dogs. Palance was our handler. If there was something amiss with him we detected it. The unit secretary, Liz Bates, was the focal point of the office. She knew everything that went on in the St. Louis Field Office.

All eyes were on her; she shrugged and went back to work. Her desk phone rang and she answered it. We watched. "Yes, sir, Steve," she replied, stood and walked into Palance's office. The group moved toward the office door and eavesdropped on their conversation.

"It had to be a TFD," Palance said to Liz. "A special agent would not do such a thing. Have you heard anything?"

"No, sir, this is the first I've heard of it."

"Well," Palance paused and thought for a couple of seconds, "Then if it was a special agent, it was Little Stevie Wonder. I'm going to address the group."

We all scrambled back to our desks and buried our heads in our paper work. Palance and Liz came to the front of the office. All eyes were on him.

Palance was carrying a type-written letter, he held it up for us to see, and began. I studied him as he stood before us; his light brown mullet was close to his head on the sides, but brushy and long in the back. He had a belly from living the good life of a DEA supervisor, plenty of cold beer with the boys and always a good meal.

He dressed the part, kind of like a television actor would dress: Polo shirt, untucked, Levis and Sperry Top Sider deck shoes. He sported a DEA seized Rolex and a large carat diamond ring.

Palance drove a 300 Z Nissan sports car, seized from a not smart, or lucky, drug dealer. It was bright red and it fit his personality. He lived a playboy lifestyle. He had money to burn, a mistress and a family, he had power, he was idolized by the young TFD's and he still had youth.

Palance was a successful example of the federal system at work. He was a government servant and he ate high off of the hog at the government trough. Another example of socialism at its finest.

It was always show time for Palance; he was a true thespian, always prepared and anxious to give a performance. His script was always memorized and he was "the star."

I figured he had had a rough night, trying to service two women and keeping them satisfied was a super human feat, something I would never consider, but I figured that Palances' ego and Id convinced him that he was a special human and he should share his greatness with the masses.

"Someone has written a letter to my wife detailing to her my relationship with my girlfriend at the United States Attorney's office." He paused and watched our eyes, seeking that ever telling look of guilt. He stopped and stared at Little Stevie.

Stevie did the unthinkable, he moved his stare downward. And to add insult to injury, he knew that he had made an incriminating move and instantly jerked his head upright and stared back at Palance.

Every special agent and most investigators have training in physiognomy, body movements and interrogation tactics.

Certain actions emit guilty responses. Little Stevie knew he
had been had.

Palance didn't accuse Little Stevie, but he knew who the
culprit was. It was time for Palance to use this incident to his
advantage. Palance's interest was stats for his next
promotion. It was time for a self-serving-speech, one that
would impress the TFD's and make them respect him even
more.

"I want all of you guys to know that I go out on a limb
for you every day of your lives. I'm the guy who protects
you from the Special Agent in Charge. I praise you guys to
the United States Attorney. I give you carte blanche to lock
up dope dealers. That is what we are here to do. That is our
mission in life. Dope dealers are filth, they lie after we arrest
them. They pee on themselves; they would come in on their
mothers for leniency. They tell their lawyers that we stole
from them and that there are discrepancies in the cash we
take from them. I stop those doubts before they are allowed
to fester. Do you guys understand what I'm saying?"

"Yeah, Steve," the group roared.

"When you guys have to fight with some piece of shit
dope dealer and use excessive force, I go to bat for you with
the SAC and the United States Attorney's Office. Am I
right?"

"Yeah," we loudly replied.

"I'm not certain who wrote this scathing and descriptive
letter to my wife, but I will find out and I will kick his ass.
I'm a DEA agent and an investigator. I just hope it isn't a
TFD. It would break my heart if I thought one of my TFD's
did this to me. Now, let's go out and do what God put us on
this green earth to do.....lock up dope dealers."

The TFD's were pumped after that production. I felt that
it couldn't have been scripted any better. It was an academy
award performance.

The dope deals were almost nightly. We all had to be in the office bright and early on every work day, write reports, take frequent breaks at the club (30 seconds away) and wait for the telephone to ring for an informant or cop to give the task force a deal for the evening.

TFD T. Anderson drove an old nondescript Ford, a junker and this car was used as the Kel car. Kel was the manufacturer of the personal listening devices placed on undercover agents, cop and non-cop.

The listening unit was in a briefcase and sat next to the driver of the Kel Car on the car seat. T. was good at running the machine and taping the conversations.

Detective Chris Wegman, an undercover St. Louis County narcotics detective was excellent in getting young dope dealers to trust him.

Wegman respected TFD Ringer. Ringer knew what he had going for himself: influential friends and relatives. Wegman would work a young dealer, gain his confidence, and then introduce him to Ringer.

It wasn't an unusual occurrence, young men and women who had the means would drive to south Florida and purchase kilos of cocaine, break them up and sell them as grams in local bars and dance clubs.

A kilo of cocaine in Miami would cost the young entrepreneur $10,000 cash. The young dope dealer would cut it at least twice, making it two kilos or more and then package it into grams. There are 1000 grams in a kilo. A gram could and would be sold for $100 in some bars and night spots.

These young kids, most from wealthy families, were making a killing in the dope business selling mostly to people they knew from childhood.

But greed sets in. They desire to be bigger dope dealers

and they get careless. They are eventually introduced to a young looking DEA cop who woos them into the dream of being a millionaire, just like their parents. Ringer had the ability to mesmerize the little stoned and wealthy drug dealers.

A deal was set up for this night in Maryland Heights, Missouri. The target was a little rich kid whose dad was a wealthy dentist. I jumped in the car with T. Anderson. We had some cold beer in a cooler, it was dark and cold outside, and we set up in a gas station parking lot to listen and record the hand to hand drug deal and buy bust of the dentist's kid. As the conversation went on, I realized this kid's dad was my dentist.

The Kel car had a good stereo and T. and I listened to hard rock on KSHE 95, "The Pride of St. Louis" sang and laughed and drank beer in the darkness.

With the extra pay on my pay stub every two weeks, my bills were paid at home and I had grown to enjoy my experience at DEA.

I was given a nick name, "The Senator." I figured somebody dreamed it up because I was older and clean cut, but I was beginning to feel like I was accepted. I knew that acceptance meant that I was becoming one of the boys. I was aware that being one of the boys was a dangerous thing.

There was so much freedom and excitement that I wondered if I could ever survive away from it. Palance and the United States Attorney's Office protected us from being hassled as long as we as a group made deals that were prosecutable and winnable in federal court.

We commanded respect as a unit. The local defense attorneys didn't even complain about our tactics. When the DEA Task Force in St. Louis, Missouri had a case on someone, their attorneys recommended they plead guilty and beg for mercy from the God-like federal judges.

Ringer hopped into the dentist's kid's car and they were talking about life in general. The little doper complained to Ringer about his family life and his sister. He hated his dad and mom and he hated his brother and sister.

Ringer had convinced this little guy that he was his friend and confidant and that he could trust him with anything. The deal was consummated; Ringer purchased a pound of cocaine from the fellow, and said, "It's as good as gold." That meant it was time for Ringer to exit the doper's car, and for the TFD's to move in and take the dealer off.

It worked as planned. The little shocked and confused druggie was sitting in the back of Reszler's "G" car wondering where he had gone wrong.

It was business as usual: the kid was slapped, shaken and forced to return to reality. "You're going to federal prison for ten years," Ringer assured him. "Where's the rest of your stash?"

"I've got some at my house in my room," the little fellow bellowed. "I'll do anything, I'll do my source down in Miami, I'll do my brother, too, I'll do anything to keep from going to prison."

Somebody stuck a "consent to search" form in his face. "We need you to sign this," Ringer advised.

"I'll sign it, and I'll show you where the dope is in my room," the little fellow cried.

Ringer took the handcuffs off of him and he signed the form. He was re-cuffed and we as a group were on our way to Creve Coeur, a wealthy West St. Louis County suburb, to the rich dentist's house to search for dope.

Most of us were intoxicated by then. We had met in the Club before the deal and drank numerous beers, just for effect. Every car had a cooler of beer. Reszler (Conan) was just starting to wobble but he wasn't as bad as he usually was.

We were guided to the dentist's house by the dope kid. It was fashionable and expansive. It was a modern ranch with a huge roof and circular driveway, in-ground pool and humongous front yard.

We could have parked in the circular driveway, or on the street, but for some odd reason we all parked on the manicured lawn. We as a group wanted to show our disrespect for the dentist and his kind. We all grew to hate the rich dope kids and their imaginable life problems.

They were pressured at a young age to be wealthy, no matter what the cost. There are limited avenues to wealth in America: hard work in a profession, become a person who labors, saves and plans, or become a crook. The slow ones choose crime.

We marched into the house and were confronted by the kid's mother. She was in shock at our presence and asked what we wanted as she observed her handcuffed kid.

"We're with DEA," Little Stevie Wonder advised her. "We have a "consent to search" for your house, signed by your son. He is under arrest for conspiracy to distribute cocaine."

The mother started to fall then braced herself and leaned against the wall. The little doper led the TFD's to his room.

Ringer and Little Stevie Wonder went into the room and the kid showed them where the rest of a kilo was hidden. It was seized.

The other TFD's, including me, started searching the rest of the house. We didn't find any dope. The dentist entered the house. He asked us who we were and what we were doing in his house.

The dentist, apparently intoxicated, stared at me through foggy lenses and said, "What the hell are you doing here?". I was embarrassed for him, and for me. "We took off your son for dealing cocaine," I advised him. "He confessed to us that he had more dope hidden in his room. We seized it after your son signed a "consent to search" form."

"Holy fuck," he muttered. He had just gotten out of jail himself for murdering a friend over a diamond debt. He got into a fight with his friend and stolen diamond conspirator, Vernon Hoerr, on a parking lot at a restaurant (Bristol) in West County. He won the fight, his friend died.

The dentist had a good lawyer, and gobs of cash. He pled guilty to a lesser charge and since it was a fight, not a real murder, he was sentenced to spend a year of weekends in the St. Louis County Jail.

I felt sorry for my dentist/friend. He had come up in a blue collar family and had struggled to live the good life and for his children to be successful. His escape from the pressures of dentistry was his yacht (The Tooth Ferry) moored in Miami. I wondered if I would ever use him as a dentist again. But I did and nothing was ever said about that fateful night.

I needed to get my feet wet in the undercover drug business. My investigative resume mostly dealt with interviewing potential witnesses or informants, or initiating surveillance on organized criminals.

Each group of cops and agents had the obligation to have the "Duty" approximately once a month. I eagerly volunteered for the duty. It meant you could come in late, and stay until 2300 hours answering the telephone.

Going home at 2300 hours was an early night on the Task Force. Usually it was 0300 before we got home and in bed, then it was back at the office at 0900, grab a cup of coffee and head for the county jail to pick up the prisoner from the night before. After that it was a morning spent at the United States Attorney's office preparing for the arraignment of the prisoner.

When the telephone rings at DEA, especially late at night, the conversations are all interesting. The callers usually start out coy and guarded. They are looking for a friendly agent to help them with their obsession....snitch on dope dealers."

Many times there is a person in their family who is involved with other drug conspirators and they wish to free their loved one from the doper association. I would sit and listen to their tales of woe and eventually their story would unfold.

On this particular evening the lady was friendly and sounded cute. She eventually advised me that she knew of someone who had been sending large amounts of cocaine through FedEx to an address in St. Louis.

She refused to give me names, but she did give me the address. The next day I alerted FedEx to the possible cocaine conspiracy and I gave them the address.

A week passed and I had forgotten about the conversation. FedEx contacted me at the office and asked me about the alert. I quickly remembered the incident. They had a package and they had opened it. It contained a kilo of white powder.

I headed for the FedEx office near the airport; accompanied by Reszler, T. Anderson, Mad Dog and Jim Bob Vollmar.

We did a field test on the powder and it tested positive for cocaine. We seized it, and I contacted the United States Attorney's office.

I was advised by an Assistant United States Attorney that since FedEx opened the package and not anyone in law enforcement, there was no problem with probable cause, and the office would issue a search warrant for the premises.

It was my time to shine. It was my chance to show the youngsters that the "old man" could still work undercover. I was given a FedEx "T" shirt and cap and the keys to a Fed Ex van.

I drove to the exclusive condo complex in West St. Louis County and parked in front of the town house condominium. Reszler, Mad Dog, Jim Bob and T. Anderson were already there conducting surveillance from a half block away.

We had exchanged the cocaine with white talcum powder and baking soda, then rewrapped the package as it was first discovered by FedEx employees.

I rang the doorbell and an unattractive young woman with huge breasts answered the door. "Package, ma'am," I said to her with a smile. She snatched the package from my hand and started to close the door.

"First class delivery, ma'am," I said to her, "You need to sign for it." I handed her the clip board with some documents at her and she signed on the appropriate line. I walked back to the delivery van and drove toward Reszler and T. Anderson.

We talked van door to car door....."Let's give her five minutes to get into the package," I said to them. It helps in the prosecution of the offender actually opens the package. Five minutes passed and we drove back to the condo with a federal search warrant.

Reszler had a sledge, which was mostly my job in the unit. I was deemed the sledge man by Palance. The sledge man hits the door right below the lock and backs away while the rest of the whacked out drug warriors charge inside with their automatics at arm's length shouting, "DEA, get down on the floor, federal search warrant."

A few months earlier, after a night of drinking during dope deals, Palance accompanied the crew on a search warrant in the French Quarter (Soulard) of St. Louis.

It was an investigative warrant, which meant it was illegal but sanctioned by a federal magistrate. An informant, known only to Reszler, advised that drugs were being stored in the house. We pulled up to the turn of the century rehabbed home and walked up the steps to the front door while some of the other guys went to the back. I was preparing to hit the door with the sledge.

Palance hesitated and touched my arm; it was a beautiful door, stained glass and hard oak and I didn't want to hit it. "Why don't we just ring the bell?" I asked Palance.

"If we do, it will give the dope dealer time to flush the product or to ready himself against us. Go ahead and hit it, but make sure you hit it below the lock, okay?"

Palance knew I was intoxicated, we all were. I was seeing two doors, but I reared back and swung at the lock with the sledge. I didn't hit below the lock, the sledge hit the stained glass and went through it. The sledge left my hands and sailed inside of the house.

"Why did you do that?" Palance calmly asked me.

"It was unpreventable and inevitable," I calmly replied.

"DEA search warrant," Palance shouted. There was no response. "Jim Bob," Palance shouted.

"Yes, sir, boss," Jim Bob said as he came running to the porch.

"Find an open window and climb in and unlock the door,"Palance ordered.

"Yes, sir," Jim Bob replied. After approximately five minutes Brown unlocked the door from the inside. I retrieved the sledge from the living room floor and we searched for drugs; there were none. We left before the owner of the home returned.

The owner of the house with the expensive art glass door did not complain, nor did he contact the SAC, or the AUSA, or the federal magistrate. It was as if the incident never occurred.

In retrospect, I deducted that the door was a cheap price to pay when the crocks come calling. He was a lucky and smart dope dealer.

The condo complex where the large breasted, unattractive woman took possession of the talcum powder dope was exclusive and I didn't wish to destroy another door if I didn't have to, "Let's try a soft entry," I said. I again rang the doorbell and after a minute the same lady who signed for the Fed-Ex dope delivery came to the door and opened it.

We forced our way inside, "DEA, we have a federal search warrant for your residence," I advised her. Her face was covered with the talcum powder baking soda mixture. She had been snorting it.

The package was on a coffee table, opened and partially used. She was in shock and I could see that she was going to go into hysterics if we didn't calm her down quickly.

"Sit down," I ordered her. "We are not going to harm you, but you are under arrest for conspiracy to distribute cocaine. Just sit and relax for now."

"That's the worst coke I've ever snorted," she replied, wiping her nose and face. I didn't respond to her comment. I took stock of her; early twenty's, dumpy, lots of makeup, expensive clothing, large diamond wedding ring, in need of a haircut and a shower.

Mad Dog was waiting for his chance to terrorize and interrogate her. He approached her while she sat on the couch and watched us search her domicile.

"Whose coke is this?" Mad Dog asked her.

"My husband's," she calmly replied.

"Where is your husband?" Mad Dog asked.

"He's at work; he sells insurance for AAA Insurance Company on I-64 in West County. He's at his office at this time," she replied.

Reszler, Jim Bob and T. Anderson conveyed the doper lady to our offices and processed her. Mad Dog and I headed for the fashionable AAA offices in West County.

We walked in, flashed our credentials to the receptionist and ordered her to tell us where the suspect, Dan, had his office. She hesitated and Mad Dog gave her his crazy look; she quickly advised us gave us directions and pointed her finger for us.

We walked to Dan's desk, identified ourselves, handcuffed him and dragged him out of his office. A few co-workers objected at our arrest of Dan. "You buy "coke" from him?" Mad Dog asked them. "We can take you, too."

The interrogation of Dan at our offices went easily. He told us the name of his source in San Antonio, Texas and he even made a taped telephone call to him and ordered up another kilo of cocaine.

I took note of Dan's descriptive rhetoric as we interrogated him. "He's my dear friend," Dan said of his relationship with the suspect in Texas. "We've been friends for years, he would do anything for me; he's the best friend I have."

I had heard these statements before. It seemed that every time we compel a drug suspect to make a taped telephone call to another suspect, they utter the same phrases, but when we explain to them that they can be the cooperating suspect in the conspiracy and only go to jail for half the amount of time of the other conspirators, they make the call. There is no honor among thieves.

The guy in San Antonio sent another kilo. The case was moving along, there was a coconspirator in California. The cocaine was coming through Mexico into Southern California, then to San Antonio, and then to St. Louis.

DEA San Antonio took the suspect off in their town. He was a businessman, not wealthy, but successful. He owned a swimming pool installation company. Business was good for him. He desired more from life.

Palance thought it would be a good idea for me to travel to San Antonio to interview the fellow. The DEA guys in San Antonio were having communication problems with him. I flew out, got a nice room in a classy hotel in San Antonio and made my way to the DEA Field Office.

The office was small, way smaller than the office in St. Louis. An agent was friendly to me, made a "G" car available to me and conveyed me to the drug suspect's swimming pool business. He was out on bond, awaiting arraignment on the charge.

We walked into his business and he ushered us into his office. He had photos of his forty foot cruiser, him and Arnold Palmer on a golf course, and photos of his young wife adorning the office walls.

The guy was shifty, like a car salesman and I could see that he had been prepped by Dan in St. Louis as to what kind of guy I was. They had profiled me. I had been kind to Dan and his wife; it is a weakness in the dope business.

I could tell the guy didn't wish to speak in front of the DEA agent from San Antonio, but he did confide in me that after he was arrested by San Antonio DEA, his name and the arrest was in the San Antonio newspapers.

DEA arrests are never released to the newspapers.

DEA arrests are kept secret so that the agent investigating the case can use the suspects against other conspirators. At this time this guy in San Antonio was of no use to anybody in law enforcement. I wondered why

Palance had sent me down to San Antonio.

The San Antonio DEA Agent left the office to make a phone call and the suspect and I were alone. "Dan told me you were honest," he began. "Someone in San Antonio has been blackmailing me. I receive phone calls ordering me to show up at a particular place with $5,000, or my dope business is going to be stopped."

I soaked in the information. This was conspiracy information and I had no defense against it. I was intrigued.

"The guy who calls me uses my nickname. It's "Buckle". I used to wear big belt buckles as a kid, and I got the nickname. Only my closest friends and relatives know about my nickname."

"So this guy uses your nickname and you deliver five grand to him. Who is the guy?" I asked.

"I never delivered the cash," the guy says. "I don't know who it is, but my friend in St. Louis gets taken off, then I get taken off and someone alerted the press about my arrest. So there is no way for me to help myself. I'm a dead fish," he said with remorse.

The DEA agent reentered the room. "I'm ready to go," I advised him. We headed back to the San Antonio Field Office. I hung out there for a while, with nothing to do. The agents were friendly to me and I had a car, so I decided to take a drive to Corpus Christi and have dinner.

I had my escape plan in place, so I decided to play my hole card before I left for Corpus Christi. "Could someone get my San Antonio suspect up on NADDIS. (narcotics and dangerous drugs information system) so I could check something out?" I asked.

A Hispanic agent quickly gained entry to the system. The guy's drug resume was before me. Nickname, "Buckle" glared at me.

"Thanks," I said, "I'm going to take a ride, I'll drop your

car off tomorrow morning and I'll be heading back to St. Louis," I advised.

I had a nice drive around Texas, slept with one eye open in my hotel room, dropped the DEA car off at the field office, grabbed a taxi, and headed for the airport. I was relieved when the plane touched down in St. Louis.

I advised Palance about my findings there, he didn't act surprised, we didn't discuss probabilities.

Dan and his wife were used by us for some small local deals. The case eventually went away. The newspaper leak in San Antonio killed the case. The United States Attorney's office in St. Louis thought the San Antonio United States Attorney should handle the case.

Dan and his wife relocated back to San Antonio. The swimming pool executive relocated to south Florida. The suspect in Southern California was identified but never arrested; lucky dope dealers who got bitten by the crocks but kept on fighting and crossed the stream.

A professional informant (a person who makes his living from snitching) entered the DEA offices and eventually was directed to the Task Force. If the information is iffy, or if the snitch is unknown, they're passed through the two special agent groups and then dumped on the Task Force.

He was now Special Agent Mike Braun's informant, the new agent from group two, the group that was convinced I was a dope dealer.

Braun was interviewing him and I was eavesdropping. Braun picked up on my interest. The snitch was telling him about a marijuana growing operation on a farm in Grafton, Illinois.

Braun relegated the case to me. The snitch gravitated to my desk and I finished the interview. I knew the area; it was

almost home to me since I grew up in Alton, just about
fifteen miles away.

Grafton sits on the north bank of the Illinois River just
before the Illinois empties into the Mississippi River. It is
about twenty miles north of the City of St. Louis and is part
of the great confluence of the Missouri, Mississippi and
Illinois Rivers. St. Louis is famous for the confluence of the
waters.

The snitch described the growing operation of the guy
who lives on a farm near Pere Marquette State Park and
grows weed there.

It was fall and I needed to get out of the office, so I
volunteered to go on surveillance with the snitch. I felt odd
volunteering, it's something I learned not to do while I was
in the Marine Corps, but I did it anyway.

I hadn't been to Grafton in a while and I was looking
forward to seeing it again. The snitch and I climbed into my
little Chrysler LeBaron Turbo, a seized car that was sporty
and ran good. I liked it!

The little Turbo wound tight in every gear, was
maneuverable and didn't look like any type of government
vehicle.

We headed toward Grafton via the Great River Road, the
white bluffs on our right and the Mississippi River running
low and slow on our left. I felt like a kid who had skipped
school. The snitch wasn't a bad guy, he had the southern
Illinois twang just like guys I had grown up with, and like
them, I knew he was ruthless. I knew that whatever I said to
him would be repeated so I kept our conversation on
business.

We entered Grafton and drove through it looking for a
road leading upward toward the high country. The snitch
was directing me and he advised me to turn right and slowly
go by the dope growers house.

The snitch panicked as we got to the farm house on our left, "Oh, no, the grower is sitting on his front porch. He sees us, he's going to kill us, he carries a 357 magnum," the snitch screams as he dives to the floor of the little car.

"I'll just keep on going," I calmly said.

"You can't," the snitch screams, "This road dead ends, you'll have to turn around and go back by his house. He's going to kill us, I know it, he thinks we're here to steal his weed," the snitch cried out in despair.

I turned the "G" car around and headed back by the grower's house. By then he was running away from the porch and toward the back of the farm house. I took the road back to the hard top highway and looked in my rearview mirror. The grower (later identified as Dana Polchowski, a Chicago native) was behind the "G" car in a Turbo Thunderbird and he's motioning for me to pull over.

I cranked the "G" car to the right and floored it. I was accelerating well but the Thunderbird was right on my bumper. If I stopped suddenly he would climb over the little "G" car.

I reached into the glove box and got the mic from the DEA radio. I tried to contact the DEA Field office in Clayton but the radio would not reach. Beautiful, safe and clean Clayton seemed like a million miles away at this point.

The Thunderbird came around the "G" car at about 100 MPH, drove about 100 yards ahead of us, then the weed grower stopped the car cross ways in the highway in an attempt to block the road.

I saw an opening and steered the "G" car through his block. The grower was standing outside of his car. I got a good look at him. He was dangerous looking, bib overalls, muscular, shaved head and low to the ground.

I floored the Turbo LeBaron again and we were doing

130 toward Hardin, Illinois, another Illinois River Town. I managed to give the finger to the grower as we needled our way past him. I was certain he would follow us but I didn't see him in the rearview mirror.

We made our way to Hardin and I headed for the States Attorney's office. My friend, Charles Burch was the States Attorney, and I hadn't seen him in a while. I needed to use his telephone to call Braun.

Charlie wasn't in so I sat at his desk and talked to Braun on Charlie's phone. "You think he chased you guys because he thought you were there to steal his dope?" Braun asked.

"Yep!" I replied.

"Okay, I'll call you right back," Braun said.

The snitch sat in the "G" car waiting for me. He refused to enter the States Attorney's office. I glanced outside occasionally to see if the weed grower had tracked us down and was preparing to kill the little snitch.

States Attorney Charles Burch entered the office as I was sitting at his desk. "What's up?" he asked. He had not heard the news that I was now detached to DEA. He thought I was still spying on gangsters.

I told Charlie about the grower in Grafton and how we eluded him on the highway. The phone rang and it was Braun. He advised me to contact the DEA pilot and make arrangements to fly to the farm in Grafton.

I called the number, spoke to the pilot and we made arrangements to meet at Civic Memorial Airport in Bethalto, Illinois. The snitch and I drove away from Hardin, Illinois. I drove him home, safe and sound, and headed for the airport.

The pilot had instructed me to contact him via radio when I got to the airport. I felt weird being friendly with the pilot, he was in group two, and everyone there was convinced I was a drug dealing cop, even Braun.

I contacted the pilot. We had a brief conversation and I

advised him of my location. The engine of the DEA surveillance airplane droned in the background as we spoke. At the termination of our radio conversation, his mic stuck open and he ended our conversation with "fucking dope dealer."

The DEA plane landed and coasted up to the terminal. I jumped in the back and we took off. The pilot had a road map and he handed it back to me as he piloted the airplane. It was a single engine high wing airplane, and it was loud.

In order to communicate with the pilot I had to use a head set and trigger it when I spoke. I pointed out the location of the farm on the Illinois River. We were flying over it in fifteen minutes.

I had a thirty five millimeter Canon camera and I took a succession of photos as we crisscrossed the farm. It was a neat farm, had horses and a lot of hay and other plants.

I observed a large patch of bright green plants that I took for marijuana. I took several photos of it and the pilot flew me back to the airport.

I showed the photos to Braun and he suggested that I do a state search warrant on the farm. I was friends with the Sheriff of Jersey County, Illinois Frank Yocum, a famous country cop.

Sheriff Yocum became famous when Tammy Evans, a twenty three year old mother of three began losing her children under suspicious circumstances.

In a two year time span she lost a two year old child to a fractured skull due to a fall, and a three week old child to sudden infant death syndrome. Another child, a three year old died suddenly and sheriff Yocum began investigating the deaths.

It was determined that the latest death was attributed to suffocation. Tammy placed her hand the child's mouth and nose and killed it.

The case was long and drawn out. News crews from around the world invaded the sleepy little county of Jersey, Illinois, and filmed whatever they could. Sheriff Frank Yocum was in most of the film segments. He became a celebrity rural sheriff.

The day after the air surveillance of the farm in Jersey County I drove to Jerseyville, Illinois and applied for a search warrant for the farm. I was armed with the photos of the green patch of the "whatever" in the barnyard. They were great photos, clear and vivid.

I was wearing Marine Corps cammies, something I never thought I would ever do. Funny thing was, I still felt good wearing them, and I still looked like a Marine.

The States Attorney for the county issued the warrant based on the photos and I headed for the farm. I had telephoned the guys in Clayton and told them to meet me there.

We met up and stormed the farmhouse. The grower was arrested. I got in his face and taunted him. He had tried to terrorize me and I was still pissed about it.

After we secured the farmhouse and arrested the grower, we walked to the patch of green plants growing in the barnyard. It wasn't marijuana, it was horse weed.

I was on the verge of a panic attack (I had been having them when I was sober) when one of the TFD's said, "I smell weed." We followed out noses to a gorgeous patch of sensimilla marijuana hidden behind the barn, 100 plants, approximately ten feet tall; $1000 a pound.

The grower did a little prison time but not much. Someone burned his house down while he was in prison. He wasn't a well-liked guy.

Reszler had been buying meth and cocaine from a banker in Clayton. Palance gave us a speech about this banker. "You see, everybody's a dope dealer," he began. "Politicians, cops, dentists, doctors, lawyers, bankers, insurance executives. If they've got money, it's from dope. It's our job to destroy them."

The majority of the TFD's believed him. Palance was an intelligent man, but I was skeptical of anything he said. I personally knew many wealthy people who were not dope dealers.

But professional people get into their particular profession to make money. After a while, in any profession, there are problems with cash flow. I wondered if any of my friends would stoop to investing in the dope game.

If money, or cash, is the only name of the game then probably most people, who are hustling for a living, have the ability to dance to the tune of the devil and dabble in dope. It's a scary thing to think about.

We as a group had the banker under surveillance when Reszler was buying dope from him. Palance decided it was time to take the guy off and see if he would do his source.

It was a bright winter day in Clayton when we took the banker off. As usual, he was in shock when we surrounded his BMW, seized his car, cuffed him and dragged him into a DEA undercover car.

He didn't have very far to go, we were on our way to our offices overlooking Clayton and I was driving his BMW to our designated DEA private parking level.

He was sitting in a chair watching us wander around our offices getting reports and laughing and joking with each other. "Is this where I get beaten?" he asked.

We all ignored him, but I thought it was amusing that almost every drug dealer in the region knew about the Task

Force and how we treat our prisoners. It gave me the impression that the drug dealers were more organized than we were.

The druggies don't know how to talk to cops and agents. They attempt to communicate with us in the same manner they have spoken to their parents and teachers. They sometimes answer a question with a question. Or they try to project their problems onto the interviewer. At night after the excitement of the "take-off," these antics always led to a beating.

This arrest was a daytime "take off" so there weren't beer cans on desks, or drug dealers being slapped silly. The Special Agent in Charge (SAC) was in his office on the next floor up. There were other regular businesses all around us, and the walls were thin. This banker was lucky.

But this guy wasn't like the typical drug dealer. He had a job, and a real good one. He was clean cut, in shape and he dressed like a banker. He was young, in his twenty's, well-groomed and he knew how to hold himself. He sat erect in the DEA office chair, and he wasn't scared.

"We're going to give you the opportunity to do your source," Reszler said to him. "You'll be going to prison, but not like your source. You are one of the lucky ones, you got taken off first. You have opportunity, the other people in your conspiracy are not lucky. You've got two minutes to make up your mind."

When the crock has you by the leg and gives you an ultimatum, a chance to save your leg and your life, but still have some scars to remember it by, you listen to the crock and not the green worm living in your dope dealing brain telling you to call an attorney first.

Almost everyone wants a deal. They know they are wrong and that they have been captured with their pants down. There's no defense against what they have done.

They want a deal and they take it; no questions asked.

The banker squirmed and looked at us and then out the window to fashionable Clayton, Missouri. It was where he had planned to have his business address. It was all going to be taken away from him.

"It's a guy I went to high school with," the banker began. "He was a greaser in high school but I was friends with him. He came from a good family but he was just, you know, different. You know what I'm trying to say?"

We all nodded in encouragement and the guy started in again. "I went away to college and I figured I'd never see this guy again. I came home and he was a member of a biker gang. They have their biker club house in Overland. It's a one percenter biker gang."

We continued to nod in the affirmative.

"I got into banking and I'm making real good money. Out of the blue, the guy calls me. We talk about old times and then we talk about money. I guess greed got the best of me, but I agreed to move some of their product for them. I knew people, professional people who desired weed, coke and meth. That's how it all started."

"Where do they get the weed and coke?" Reszler asked him.

"Somebody in Florida," he stated. "But they cook their own meth at the club house in Overland. It's actually in a shed at the rear of the clubhouse. There are always a bunch of Harleys, you know, choppers parked in the driveway and on the lawn."

Palance was listening to our conversation, he wandered out of his office. "Call the guy and tell him you need more product. Set up a meet…..tell him you've got some cash for him. Do you owe him any money?"

"Yes," the banker replied, about $5,000."

"Do you have his money?" Palance asked.

"Yes, I have it, and I'm about due to meet with him and give it to him. It's how we work…..he gives me product and I give him cash after I sell it."

"How many other old friends does he have working for him?" Palance asked.

"I don't know. I think mostly he and his biker gang peddle their dope at bars and such," the banker answered.

Reszler hooked up a phone with a recorder and made the spiel into the tape….."This is TFD Johnny Reszler, assigned to the St. Louis Field Office. This is a call from defendant Randy Goins to drug conspirator Jess Grimes at 1130 hours."

Reszler dialed the number.

"Yeah," the voice said.

"I need a meet and swap," Randy the banker said.

"Okay, I'll meet you at the Galleria, parking lot, same place, one-hour." He hung up.

"It's a place at the south end of the Galleria Mall parking lot," Randy the banker advised. "It's secluded and there aren't any surveillance cameras there."

"Okay," Palance loudly said, "saddle up. Jim Bob, you and T. Anderson go to the parking lot and look for counter surveillance. Set up with a camera and get situated where you can photograph this meet."

The TFD's began their scramble while Palance planned an attack in his supervisor brain. "Where is the cash you're going to give to Jess?"

"In the trunk of my car," Randy said.

"Reszler, quickly get the cash from his car. Bring it in here and Zerox the bills, then give it back to the banker."

Reszler took off for the garage. Palance was looking at his Rolex. "What if you're a few minutes late?" Palance asked.

"I've never been late," he replied, "I don't know. He might leave."

"What will he be driving?" Plance asked.

"Either a Harley chopper, or an old grey pickup truck," Randy replied.

Palance got on the air, "Jimmy---old Harley or old grey pickup---scumbag biker."

"Ten-four," Jim Bob replied.

Reszler was copying the funds seized from the trunk of the bankers BMW. "Finished," Reszler said to Palance.

"Wire Randy," Palance ordered.

Randy was the new, almost friend, of the task force. If it had been nighttime he would have been given enough beer to loosen him up and he would have been treated like one of the boys, after he was slapped into reality.

Randy the banker was taking this action in and he was liking what he saw. "I wish I would have tried for DEA instead of banking," he mumbled to the group. "This shit is fun!"

"Damned right it is," Reszler replied.

"Testing, testing," Reszler was saying to check Randy's wire. "It's set up," Reszler said.

"Okay, let's go." Palance said as he gave Randy the keys to his BMW and the $5,000 seized from his BMW trunk. "This will be the last time you drive her," he said. "We're seizing it after this deal."

"Okay," Randy replied. "But I'll get leniency from the United States Attorney, right?"

"For your cooperation, yes, "In fact, I might even talk to the U.S. Attorney and ask him if you can keep your BMW. No promises though."

"Thank you, sir," Randy replied.

"Head out," Palance said. Palance knew the basic

principles of manipulation, "Give the sucker hope and always tell them what they want to hear."

Reszler and I followed Randy as he drove down Brentwood Boulevard toward the Galleria shopping mall. It was fashionable and exclusive and had a huge parking lot.

As the BMW pulled into the lot we could hear Randy on the Kel clearing his throat so he could sound confidant and believable.

He pulled up to the side of an old grey pickup, driver's window to driver's window.

"C/I has made contact with target," T. Anderson said.

"What's up, man?" Randy said as we listened to the Kel.

"You got my money?" The scummy biker asked.

"Yeah, $5,000, here it is." He handed the package of cash through the window.

"Here's your next order," the scummy biker said as he handed Randy the package of dope. "See ya," the biker said as he slowly drove away from the scene. Randy pulled away from the parking lot and headed back to the DEA offices.

We all headed back to the office. Randy the banker was waiting for us in the garage with the package of dope. We went inside, took the elevator and walked into the office packed with desks.

Palance came out of his office, "It went well," he'd been listening to the radio chatter. "I've spoken to the United States Attorney. "You are going to be booked, and then released on your own recognizance. You can go back to work and you can keep your BMW. But you are not off the hook. You will be compelled to testify against your friend, Jess the biker, in a court of law. Can you do that?"

"Yes, sir," the greedy banker replied.

"You will get some jail time…. it'll be in a medium security federal lockup. But it won't be what your biker friend is going to experience."

Randy the banker shook his head in dismay as Palance preached to him.

"Get him booked, fingerprinted, photographed, and conveyed to the United States Marshall Service for Arraignment," Palance said.

V.

MIAMI BEACH BLUES

Things were changing in the Task Force. The Drug Enforcement Administration St. Louis Field Office moved from its location at the Chrome Alloy Building to another office building in Clayton, Missouri.

It wasn't a big move, just a couple of blocks away at a new office complex above the Missouri State Bank Building, overlooking Maryland Avenue and the St. Louis County Courthouse.

The building was newer, had better and more secure parking and better views from the offices. Another plus was that our offices were big and wide and our desks weren't stacked on top of each other. On the down side, there was no more Club for the TFDs and agents to drink and eat at before and after drug deals.

It was a sad day for Reszler and Special Agent Mike Schweig; they pretty much lived at the Club. It was a sadder day for the owners of the Club; they were out of business six months after we moved.

Reszler wasn't able to keep track of his Club employee girlfriend, Maya, and they quickly broke up.
But Reszler had cultivated another Clayton office worker, a beautiful mulatto girl who worked for county government.

There were trendy bars and restaurants in and around Clayton and close to our new DEA offices at street level, not stuck high up in the air like the Club, and Reszler met the mulatto gal at one of them.

It isn't an unusual experience for young people to meet one another at night in bars. They are always looking for a "hook-up" and some of the Clayton movers and shakers knew who the brash young undercover cops were and where they ate and drank. There was always a young chick stalking a young cop, or agent, waiting to be recognized as a possible girlfriend.

Reszler had a small apartment in south St. Louis and this beautiful mulatto gal moved in with him. Reszler allowed the move in at a weak alcohol/sex fueled moment and he regretted his indiscretion as time went on.

Reszler's sights were set on a lovely pin-up model who loved cops. Her photos were everywhere in the St. Louis area, on calendars in auto parts stores, barbershops, taverns, anywhere where men congregate. He pined for her, even though a special agent in group two was also interested in her. She was young and cute with a killer hard body.

Reszler was cooling his heels waiting for the group two agent to be transferred, or for the pin-up goddess to tell him that she didn't wish to talk to him anymore. Reszler wasn't going to get involved with any chick who was attached to an active DEA employee but he always had the model on his mind.

I had broken my left hand in an off-duty incident (too much beer and too much mouth) and had a cast up to my elbow. I didn't miss any work, but I was, in Palance's mind, damaged government property and a liability to the task force.

Palance sent me to Miami to pick up a large motorhome. Since we, the task force, did so much marijuana cultivation in the boonies in southeast, Missouri (Mark Twain National Forest) Palance figured we needed a motorhome.

Palance hit me with this news as he handed me the airline ticket and a wad of expense money ($100 bills). We all had credit cards with fake names on them, provided by the fed, as well as phony driver's licenses for the states of Illinois, Missouri, and Florida.

I called my wife and told her the news. She was leery of DEA, the police department, and by that time, me. I was drinking again, most every night, and I was aware of the fact that I had changed in demeanor and in my physiognomy. I sent messages of aggression and violence without really trying.

I had been working out regularly at work (there was a gym for agents and TFD's at the facility) wore tight fitting Polo collared shirts and flowered Miami Vice shirts, had longish hair and actually did not care if I lived or died.

I had never been an office cop. I was for most of my duty in the Marine Corps a machine gunner. I had always pushed the envelope in everything I did and I was pondering my mortality at the age of forty three.

I had come to the conclusion that if I died in my mid-forty's, I didn't wish to die in bed lying next to my wife, or kneeling before a commode, or at the bottom of a stairway broken and bruised, or in a hospital being prodded and violated by doctors.

I wanted to die on a DEA drug deal with Reszler, Mad Dog and T. Anderson, preferably shot in the heart. That is how the DEA lifestyle creeps up on the unsuspecting detached cop.

I figured I'd be going back to the police department at some point in my career and returning to mediocrity was a fate worse than death

I was telling my wife my story about the Miami trip and Reszler was standing in the middle of our big office telling a story about his "G" car Trans Am:

"So I'm drunk, with a beer between my legs," Reszler begins," "And I'm thinking about the damn seat in the Trans

Am, the one I took away from that fat fucking Canadian.....the back was broken and you never knew when it was going to give away and send your ass into the backseat." The crowd was smiling and laughing along with him.

"So, I'm on I-55 coming back from Sikeston doing about eighty, when I look in my rearview mirror and a damned Missouri State cop is pulling me over." The crowd is on the edges of their seats.

"I tuck the beer deeply into my crotch and roll down the window as the guy comes to my door."

"Evening sir, can I see your driver's license and registration and proof of insurance?"

Now the crowd is serious and watching every move Reszler makes, and I'm talking to my wife and listening and watching Reszler at the same time.

"So I reach into my back pocket for my wallet and the damned seat back gives way and I fly into the backseat with the beer between my legs landing on my chest and spewing foam all over my chest and neck."

The room started laughing and watching as Reszler demonstrates during his skit. I was laughing and my wife figured I was laughing at her as Reszler continued his story.

"The fucking highway patrol cop was spit shined and stood erect as he watched me slithering around inside the fucking General Motors piece of shit car with beer flying around. I figured my ass was grass, so I reach back and bring the seat back up and I'm flitting around with my driver's license trying to find the Missouri state license. The Florida license falls out as well as the Illinois license and the highway cop is watching as I fumble them."

I'm laughing and my wife hangs up on me. I wait and listen to the culmination of the story before I call her back.

"How many drivers' licenses do you have, sir?" The fucking highway cop asks."

"Sir," I began, "I'm an undercover agent for the DEA, and I'm trying to follow a damned dope dealer who was just a quarter mile ahead of me. If you let me go, I can still catch up with him."

"Show me your credentials," the highway cop says.

"I hit him with my creds and he says," Drive safely and have a nice evening, turns and walks away."

By now everyone is falling out of their chairs laughing. Palance walked out of his office, laughing; "I just made an appointment at the Pontiac Dealer in Creve Coeur. Take the Trans Am in tomorrow morning and they will replace the seat."

I called my wife back and continued my tale of woe and the Miami trip story. "It's just a turnaround trip," I continued. "I'm flying down and driving right back."

She wasn't impressed and I didn't blame her, but the extra DEA money on my pay stub came in handy. I felt I was shirking my family responsibilities, but I rationalized the situation. I had to make a living. Being a cop, federal or local, was my forte.

Another St. Louis City cop came to the unit. This guy's dad was a prominent lawyer. He had instant status within the unit. Since his dad was more important than the other TFD's relatives he was placed at the top of the totem pole of city cop TFD's. His name was Detective Sultan and he was welcomed with opened arms by the DEA establishment.

Special Agent Michael Braun who had been officially transferred into the Task Force, was one of the guys impressed with Detective Sultan.

Braun was destined for stardom in the Drug Enforcement Administration. He was tall and tight, an ex-

Marine, an ex-Cape Girardeau, Missouri cop and an ex-Illinois State Police Investigator. He sported a $5,000 Rolex Submariner and dressed the part of a high spending government bureaucrat.

But his true claim to fame was that he finished number one in his Special Agent academy class. In essence, this fact meant that he had the option of being transferred to any field office in the world to begin his career with the federal government. He chose the St. Louis Field Office.

To the TFDs, who were constantly dreaming of getting out of St. Louis and living near the beach, or the mountains or the desert, Mike's choice of duty assignments was odd and unusual.

Braun's personal mission was to make friends with and lead errant TFDs. In reality he needed a few TFDs to maintain his cases while he was travelling to South America for headquarters DEA.

DEA had a special operation going on in South America (Operation Snow Cap) and they moved their future stars back and forth from their duty assignments to Snow Cap assignments.

The powers that be in Washington recognized Braun's potential and they continually gave him resume building dangerous and important missions overseas to draw attention to him and his potential greatness. He was foot loose and fancy free, newly divorced and dating a cute and smart Assistant United States Attorney, one who prided herself on enhancing the careers of the TFDs and other agents.

Part of Braun's self-serving rhetoric was the line: "They say that the most stressful times in your life are divorce, job change, and relocation. I did them all at the same time."

Even though Braun was an Illinois Investigator, he lived

just across the Mississippi River from his hometown of
Cape Girardeau, Missouri.

Cape was Braun's wife's hometown also and life was
fairly good for them. He had a son, a house and they were
living the mediocre lifestyle of southern Missouri and
southern Illinois, always just minutes from good old Cape.

In Braun's mind, mediocrity was a curse and I can
personally understand his thinking. Braun applied for DEA
without telling his wife. DEA hired him and he was on his
way to acceptance when he advised his wife of his
intentions.

Braun's wife didn't want to leave her hometown, she
balked. He quit his Illinois State cop job and headed off to
the DEA academy. Divorce came quickly.

Braun was obsessed with a big-time dope dealer who
came to town occasionally to drop off a load of cocaine.
He had an informant who would contact him, covertly, and
tell him that the dope dealer was in town and where he was
at this particular time. Braun would get the entire unit to
head for the guy's location and initiate surveillance.

The dope dealer was a big-time body builder and he
worked out at a gym on Clayton Road across from the
Galleria Shopping Mall.

Braun would have us on surveillance at the gym, and if
the guy left he would have us follow him and report back to
him what his location was. Rolling surveillance is next to
impossible. Traffic plays big in rolling surveillance.

At times traffic is the cop's friend, it hides him from the
rearview mirror eyes of the bad-guy. But traffic also is your
enemy. If you get caught at a light, it is almost impossible to
make it through the intersection and resume the surveillance.

Needless to say, we lost the guy more than we spied on
him. We would contact Braun on the air and advise him that
the target was lost. Braun would become furious. He was

obsessed with the guy.

He would contact the informant and try and get a new location on the dope dealer while we waited for him to hit us on the air and give us better info. It was a rat race to try and get to the new location before the guy left for parts unknown.

I left for my turnaround trip to Miami. I debarked with my carry-on bag and walked toward a taxi in a long line of taxis. It was dark and I was tired and I just wanted to get to my hotel, which was on the Miami River, and get some sleep. I was certain I was going to be on the road in the motorhome on the following day.

I asked the taxi driver if he would take me to the hotel, "Yes," he replied, and I jumped in the back. A taxi driver from the line of taxis behind the one I was in stormed up to my taxi driver screaming at him and threatening him.

The two taxi drivers were speaking in Spanish, cursing and making motions with their hands and I could see that my taxi driver was afraid. The scenario spelled violence for me, so I jumped out of the taxi and confronted the screaming intruding taxi driver. He took a long look at me and then walked back to his taxi. I was surprised. I was usually underestimated in disputes and was accustomed to fighting.

I climbed back into the back seat of the taxi and told the driver to "take off" and he did. I had not considered the cast on my left hand before I jumped out of the taxi, but I was considering it now and I felt stupid. I was in no condition to fight with anyone, it's how I broke the bone in my hand to begin with.

I checked in to the hotel and awoke early, took another

taxi to the DEA field office and checked in with the group supervisor that had the keys to the motorhome. I was given a ride to a storage facility and took possession of the vehicle.

I inspected it; it was not drivable. It had been stored in Miami for a long time, there was weed residue throughout, and the interior was covered in mold. I called Palance and told him my dilemma.

"Drive it anyway," Palance said.

"No," I'm not driving it," I replied.

"Call me back in an hour," Palance said.

I cooled my heels at the storage facility and called Palance back.

"It's going to be cleaned by DEA sometime this week, but you'll have to wait for it. Get some more expense money from the SAC in Miami and wait it out."

"Okay, I replied. I headed back to the hotel. There was a nice pool right on the Miami River and I figured I'd lay out in the Miami weather and watch the boats go by.

The weekend was looming. I called my wife and asked her if she could get someone to watch the kids and come down to spend the weekend with me. She did.

I sat in the hotel lobby as she got out of a taxi and joined me. I had rented a car, another nifty Chrysler Lebaron Turbo and it was in the hotel parking lot. As soon as my wife got into the lobby hightailed it to the parking lot, climbed into the Lebaron and headed for Key West.

In the 80s, in Miami, or in Key West, a person could be blindfolded, given a rock, turned around in a circle ten times, told to throw the rock and they would hit a dope smuggler. I was again suspected of being a drug dealer.

Every restaurant we went into, every establishment we frequented, people looked at me as if I was a dangerous predator. But I never got stopped by any south Florida cops, and I was never the recipient of rudeness. Folks were leery of me.

We had a great time in Key West. We went deep sea fishing on the charter boat "Wild Bill." I asked the captain how he came to name his boat "Wild Bill."

He told me he named it after his late son. I asked him what happened to his son. "He got into the drug business and got killed, on this boat, just about where you are standing. They killed him and tossed him over the side."

The captain didn't know me or what I did for a living. I pried further into his story. "Who did it? How did your son get involved in drug smuggling?" I asked.

"Down here, if you own a boat that means you have the ability to navigate, operate in these waters safely and you know where uninhabited islands are. The smugglers who deal in large loads of weed, and cocaine need people with those skills and they need your boat," he replied.

"So they approached your son with a sweet deal and he took it?" I asked.

"Yeah, he wanted to get rich quick and he got greedy. He hid some dope on an island for it to be picked up at a later date. He was suspected of dabbling in the load, taking some of it for his own business. They caught him and murdered him."

The story of a murdered son, the dope game, and the hard scrabble life of a Florida hustler put a damper on the perfect day with its perfect water and sun.

The people I dealt with on an everyday basis had the ability to murder for drugs. It's a serious business. Palance was right: drug dealers are filthy vermin that should be exterminated.

I spent my expense money on fancy restaurants. We caught Dorado and the mate on the boat cleaned them for us. I had a cooler full of fish on ice, and my plan was to walk my wife onto the airplane with the fish. It didn't work; the airlines would not allow the cooler on board.

So I was walking back into the parking lot in Miami, broken hand, which was hurting like hell because I was using it to catch fish in Key West, hung over from drinking like a drug dealer in paradise, and pissed off because I was stuck in Miami and probably would be for the next two or three days.

I laid around the pool during the day, and I would go out to eat at night. I was in Joe's Stone Crab in south beach and had an excellent meal (stone crabs) when I paid the tab with a hundred dollar bill.

"Can I keep the change?" the waiter asked.

"Fuck no," I replied. "You think I'm going to give you a $65.00 tip?" Real dope dealers tip big.

I tipped the guy $5.00 and walked out into night time Miami. I could have gone bar-hopping, but I chose not to. I headed back to my hotel and watched television. A day passed and I was called at the hotel and advised that the motorhome was now ready. I had been nursing the Mahi Mahi (Dorado) changing the ice a couple of times a day, making certain the fish did not waste away.

After returning the rental, I called for a taxi to take me to the storage facility, it didn't show, so I walked out into the road and flagged down a taxi.

The Cubano driver gave me the once over and I climbed in. We were on our way to the storage facility and the driver asked me, "What's in the cooler?"

I figured it was none of his business so I thought I'd screw with him for a while, so I said, "Why do you want to know?"

I had pushed his buttons and he was really curious now. I figured he was an informant for some kind of a cop down here in paradise. He'd pigeonholed me as a drug dealer carrying dope in a Styrofoam cooler and he was chomping at the bit to see if he was correct in his assumption. To him, I was potential "cash on the hoof."

He pulled the taxi to side of the road, and turned toward me in the backseat, "If you want me to take you to your destination you will have to show me what's in the cooler," he said in broken English.

I was amused at his actions, so I said, "It's fish!"

"Fish?" he replied. "I like fish, can I have some?"

"No," I replied.

He began driving again and we were nearing the facility. I could see that he was still intrigued with me and the cooler. He stopped and I climbed out and paid him. "Can I see the fish?" he asked.

I thought about this stooge, and I actually didn't wish to stymie him anymore, so I lifted the lid off of the cooler and allowed him to look inside. "Mahi Mahi," he mumbled, "Are you sure I can't have some?"

I walked away from him and into the storage facility. There was a message for me from the St. Louis Field Office. A new agent who had just been transferred into the St. Louis Field Office from the Miami office wanted me to telephone him in St. Louis.

I made the call. He asked me to go back to the DEA field office and pick up a large box with his personal property inside, stick it into the motorhome and bring it back to St. Louis for him.

I walked to the motorhome and inspected it; nothing had been done to clean it up. The marijuana residue, which would have been ten or twelve pounds if it had been collected and weighed, was still in the back.

I wasn't going to fight with DEA anymore concerning the condition of the motorhome. I climbed in and headed for

DEA Miami to fetch Special Agent Mike Duda's property.

I flashed my way through the security at DEA and made my way up to the third floor via elevator. I walked into the group office, which was big and spacious like ours in St. Louis, and I spied the big box waiting for me in the middle of the office.

My hand was really hurting me at this point and I fought to drag the huge box out of the office and onto the elevator. There were approximately fifteen special agents, male and female, sitting at their desks dabbling with reports and talking on the telephone, but none of them offered to help me. They could see that I was having a problem moving the huge box with my right hand and trying not to use my freshly casted left hand.

I got the box onto the elevator and into the parking lot, and now I had to lift it to get it into the motorhome. By the time this maneuver was completed, I was hurting big-time.

I got on the road late and figured I'd take the scenic route back to St. Louis. I took A1A whenever I could, then switched over to the interstate around Merritt Island. I wasn't out to break any records, it got dark and I stopped for the night at a motel and had a good night's sleep.

I slept late, had breakfast and started my trek north. The motorhome would only travel safely at fifty five MPH, I figured the tires were out of round for sitting at the storage facility.

My fish were still on ice and not smelling and when I stopped for gas in north Florida, I tossed a six-pack of Heineken on top of them.

It was a long and grueling drive back to good old St. Louis. It had gotten dark early and I'd stopped for some fast food just to keep something in my stomach. The motorhome chugged and bounced all the way north.

I got into southern Georgia at around 10:00 p.m. and my

hand was hurting so badly that I could hardly raise it to put it onto the steering wheel. I figured I'd broken it all over again. I'd had broken hands for most of my life and it was not something I was unaccustomed to.

I popped a Heineken while tooling down I-16, just north of Statesboro, which is the point where the exhausted driver going to St. Louis figures he's not going to make it and it's time to search for a motel.

The Heinekens had been sliding down and before I knew it, I was out of beer and feeling euphoric, so I stopped at a gas station near Metter and purchased another six-pack.

I cruised in the darkness drinking beer, singing along with the stereo (Hotel California) and wondering what life was going to bring to me, when the traffic abruptly stopped. I could see flashing cop lights ahead of me and the cars were inching along.

"It's a damned sobriety check point," I mumbled to myself. There were empty Heineken cans in the cooler. I rolled down the electric passenger side window and started tossing them out onto the side of the road. I knew that I would never pass a sobriety check. I was wasted, but able to drive. I couldn't have stood on one foot nor done any other maneuvering.

The traffic kept inching forward and I thought about the weed residue in the back of the motorhome. "FUCK," I yelled, "Fucking DEA, now I'm probably going to jail in fucking southern, Georgia, the armpit of the world for a drunk Yankee cop."

I thought about my wife, she would be happy if I got pinched. Maybe it would bring some sort of harmony to our lives if I was tossed back to the department from DEA. But I would probably be suspended by the department, and maybe fired.

"Maybe it wouldn't be a bad thing," I mumbled. "Maybe it should happen this way and I can stop being crazy and start living like a normal human being."

The traffic inched forward and finally I was at the cop cars. It wasn't a sobriety check-point, it was a fatal vehicle accident. There was a dead body covered with a blanket lying on the shoulder of the road.

The traffic sped up and again I was tooling along at fifty-five MPH feeling like I'd won something at a raffle. I popped another Heineken and by the time I got to my house, I was mellowed.

My wife wasn't surprised that I'd gotten drunk while driving home, it was a common occurrence. I hardly ever came home sober.

I drove the motorhome to work the next day. Palance inspected it and observed that there was a place for a portable generator at the right rear of the vehicle, the space was empty. Instantly Palance suspected that I had stolen the generator.

He made no verbal accusations, but he inquired about it and then had a difficult time letting go of the fact that the generator was not there when I took possession of the motorhome. I was embarrassed and humiliated.

Palance had prejudged me from the beginning of my DEA experience, and he was using "Be one of the boys" as his precursor in suspecting me of stealing. I looked at him with pity.

My friend from Intelligence called me again. He had some news on Latchkey: An informant advised him that Latchkey's employee at his restaurant, George Fletcher, had been renting vehicles at the Dollar Rental Agency on Brentwood, driving to Miami and returning with kilos of cocaine in the trunk. I thanked him for the information, but in reality, he wanted me to give him some federal information on this drug conspiracy. I had nothing to give him.

The days had become long at the DEA St. Louis Field Office. The deals had slowed and the TFD's were thinking of their futures instead of dope dealers.

Palance thought it was time to take off the scummy bikers who had awakened the greed in the clean-cut banker. It was late afternoon when we made surveillance on the biker club house in blue collar Overland, Missouri.

Palance had given me a newly seized one-ton Ford conversion van. I liked the van, it was comfortable and I could haul my kids and dogs around in it. It was purchased and owned by some goofy dope dealer with every available option, including a raised roof, until he tried to sell dope in it. Now it was DEA's, and mine.

I kept making passes by the biker clubhouse and reporting back to Palance via closed circuit DEA radio. The Harleys were starting to accumulate on the lawn, all lined up in military fashion,

I was nursing a beer, and after it got dark, I set up at a good location where I could see everything going on in front of the biker hang out. The other TFD's were set up at a bar near the clubhouse, drinking and shooting pool. Palance was at his office.

"How many Harley's are parked on the lawn?" Palance asked me.

I quickly counted them, "ten or eleven," I advised him. "All lined up in a row, some of them real nice bikes."

I could read Palance; the more people at the location meant more arrests which meant more stats for his promotion. The Harley's would be seized and sold and that meant more cash for the government, and alas, more stats for Palance.

Palance and the TFD's, most of who were wasted, showed up in the neighborhood. They parked their "G" cars on the street down from the clubhouse and I pulled the big conversion van onto the driveway.

The scummy bikers didn't know who was in their front yard near their worshipped Harleys so they came out in force spoiling for a fight.

It was a poor choice for the bikers. The TFD's struck first, fist fighting with the bikers on the lawn and getting the best of them.

Palance yelled DEA, search warrant, and the bikers, who were losing and confused, stopped their aggression. The TFD's did not; they kept beating the bikers.

I leapt from the van and started kicking and hitting with my right hand (my left hand was still in a cast, and killing me) while the bikers pleaded with us to stop beating them. When the bad guy is losing the battle, he becomes the underdog.

"Enough," Palance said. "Cuff them and put them in the back of the conversion van."

The bikers were in the back of my van, sitting on top of one another, beaten and confused, pleading with me to take them to the emergency room. The TFD's and Palance went to the rear of the clubhouse to the shed where the meth was manufactured. They found a meth lab and a sizeable amount of meth and then entered the house and found meth and cocaine.

After about an hour, Palance and the TFD's exited the house and Palance advised me to head for the office with the prisoners.

I was still pumped up over the fight and the other TFD's were also. Besides being half drunk we, as a group, were in fight mode.

I had grown to hate scummy bikers, and I hated their loud and obnoxious Harleys. Instead of pulling straight out into the street I cranked the wheel and backed into the yard. I rolled over every Harley parked on the lawn.

I could hear the Harley's scrunching under the wheels of the one ton conversion van, and the beat-up bikers in the van could hear their precious bikes being pulverized as they banged under the floor boards of the big van.

"Sir, sir, please stop," they were shouting.

I stopped, put the van in "drive" and pulled forward crushing the bikes a second time. I came to a stop in the driveway with the bikers screaming and threatening to kill me.

I climbed out of the van and Palance quickly closed on me, "What the fuck is wrong with you? Why the fuck did you do that?" Palance screamed.

The TFD's were stifling laughter, "I don't know, it's just something I always wanted to do," I replied.

Palance was massaging his temples as he walked in circles in the driveway......"Okay," he finally said, "Here's how it is going down, you were backing out and you didn't see the Harleys and you accidentally ran over them. I'll get a flatbed truck here and we'll have them conveyed to the impoundment lot. They can be sold by the government for parts."

"Okay," I replied.

We headed for the office, booked the prisoners and housed them in the St. Louis County jail for safekeeping. They would be arraigned in the morning.

The scummy bikers were super polite while in our offices, although they stared at me with hatred, something I had grown accustomed to. They said "yes, sir and no sir," and did not make any overt moves or say anything that could have been construed as inflammatory.

I thought about the demeanor of the beaten bikers. If the tables had been turned, if we had been unarmed and out-numbered and if we weren't the federal cops playing junior "G" man, they would have beaten us to death and disposed of our bodies.

The DEA phones were ringing again with informant information, most of it anonymous. Someone called and advised the duty officer that there was suspicious activity at a farm in Paris, Missouri. Paris is northwest of St. Louis, about a ninety minute drive.

Ronnie Been, a semi-new guy from the city and his partner, Detective Sultan, drove to Paris in a seized pickup truck. Both were accustomed to knocking on doors, speaking to inhabitants, and getting answers. It's what cops do.

Ronnie had lived a charmed life, like the rest of the TFD's. He had an influential and high ranking brother on the city P.D. His brother took care of him.

Ronnie and Detective Sultan parked the pickup and walked to the front door of the old farmhouse, knocked on the door and waited.

A man in bibs answered the door and asked them what they wanted. "We're with DEA," Ronnie Been replied, "We'd like to come in and have a talk with you."

The farmer slammed and locked the door. Ronnie and Detective Sultan stood in disbelief; they were important guys, and they were representing the United States Department of Justice.

"Sir," Ronnie Been said as he banged on the door, "Please unlock the door or we are going to kick it in, we need to speak with you." There was rustling inside of the house, loud voices and then a door slamming at the rear of the house.

The TFD's heard additional noise from the rear of the house, like someone running. Ronnie and Detective Sultan pulled their pistols and carefully walked to the rear of the farmhouse. The rear door was unlocked. They carefully entered, the farmer had vacated through the rear door.

There was a path leading to cornfields at the rear of the farmhouse. Ronnie and Detective Sultan followed the path. Inside of the rows of corn was a large marijuana field, acre after acre of bright green marijuana.

A large pickup truck blasted by them heading for the main road at the front of the farmhouse, it had two occupants; one of them was the farmer who had opened and slammed the door on them.

Ronnie and Detective Sultan ran back to the farmhouse; by the time they arrived the truck was miles away. They entered the farmhouse, found a phone and called Palance.

Palance mounted up the entire Task Force and we headed for Paris, Missouri. There was a large barn adjacent to the farmhouse and it contained approximately five tons of cultivated sensimilla marijuana, bailed into 100 pound bales. At the time it sold for $1000 a pound on the street.

We began the arduous task of bringing the marijuana out into the barnyard and burning it. It was difficult to burn and each bale had to be prodded with a pitch fork, broken up into pieces in order for the weed to burn.

We worked all day, dragging the weed out, breaking it up and burning it. We all had contact highs, the burning quickly turned into a game, cold beer to drink and expensive weed to breathe. We drove back to St. Louis laughing on the radio and making jokes about a mandatory police department drug screen.

The investigation began: the farmers who had lived in the house left nothing behind revealing their identity. But there were fingerprints, which ultimately led to their capture.

The owner of the farm was located. He advised us that he had rented the farm, sight unseen to two brothers from Kentucky. He had their names, but they were phony.

People with land and a house on it advertise their property for rent in local farm community newspapers. The landlords seldom meet the renters. Money is exchanged via mail, or cashier check; the door key is left in a mailbox. The landlord doesn't care about what goes on at his property; he only cares about the monthly rent being paid to him, preferably in cash.

The Kentucky brothers were well prepared for a visit by DEA. Neighbors advised that the pickup used in the escape was well stocked and hidden in the corn fields.

Customers came frequently and left with loads of weed, many with out of state license plates. Apparently the brothers kept their cash in satchels so that when DEA did come calling they could grab the bags and hightail it out the back door.

By all appearances they were smart dope dealers; they got away from the scene. They had planned for every possible government intrusion into their dope dealer lives, but they still got caught.

But their cash was not seized. Their homes and vehicles were modest. The farm was not theirs; the government did not seize it. They played dumb, got good lawyers, didn't cooperate with the government and did some federal time. When they got out they were wealthy folk, probably living in Florida or California. Smart dope dealers! The crock lunged and missed.

VI.

ATTACK DOGS DON'T STOP DEA

Group Supervisor Palance was overheard telling his secretary, Liz, that the "boys" should go back to Sikeston, and to prepare to get some travel orders and vouchers prepared for the trip.

There weren't many secrets in the Task Force, and like me, most of us did not desire to return to Sikeston, Missouri.

The TFD's were on the phone calling informants trying to set up deals. I glanced over to Little Stevie Wonder. He was stoic but looked scared. I figured he knew that it was just a matter of time until Palance paid him back for the letter to his wife.

There is nothing more painful than payback, especially in law enforcement. Cops and agents go to great extremes to punish their alleged enemies, it's one of the reasons people in this profession seek promotion.

Palance's United States Attorney's office girlfriend walked into the office, crying and wiping away tears. Apparently she had gotten served with a subpoena from Palance's wife's lawyer. Liz and she hugged, then she walked into Palance's office, the door closed.

The TFD's were still hammering the telephones. I wondered if I could scare up a dope case. I noticed that most of the TFD's were calling cops in other jurisdictions. Rural cops usually know who their dope dealers are and they know that if DEA can take one of them off, drug proceeds will come to their police department.

The TFD's were going back and forth to the coffee

machine and spilling coffee as they trudged to their desks. It was business as usual: write reports, talk and joke, act important on the telephone and have phone sex with a DEA girlfriend who could possibly become an informant.

I dialed my old friend Sheriff Frank Yocum, from Jersey County, Illinois, the scene of my latest marijuana/horseweed caper. I need a case," " I advised him.

"I'm doing a state warrant tomorrow in Fosterburg, Illinois. That's close to where you grew up. You want to come along?"

"Yes," I replied. "What's it all about?"

"A woman scorned," he began. "Drunk doper wrecked her car in Jerseyville. Ran the tires off of the wheels and got locked up. Says she can do the biggest doper in Madison County. It's out of my jurisdiction, but I can still do the warrant. Interested?"

"Yeah, who is the biggest dope dealer in Madison County?"

"Freddy Hawk, heard of him?"

"Nope, but that doesn't mean anything. Who's the informant?"

"Mickey Masters. Heard of her?"

"Nope! Where do you want to meet?"

"We can stage at the state hospital, in the rear in the parking lot. Know where it is?"

"Yes, what time?"

How about noon?"

"See you there." He hung up before I could ask him any more questions.

The TFD's and agents were starting to head toward the door for an early lunch. I followed them to a restaurant/bar across the street from our office building. It was a laid back morning. Things didn't start popping until dark. I wandered over and sat at a booth with Reszler T. Anderson, and S/A

Mike Schweig.

There was small talk about Palance and his girlfriend. "Instant gratification is the name of the game at the federal level," Mike Schweig said while looking at me. I felt he was tutoring me because he felt I was naive. I've always been underestimated, it has worked in my favor for my life so far on this green earth.

The place started filling up with business people from the offices in the surrounding buildings. These establishments were the watering hole of the jungle. There were secretaries with their bosses and other matchups that the casual observer could tell were unusual or naughty.

Some special agents from the other two groups filtered into the watering hole. Group two guys sneered at me. They didn't know that I knew the whole story of why I was targeted. I felt they hated me because they jumped the gun and sacrificed me for having a screwball for a relative. I ignored them.

I wasn't eating lunch so I saw my opportunity to maybe have a sit down with Palance about tomorrow. I sauntered back over to our office. Liz was still at her post outside Palance's's office. I walked around her and entered his domain.

"Hey, I've got a deal tomorrow at noon. Is it okay if I take some of the TFD's with me?"

He watched me as if he was surprised, staring up at me as I stared down at him. "Tell me about the deal," he softly said. The tone of his voice took me off guard. He was calm and collected. I attributed it to him not having to sneak around anymore to be with his girlfriend. Everything was in the open now.

"Sheriff buddy of mine in Jersey County, Illinois, Frank Yocum, he helped us with the Grafton weed case."

"Yeah, I know who you are talking about," he replied.

"He's going to execute a state warrant in Madison County, Illinois. It's where I grew up."

"What's the name of the target?" He asked.

"Freddy Hawk," I replied.

"Who's the informant?" He asked.

"Mickey Masters," I replied.

"Liz," he called out. Liz came running in, "Yes, sir, she anxiously said.

"Put two names in NADDIS for me please, Freddy Hawk and Mickey Masters, Alton, Illinois area."

"Yes sir!" Liz exited the office.

Palance continued to stare at me, as if he was amused. "You know, you're not that bad of a guy, as I see it. Why do people hate you so badly?"

"I have an independent attitude," I replied. "It's an east side curse." He accepted my explanation. Liz rushed back into the office.

"Freddy Hawk is a small time weed and coke dealer in Southern Illinois. His brother is a big time weed and cocaine dealer in Southern Illinois. Mickey Masters is not in NADDIS." Liz walked out.

"I'll give you the whole crew," Palance continued. "I'm not going but I'll put Special Agent Mike Schweig in charge. Where are you guys staging?"

"The Alton, Illinois State Hospital," I replied. "It's a mental hospital. There's plenty of nuts in the Alton area to keep it filled. The back of the hospital faces Fosterberg Road.

Palance laughed, "Okay, good luck."

I walked back into the offices. The TFD's were going back and forth from the restaurant/bar across the street, and then to the office. Reszler missed his Club girlfriend Maya, and he would speak kindly about her to anyone who would listen.

I'd heard most of the stories about the two of them, they were lovers, but they were more than that, they were drinking buddies.

Reszler had a small cruiser at the Lake of the Ozarks, and his parents had a small lake house with a dock. He and Maya would go to the Lake for a weekend and get so drunk that Reszler couldn't find his way back to the lake house.

After some help from passing boaters, Reszler would finally bump his way back to the dock, but then the real trouble began. They weren't able to climb out of the cruiser, onto the dock, and into the lake house. They were incapacitated on the deck for hours until the booze partially wore off so they could make it to the house.

Cop stories, booze stories, and DEA stories were told over and over again to anyone who would listen. I sat at my desk and wondered what was in store for me. I had refused to turn into a TFD, but I realized the DEA machine was larger and more powerful than anything I had ever come up against, even the Marine Corps. My resistance was futile. I had become one of the boys.

The Marine Corps stays with the former Marine for a lifetime. I figured the DEA experience would be the same way. I heard a female agent talking at the Club. "Is there life after DEA?" she asked a friend/agent.

"Doubtful," the agent replied.

Reszler and I were riding together toward beautiful and quaint Alton, Illinois. I was giving him directions and he was relaying my directions to the other DEA "G" cars following us.

We came across the Lewis and Clark Bridge, "Hang a right," I told him, he did and we motored on. I silently reminisced about the old town, the place of my youth. It was as if he sensed I was thinking of better times, the times of dreams and plans that mostly never come to fruition.

"What kind of a town is this?" he asked.

"It was a good town at one time. Everybody had employment if they desired it. There was the Glass Works, Laclede Steel, Alton Box Board. Retail stores in the downtown area that actually made money. It was bustling."

"It looks like a shithole now," he said, "What happened?"

"The factories closed," I replied.

Reszler reminisced about living in North St. Louis County, just across the Mississippi River from Alton, Illinois. He told story after story, and they were funny, but he was a story teller.

He reminded me of a kid who grew up being doted on, the only son in the family and the family member who was going to make something of himself.

He talked about how he and a friend beat up two black pimps in the tunnel of love ride at an amusement park near his house. "The pimps made a fatal mistake: they came to the amusement park with their white girls," Reszler droned on.

I laughed, "That's a funny story," I replied.

I analyzed the pimp beating. If everyone hates pimps so much then why are pimps in charge of almost everything? The federal supervisors are pimps of us cops.

Politicians, state and federal, are pimps of the cops and agents. Supervisors are pimps in the police department. We pimp the wildebeest when we get our fangs into them. Everybody is pimping someone, but cops get pimped more than wayward girls on the streets, especially at DEA.

Reszler was still laughing and rambling about his youth. "I knew right then and there that I wanted to be a city cop. I told my dad what I wanted. He introduced me to Doc Cooper, the department surgeon. You know his brother in law was the governor. Doc Cooper liked me instantly. I got into the Cadet Program and worked for him in the medical division. He made sure I got big and strong, he gave me his magic muscle pills, and I still use them. You ever use them?"

"No," I replied.

"I got into the academy as soon as I turned twenty one," Johnny continued, "and after three years I got on the Task Force."

"We're coming up on the state hospital; turn right into this parking lot."

I tried not to categorize Reszler, but I was a cop and it's what we do. "Spoiled cop's kid," I muttered to myself."

Frank Yocum was waiting for us, giant belly and the ever present cigarette. I climbed out of the hot rod and shook his hand.

"You're a fish out of water working drugs," he mumbled.

The TFD's led by Special Agent Mike Schweig, pulled into the lot in a queue. TFD Jim Bob, blonde and squat like a fullback, climbed out of the big surveillance van (the van I used to roll over the Harley's, Palance took it away from me after I ran over the Harleys) along with Special Agent Monica Rose, in attendance to wire the female informant.

Ringer and Ronnie Been arrived in Ringer's Chrysler "G" car. Everybody stood in the lot and waited for direction.

Sheriff Yocum motioned to a female sitting in his unmarked sheriff car to get out and come to the van. She did and everybody stared at her.

Staring is a common occurrence for undercover cops when dealing with informants. They are trying to get a feel for the informant, their lives might hinge on whether he or she is telling the truth, or if the cops are being set-up.

"This is Mickey Masters," Sheriff Yocum said. "She advised me she could buy cocaine from Freddy Hawk's girlfriend at Freddy Hawk's house, which is right up the road. Did you all bring buy money?"

"Yeah, Sheriff," I replied, "$3000 enough?" There were patients from the mental hospital waking around the grounds. We were a curiosity to them. They circled us, and some of them would walk to us and ask us for cigarettes.

Alton was always known as that weird town where the crazy house is. It housed mentally ill folks from the southern tip of the State of Illinois. It was tongue in cheek for the citizens of southern Illinois, but in reality most of the citizenship had had relatives housed there.

"Did you bring a wire?" Sheriff Yocum asked.

"I've got it," Monica Rose said standing in the opening of the sliding side door of the van. Come inside young lady and I will place the listening device on you."

Mickey Masters was a country doper. Used up body, dead skin and hair, skinny and dirty looking with needle marks on her arms and a red bulbous nose from snorting cocaine. She was dressed country western with cowboy boots and a denim jacket.

She walked past everyone staring at her and entered the van. Monica slid the door closed. In about two minutes, Monica stuck her head out and said, "I'm testing, you all turn your radios on and tell me if we're transmitting."

The group turned on their miniature radios and listened. "Testing, testing, am I getting out?" Monica asked.

"Loud and clear," several TFD's responded.

"You need to sign this document stating that the United States Government is giving you $3000.00 in funds to buy cocaine from someone," Monica advised Mickey Masters. She signed it and Monica relinquished the cash to her.

"I need to tell you guys something," Mickey Masters said. "Vicky Bass, the girl I'm buying from has two big attack dogs. If she gives the order to attack they will rip you guys apart. One's a Doberman and the other is a German Shepard. They are protective of her. You will probably have to shoot them when you come in."

"We've got shotguns," Mike Schweig loudly said. "A couple of dogs won't stop the Drug Enforcement Administration. Young lady, your job is to buy the dope and get out of there. Don't tarry, understand?"

"Yes, sir," Mickey Masters replied. She went back to Sheriff Yocum's car, got in and closed the door.

"Are we ready to roll?" Schweig asked with a smile.

"Not yet, we're waiting for her car to arrive. I had to pay to have tires put on it. It'll be here in a couple of minutes," the sheriff replied.

"Car, tires, what's going on?" Schweig asked.

"This gal we're buying dope from, Vicky Bass, I had a stealing case on her in Jersey County. I was trying to be reasonable, so I let her go on her own recognizance. Her boyfriend Freddy Hawk, picked her up at my office and assured me that he would make certain she showed up for a court appearance on the stealing charge."

"Don't tell me, she didn't show, right?" I said with a smile.

"Right! I telephoned Freddy's house, they told me to fuck off, advised me that they didn't live in my county and that they were friends with the sheriff in their county and then hung up the phone. I just waited for my chance to get them. Mickey Masters was drunk, driving on her rims after she blew out every tire on her car. She wandered into Jersey County and got stopped.....the rest is history. I've got the search warrant in my fat little hand."

An old Chevy Impala rolled onto the lot with a sheriff's deputy driving it. Mickey Masters observed her car and climbed out of the sheriff car. She walked to her car and checked the tires, "Nice," she said. "Is it time to go?"

"Yep," Sheriff Yocum said. She climbed in and headed for the house.

"Everybody in the van," Schweig shouted.

"I'll stay in my car," Sheriff Yocum advised.

"We'll follow you and communicate by radio," I said as I headed for the van. We drove about half a mile and were in the boonies. The place wasn't foreign to me; I'd been around the area for what seemed to be a lifetime. It seemed I was always being drawn back.

Mickey made a right turn onto a gated driveway with the gate open and headed up a long and winding gravel pathway. We drove past the driveway and ducked into an opening alongside the roadway just down from the house. We could see the A frame style house through the trees. It reminded me of Colorado.

We listened to the monitor as Mickey Masters stopped her car and attempted to get out. The dogs were on her, barking and growling so she shut the door and waited.

"Back," a female voice said. "Down, go to your rooms," she said. "Fucking dogs! Hi, Mickey. Did you come to buy?"

"Yep, can I come inside?"

"Yeah come on inside, the dogs won't bother you unless I tell them to."

We listened as the car door opened and then shut and footsteps of the two women walking up the stairs of the porch, and then to the inside of the A frame.

"How much do you want to buy?" Vicky Bass asked.

"I've got $3000 in my purse, how much will that buy today?"

"$3000 will buy half a pound today, we've got a lot to sell. $3000 will make you $10,000, show me the cash."

There was some rustling and steps, and finally Mickey had the dope and Vicky had the money. "You want to do a line?" Vicky asked.

"Yeah, Mickey replied. There was snorting on the radio.

"I figure I owe you at least a line since I stole your old man right from under you. I feel bad about it and I want to apologize."

"I accept your apology, snort, snort," Mickey replied. "Does he beat you?"

"Yeah," Vicky replied, "But not like he used to beat you. He doesn't load up on me with his fists like he did to you, snort, snort."

"Where is Freddy?" Mickey asked.

"He's out doing something, I'm not sure where or what. But he treats me well, I mean with the dope business I get just about anything I desire."

"Tell the sheriff we're going to hit the place," Schweig advised.

I keyed the radio and advised him. "Fine," he replied.

Schweig drove the van up the winding hill which led to the rear of the house and a large wooden back porch.

We slid the side door of the van open and we jumped out into the graveled parking area of the property.

The attack dogs charged at us, we pointed twelve gauge shotguns at them and they veered off and ran toward the barn. "A dog will always choose the winning side," Jim Bob shouted as we ran up the steps to the front door.

Vicky Bass came charging at us, stoned and angry, "Attack, attack," she shouted at the retreating dogs.

"DEA, get down, search warrant," several of us shouted at her. She took a wild swing at me with a right cross. I ducked and she fell down on the porch deck still yelling attack at her missing dogs.

I handcuffed Vicky and dragged her by one leg into the living room of the house. She took a look at Mickey Masters and shouted, "Narc, you fucking narc, I'll kill you for this."

Mike Schweig handcuffed Mickey for effect and marched her out of the house. Sheriff Yocum took charge of her and sat her in his car.

I took a quick inventory of Vicky Bass and the house. Vicky could have been cute if she wasn't a stoner. She was petite, blonde and blue eyes and was dressed in a cowboy outfit, much like Mickey Masters. The attack dogs wandered into the house and curled up next to their mistress. A lot of good you two fuckers are," she scolded them. They quickly napped.

The house was country western as well, large oak furniture and a loft with knotty pine stairs and wall coverings. It was an expensive piece of real estate considering the acreage and barn. The TFD's started the search. The government buy money and the half pound of cocaine was still on the coffee table in front of the couch. Schweig seized the cash, and the dope was temporarily left on the table.

"Where's the rest of the dope and cash?" Schweig asked Vicky.

"Fuck you, you fat piece of shit narc," she replied.

"Thank you ma'am," Schweig said.

I wandered into the kitchen. There was a pantry attached to it and there was a large floor safe in the pantry. "Safe in here," I loudly said.

"Car coming up the drive," Reszler shouted. I ran to the porch and observed a scrubby bearded man sitting in an old Chevy with a confused look on his face. I walked to the car and placed my little revolver in his face, just like every other good little DEA operative, and ordered him to step out. I searched him and he had a .25 automatic in his jacket pocket. I seized it and placed it in my pocket and hooked him up.

"Who the fuck are you guys?" He asked.

DEA," I replied. "We're doing a search warrant on your house. Schweig and Reszler joined me at the car.

"What's your name, man?" I asked.

"Freddy Hawk," he replied. "Did you guys kill my dogs?"

"No, they're inside sleeping next to your girlfriend."

"A lot of fucking good they did," he mumbled.

We marched him into the house and back to the kitchen. He was watching and looking at everything going on inside his house.

The TFD's were into every nook and cranny of the house. Some were sticking cash into their pockets at every chance. Freddy noted it as we sat him into a kitchen chair near the floor safe. He'd been drinking beer, I could smell it on him, and it was just noon. He lived the life of a wealthy country drug dealer. He had no itinerary or schedule to meet, he did what he wanted when he wanted. The cash flow kept him fat and sassy.

"Open the safe," I ordered him.

"Nope," he replied. He kept watching the TFD's from the kitchen doorway searching his living room.

Schweig came into the kitchen. "We have a search warrant and I'm ordering you to open that safe," he said while pointing.

"Let me see the warrant," he replied. I obtained the warrant from the van and held it up for him to read.

"This is a state of Illinois warrant, it ain't a federal warrant, and it doesn't say anything about my floor safe so

I'm not going to open it."

"I'm calling Palance," Schewig said and walked into the kitchen. He returned in five minutes, "Palance says to pay a moving company to move the safe to our office and we'll have somebody from Chicago open it."

"Not without a separate warrant," Freddy Hawk exclaimed. Mike walked out of the room.

It was a standoff, but Freddy showed his weakness. He was squirming in the chair. He needed to relive himself.

"You guys want me to cooperate, right?"

"Yeah, Freddy," I replied.

"Okay, I'll cooperate, but I need to use the toilet." I studied him. Marine Corps field jacket, jeans and boots and a seven day growth. Long stringy hair, but he wasn't dirty, he didn't stink, and his clothing was clean.

I unhooked him and he went into the bathroom while I stood behind him in the kitchen. He finished and walked into the pantry and opened the safe after playing with the combination. He returned to the chair and I hooked him up.

"Safes open," I again shouted toward the living room. Schweig came in and seized cash and drugs from the safe. How much cash is here, Freddy?" Schweig asked.

"Twenty thousand dollars," Freddy replied. "There's a kilo of cocaine there also."

"The United States government is going to seize your cash and the dope." Schweig took the dope and cash and left the kitchen area.

"Let's talk about cooperation," Freddy said to me. "You guys want me to do my source, right?"

"Yeah," I replied.

"Okay, I'll do it, but first I want to call my attorney and advise him what I'm doing. Is that okay?"

"Schweig," I shouted. He came into the kitchen, "Freddy wants to do his source for leniency but he wants to telephone his lawyer first. That okay?"

"I'll have to call Palance, I'll be back," He said as he walked away.

"Okay, you guys are seizing my cash and dope, I understand that, but some of those guys out there are stealing my house cash. I've been watching them and I've seen them sticking my cash into their pockets."

I was embarrassed and Freddy noted it. "You haven't been doing this for long, have you?" He asked me.

I didn't answer him. "You're no kid, and you're not a federal agent. You're a loaner cop, detached to the feds to play kid agent for a few years. Right?"

I nodded in the affirmative. Sheriff Yocum walked back into the house. I heard his voice in the living room, "Hello Ms. Bass," he said. "How nice to see you again; you want to tell me to go and fuck myself, now?"

"Yeah, go and fuck yourself," Vicky shouted.

"Vicky, shut your fucking mouth," Freddy shouted from the kitchen. Sheriff Yocum walked into the kitchen, looked at Freddy shackled to the chair, and smiled.

"I'm out of here," the Sheriff said, and walked out.

"He was the affiant on the state warrant, wasn't he?" Freddy asked.

"Maybe," I replied. Freddy's knowledge of the justice system intrigued me. "How do you know so much about the system?" I asked.

"I had a good civics teacher in high school," he replied.

Schweig walked in. Palance said if he wants to do his source, he can, but we're letting the cash walk and we're using his cash. Who's your source?"

"Little John Gipson," Freddy replied.

Schweig was making faces and in deep thought. "You guys know him," Freddy said. "He's been taken off by DEA from St. Louis before. He's a heroin dealer, lives in Los Angeles, now he's dealing in coke."

"Yeah, I remember him," Schweig said. "Big dope dealer. You can do him?"

"Yep," Freddy replied.

"I'll be right back," Schweig said.

"Can I telephone my attorney, now?" Freddy asked.

I unhooked him and he walked to the wall phone in the kitchen. He dialed it and waited.

"This is Fred Hawk, I need to talk to Harvey," he lowly said. He waited, "Harvey, I've been taken off by DEA. Yep! Yep! State warrant. Yep, nope, I told them I was going to cooperate and do my source. Yep! Nope! Leniency for me and Vicky, I'll call you when this is over." He hung up and stood and looked at me.

"I'll sit back in the chair but do you have to handcuff me? I'm cooperative." I nodded, Freddy sat and brooded, un-cuffed.

Schweig came back into the kitchen. "You can call Little John Gipson and have him deliver a kilo, right?"

"Yep!" Freddy replied.

Schweig hooked up a Pearl recorder to the wall phone. "Okay," Mike replied, "Do it!"

Freddy got up from the kitchen chair and walked to the wall phone, he dialed and waited, "Hey my brother, I'm in need of another "K", can you accommodate me? Yeah, cool, same price, $18,000, hour and a half, right , I'll be waiting. Bye!" Freddy sat down in the kitchen chair.

Schweig walked out of the kitchen, "Okay everybody we've got a controlled delivery of a kilo of cocaine. The target will be here in one hour."

The group looked at him as if to say, "So, what's the big deal?"

"We need to video tape this transaction," Schweig

mumbled. He walked around in circles looking to and fro in the ski cottage. "The loft, some of us can hide in the loft. We'll put the camera right behind the couch. The rest of you guys hide in the bedroom."

Freddy Hawk listened with a smile on his face. "Can I make a suggestion?" he asked.

"Schweig," I yelled, "Freddy wants to make a suggestion, can you come into the kitchen?" Schweig came in,

"You can hide your government cars behind my barn, and there's a tack room in the barn that some of you guys can hide in," Freddy suggested.

"Great idea," Schweig said and ran out of the kitchen.

"I need to get Vicky up and presentable or this deal won't go," Freddy said.

I nodded; he stood and walked to the living room where Vicky was snoozing with the dogs.

"Get out of the way you useless piece of shit," he said to the German Shepard. The dog growled and raised its lip and Freddy kicked it in the head. It took off toward the locked front door, circled and laid down. The Doberman calmly stood and walked away from Vicky.

"Vicky, wake the fuck up," Freddy said as he shook her.

"I had this terrible dream that we got taken off by DEA," Vicky mumbled.

"It ain't a dream," Freddy said.

"What? Oh, fuck! She raised up and looked at the TFD's and Schweig, "Narcs, you fucking narcs, get the fuck out of my house." She stood and started swinging at the group. Freddy slapped her, grabbed her by her shirt and shook her.

"We're the fucking narcs, now, Vicky. We're setting up Little John. He's bringing a kilo of coke over here and were going to buy it, for DEA. It'll be on tape and we'll get leniency. You understand?"

"Oh, fuck, we're narcs? Oh fuck!" she replied.

"Now get your ass into the bathroom and make yourself presentable to Little John. Do it now." Vicky wandered off.

Schweig walked into the parking area behind the house and returned with a portable camera. He set it up on a table, next to a lamp. It was not visible.

The TFD's were walking toward the courtyard to hide their "G" cars. In five minutes they returned.

There was still an hour to kill. "Crown Royal, anyone?" Freddy asked with a grin.

"Yeah, I'll take a glass," Schweig replied. Freddy poured him a stiff one.

"There's a couple of cases of cold beer in the fridge if you guys want one," Freddy said. Everybody was drinking Crown Royal chased by cold beer. Within forty five minutes, everybody was drunk.

The wall phone rang and Freddy answered it. He handed the phone to Schweig, it was Palance. "Yes, sir, Steve, I understand, we'll take care of it." He hung the phone up.

"Okay everybody, it's official, we're letting the money walk, everyone clear?"

"Yeah," the TFD's mumbled.

"I'll be in the loft," Schweig continued. Most of you guys hide in the barn with TFD Been. Reszler and T. Anderson, you guys hide in the bedroom. Everybody be alert. This guy's a class one violator, probably armed and he knows the system. Ringer and Been, listen to the Kell on your radios."

"Yeah, yeah," they mumbled.

"Car coming up the hill," I yelled.

"Everybody get into place," Schweig yelled as he activated the video camera and scrambled up the loft ladder.

There was a tap on the door. Vicky, who by then had made herself up and was looking good, opened the door and flashed her big blues at Little John. "Come in, John," she seductively said.

Little John Gipson, black and cool, carrying a grocery bag, and wearing an $800 leather jacket calmly strolled inside. He kissed Vicky on the lips, palmed her butt and said, "When you gonna leave this cracker and come with me. I'll put some color on your ass."

The front door was still open when Freddy approached them. He looked outside, "I see you drove the 38 Chevy this evening, my brother," he said as they shook hands.

"Yeah, I spent a load on it, I figure I might as well drive it as much as I can," John replied. Vicky and Freddy plopped onto the couch, John Gipson sat in a chair across from them. He set the grocery bag on the coffee table. "Crown Royal?" Freddy asked.

"Yes, my brother," Little John replied.

The greetings and salutations were complete and the drinks were being downed. Little John was flirting with the now cute Vicky and the dogs were circling the group no doubt wondering when the fireworks were going to begin.

Freddy began counting cash and laying it on the coffee table. "$18,000, my brother," he said. Dope in the bag?"

"Yes, my brother," Little John said. He pushed the grocery bag toward Freddy, looked at his wrist watch and said, "I've got to run." His demeanor had changed. He began nervously looking around the room and up to the loft. He put his hand on his waistband as if he had a weapon, stood and backed toward the door.

Freddy Hawk and Vicky had looks of fear on their faces, they figured he'd heard something or observed one of the undercover government cops. Little John backed out of the doorway climbed into his customized 1938 Chevy and tore out down the gravel driveway.

Schweig climbed down from the loft with the camera and tripod, cassette in hand. "We've got everything we need," he said. "Good job, Freddy and Vicky. But you'll still be spending the night in jail. You'll be arraigned in the morning and bond will be available."

"Make sure my dogs are out of the house," Freddy said. "They'll survive for a day or two until I can get us released. They'll survive. There's a creek down at the bottom of the hill, and rabbits for them to chase and eat."

Joe Ringer and Jim Bob cuffed them and placed them in the back seat of their Chrysler "G" car for the ride to Belleville, Illinois.

The dogs were shooed out of the house. They stood on the porch and watched as their masters were carted away by the narcs.

A month quickly whizzed by and Little John Gipson had not been arrested. S/A Braun informed me that he had a federal search warrant for John Gibson's mother's house on Brown Street in Alton, Illinois. We were going to execute it this evening. Our beer drinking/golfing buddy AUSA Cliff Proud was going to be in attendance.

It was a typical DEA raid. We stormed in after kicking the door as John and his mother and some other family members were watching television.

John Gipson had twelve children from two women. Most of them lived in his mother's home on Brown Street and most of them were in attendance when we entered. We knew about Little John's children and girlfriends, but with that many people screaming, crying and running to hide, it was hectic.

Little John, having lived most of his life in Alton, Illinois knew how to milk the state system of Aid to Dependent Children. He refused to marry the two women he had the children with, but he had them legally change their names to

Gipson so they could live in his mother's house and act like her children instead of Little John's concubines. That way they qualified for lucrative state checks every month.

Little John was a wealthy heroin and cocaine dealer and lived high off of the hog in California as well as Illinois. He chose to let the state of Illinois pay the way for his twelve children.

I always felt badly after a drug raid where children are present, but I often wondered if their screams and tears are manufactured. Many times their actions looked scripted.

We found dope and cash and there was a kilo of cocaine in the trunk of Little John's customized 1938 Chevrolet. We seized it.

During the search we found scores of custom made golf clubs hidden in a crawl space in the garage. We wondered about them and later found out that the son of a golf shop owner had a heroin addiction and was stealing his dad's inventory and trading golf clubs for heroin.

By the time we concluded the search it was late. Cliff Proud advised us that we could house John Gipson for safe keeping in the Alton, Illinois jail overnight and that since I lived north, I should convey him to federal courthouse East St. Louis in the morning.

I agreed, and John Gipson was nestled in the Alton jail. Braun was concerned about this revelation because the Alton jail wasn't a federally approved incarceration facility, but Cliff Proud approved it so we did it.

I picked John Gipson up in the morning. He was cuffed and sitting next to me in my little LeBaron. There was no conversation but he was amusingly staring at me as I drove toward East St. Louis, Illinois.

I don't mind talking to people who I arrest, but dope dealers are a different breed of criminal. They have cash hidden somewhere, cash that is destined for a big-time trial lawyer who will defend them in any way he can.

Everything that is said between a defendant and a government agent is regurgitated verbatim to a defense lawyer. The agent will be beaten with information while on the stand testifying against the defendant.

I figured I'd stop any conversation before it started. "Don't ask me any questions," I began. "I'm not going to converse with you or be your friend."

Little John stared and cleared his throat. "Your name is Tim Richards. You lived at 1106 George Street in Alton when you were a kid, across from the basketball court at Lincoln School. You and I used to play basketball together. You were pretty good as I remember, for a white boy."

I was the one staring then. I nodded and smiled. We had a brief conversation about the old neighborhood. We both went to Lincoln grade school but he was a couple of years ahead of me.

Most of the conversation between me and John Gipson centered around his 1938 Chevrolet. He bought it as an original car and paid large sums of money to have it turned into a customized show car. He flat-bedded it to his home in Southern California for the custom paint job but had most of the work done in good old Alton.

John's lawyer, Frank Fabbri, was a popular defense attorney with the black dope dealers. He was always in the federal courthouse wandering the halls, waiting to go into court.

Frank Fabbri looked like a sleaze-bag lawyer. He dressed the part, gaudy suits that didn't quite fit him properly, he chain smoked outside of the courthouse, he was white and had a black wife, and a black girlfriend, and he always had a wise crack to throw at anybody within earshot.

But in reality, Frank Fabbri was a nice man. He was a

hard-working man and intelligent. He handled John Gipson's plea and John went away for a paid federal vacation.

Frank purchased John Gipson's beloved 1938 Chevrolet on the courthouse steps for a fraction of what it was worth. He drove it daily and it was his trademark. It was a one of a kind car, and Frank personalized it with the license plate, snub-38.

VII.

NO SUCH THING AS FAILURE

The deals were day and night and the young fed/cops were bringing in loads of money from seized assets. We seized cars, houses boats, motor homes, jewelry, cash and any other kind of asset we could get our federal hands on. Little Stevie Wonder even seized a doll collection from a farmer in the boot-heel.

Word was getting back to the police department that we were running wild throughout the states of Florida, Illinois, Iowa, Kansas, California, and Texas, doing whatever we wanted to do when we wanted to do it. The governing class at police headquarters was concerned to some degree, but we were giving the department millions of dollars for them to spend as they wished.

Somehow the word got to the chief of police that some of us might be using controlled substances. There was a drug screening order that had been drawn up in the mid-seventies stating that when a member of the department was ordered to report to the medical division for a drug screening that he or she would report to that venue immediately for screening. There was no excuse accepted.

Some of us were ordered to report for a drug screening. The young cop would telephone the chief's office and tell them that he was too busy with federal drug asset forfeiture to report. The chief's office accepted the excuse. Money talks in the cop and crook business.

The federal agents were also screened for drug usage periodically. They griped that they had to go but the cops didn't have to. We burned marijuana throughout the mid-west, inhaling much of it. No TFD ever took a drug test.

The rumor mill was spinning tales about Group Supervisor Palance's promotion. Word had it that he would be promoted soon and would leave the group for greener pastures in Washington, D.C.

At about that same time Reszler was graduating from "Hootie Owl" Tarkio College. Like wild animals, the group sensed that things were going to change for the cops and agents in the task force. Without Palance to protect us from the Special Agent in Charge (SAC) the United States Attorney and hundreds of defense lawyers, the job for us was going to change, and not for the better.

Being the old man of the group I had the opportunity to monitor some of the TFD's. Reszler was my closest friend in the group. We even double dated a couple of times. He would bring his pin-up model and I would bring my cute wife.

I noticed a change in him. He was on his way to being a full-fledged DEA agent. The TFD's hated most of the federal agents. We imitated and mocked them. We had private obscene names for them. We did all of the work in the task force, the agents got all of the credit. The police department reaped the benefits of the seized assets. The cop gossip over beer had the governing class at police headquarters pilfering what they could. I tended to believe it.

We kept on kicking in doors and seizing assets for the city, state and federal government. It was almost a joke among us. We stole the assets from the drug dealers and handed it over to the thieves at police headquarters to squander among their political friends. It was all done legally through the United States forfeiture law.

We knew we were the whores in this money grab, but we never complained because the position of TFD was better than any other job within the system. We had cars, freedom, money and a chance at stardom. And we never had to take a drug test.

The deals started slowing down for the group. I figured it was because we all knew that Group Supervisor Palance was leaving the unit.

Little Stevie Wonder had a deal for the evening out west in St. Charles County, Missouri. It was a buy-bust, most of our deals were buy-busts or search warrants.

Little Stevie Wonder had an informant who told him he could buy cocaine from a source, so Little Stevie got the group saddled up and we headed out to the boondocks, in the dark.

We met up on a farm field near a blacktop road. Little Stevie wired the informant and gave him government funds for the buy. "Now just say it's as good as gold, and we'll swoop in and arrest the dealer, understand?" Little Stevie said.

"Yes, sir," the informant replied.

The informant took off in his pickup and we followed him for a couple of miles until he pulled over to the side of the road. We all pulled over and listened to the conversation.

Reszler and I started walking alongside the road trying to get close to the deal so we could grab the dealer when the deal was consummated.

"It's as good as gold," the informant loudly stated. The tone of the informant's voice spooked the dealer and he took off running down the blacktop road with the federal cash in his pocket.

The federal government doesn't give a damn about some

stupid substance that is illegal in the United States and that a bunch of weirdos want to ingest into their bodies. The government cares about cash. If buy money isn't supposed to walk, and it does, then the agents have a lot of explaining to do. Scrutiny is not the friend of narcotics investigators.

"Get him, get him, he's got the buy money," Little Stevie Wonder screamed.

Reszler and I ran after the guy shouting for him to stop and that we were DEA agents. He continued to run down the dark road with dense foliage on both sides. We chased him for a couple of hundred yards, slowly gaining on him from what we could see. Finally we caught him and knocked him down.

We cuffed him and dragged him to his feet. The guy had soiled his trousers and he stunk like a dead and bloated rat. I could see the humor in the event. Little Stevie Wonder would have to transport him back to our offices in beautiful Clayton, Missouri in the back seat of his G car.

I glanced at Reszler expecting a smile or laugh. Little Stevie was actually an okay guy, but he was an agent and our enemy. Reszler did not see the humor in the event. I could tell he was upset. "What's up?" I asked.

"I'm growing tired of this bullshit," Reszler replied. "Fucking deal after deal, it never stops. And now this asshole shits his pants. I'm just tired."

"Resz," I began. "You'd better rethink your decision to take an agent job. You'll be doing this shitty job for the rest of your life."

"I know, man, I really don't want to be an agent. I hate the fucking agents. I don't want to be like them. But I don't want to go back to the department, either. What's going to happen when Doc Cooper retires? I'll be up for grabs, riding around in some black district conveying Willie and Willa

Mae and their chillins to the hospital."

We handed the shitty dope dealer over to Little Stevie Wonder, climbed into our "G" cars and headed back to Clayton.

I wasn't the only one who had observed a change in Reszler's attitude. Group Supervisor Palance monitored each and every one of us. We were his whores and we worked for him like he was the king pimp; for in fact he was.

Palance loved and cared for every one of us because we worked for him. We didn't have to. Some guys have come to DEA and just went along with the crowd to get along. Go along and get along. But as a group there wasn't one slacker.

Palance mesmerized the young cops. He talked with them about women, of which he was an expert, about cars, duty assignments, their parents, how to act undercover, how to sell oneself to the unsuspecting informant or dope dealer. But the common denominator was hatred for drug dealers. We all hated dope dealers.

Before most deals Palance would give us a pep talk about safety, and he would intertwine his speech with negative descriptive sayings about dope dealers. "You know these guys are pussies," He would say. "They would snitch on their own mothers if they were given the opportunity. These big rich dope dealers with their steroid muscles, "no offense Reszler," piss their pants and shit on themselves when we arrest them." The group would laugh.

Palance was the consummate pimp of young alcoholic cops, and his style of leadership worked well for him. The St. Louis Task Force had stats that were intriguing to other group supervisors in the country. Other agents started bidding for Palance's job. They were waiting for him to be promoted and leave, and then there would a fight for leadership of the St. Louis Task Force.

What most of the applicants wanting Group Supervisor Palance's job did not know was that we worked for him because he knew what motivated us as a group, and as individuals. He had a knack, everybody's good at something. Would the group work like whore dogs for someone they didn't know, or did not trust? Doubtful!

I watched Palance work his mesmerism on individual young cops. He cornered Reszler one afternoon before a deal and after a federal pep talk. "You okay, Conan?" he began. "You've been acting kind of down lately. New girlfriend okay?"

"I'm okay," Reszler countered. He didn't wish to give any details of his life to Palance. He already knew too much about all of us. He whisked away with a smile, but Palance wasn't satisfied with Reszler's response. He stared at his gait and read his body language as Reszler walked away. It makes us all open books.

Physiognomy is used by every good investigator. The feds go to local police departments and give classes on it. I took a couple of the classes. I use it daily.

Body language tells a lot of the story about individuals. The problem arises when the cop/investigator can't control it and everyone he comes into contact with, wives or girlfriends, friends, or relatives, become a subject of physiognomy. It's a slippery slope. Palance was at that stage of the art form.

I learned a lot from Steve Palance. One of the most important things I learned was, in his eyes there was no such thing as failure. As long as you tried you did not fail. That philosophy eliminates the fear of failure.

I never could figure out if he learned that in DEA school or in the hard scrabble world of undercover drug deals, but it impressed me. It was kind of a scaled down version of "dope dealer today, dope dealer tomorrow."

But what Palance might not have taken into consideration with Reszler was that Reszler's tenure at the DEA task force was drawing to an end. We are only loaned out for three or four years, unless you are closely related to an important person.

Reszler was not. His "ace" was the department surgeon, Doc Cooper. Doc Cooper was on his way out and it was common knowledge that his power within the St. Louis Metropolitan Police Department was limited. His brother in law, Governor Warren Hearnes was no longer in office.

There is a transitional period for VIP's in the region. Some don't lose all of their power at once. It slowly dwindles until their names become jokes. Such was the case with Doc Cooper.

Reszler's dilemma was the fact that he had been living like a diplomat in the glamorous and exciting world of federal law enforcement. With one phone call he could go from glamor and intrigue to mediocrity and boredom. It's the horror of big-city small time politics.

Reszler knew it was coming and the only way he could combat it was to be hired by DEA, which meant he would have to conform and be one of the "prick" federal agents instead of one of the beer drinking, bad attitude, independent acting, uncontrollable, unaccountable, spoiled city cops playing junior G-man. It was a sobering realization for all of us.

In St. Louis, and in the game of law enforcement, there was no better place to be. But it was a mirage, a foggy booze induced dream that pushed us forward, blindly hitting doors with sledge hammers, fighting bikers and businessman, working strange hours and taking the abuse that a federal agency deals to small time cops playing fed.

It wasn't real and we all knew it. It was time for Reszler to fish or cut bait, and a sobering decision making time: become an agent or go back to mediocrity.

Nobody likes to face reality, especially spoiled, entitled cops. Reszler was worried more about career than mortality, and it showed in his demeanor.

Jim Bob, the county cop who was a hero had been living in a motel in Springfield, Missouri with Detective Horowitz, acting like wannabe drug dealers who were trying to buy some big-time marijuana to take back to St. Louis and sell.

Palance gave them carte blanche, expense money and the blessing of the SAC to take as much time as they needed as long as there were people to lock up and assets to seize when the dust settled.

I got a call at bedtime telling me to meet the crew at the office and that we were going to Springfield, Missouri for a deal. I didn't want to go and I advised Detective Horowitz of that fact. He said Palance told him that everyone was going. "Is Palance going?" I asked.

"No," he replied.

I thought about my decision and then told Horowitz I would meet them. I had been refraining from beer and was semi sober for the first time in a couple of years. I was concerned about the road trip with the boys. It usually turned into a rolling drinking and pissing contest.

I quickly packed a bag and said goodbye to my wife, kids and dogs. I had been living this lifestyle for more than two years and I knew the end was near. My problem remained static: where do I go after DEA? Is there life after DEA?

I met up with the boys and we headed southwest. I jumped in with Detective Horowitz who had been rewarded with a new Buick "G" car for his stellar ass kissing tactics with the DEA bosses.

It was late, after 10:00 and we had the roads to ourselves. There was a convoy of about four cars and we were talking on the closed circuit DEA two way radios.

We were all drinking beer as we bore through the dark night. Horowitz started the racial slurs on the radio; it didn't take much for everyone else to join in. They were imitating Amos and Andy and playing the skit to the tune of DEA and our SAC.

The skit was disgusting and it dragged on and on, everyone trying to outdo everyone else. Nothing is as racist as a St. Louis cop.

Someone from the St. Louis Field Office got on the air and said, "You guys are broadcasting out. Your conversation is getting out," which meant the SAC or anyone else in St. Louis was listening. The DEA brass monitor the radios. They are always intent on knowing what is going on with their agents and cops.

The radios aren't set up to broadcast long distances. They are car to car short range radios mostly used for surveillance and communication between vehicles. But on this night they were hitting the air waves and going long distances. St. Louis was listening.

The boys didn't stop with the racist shtick. As I suspected, the pissing contest had only just begun. It continued on and on, and if the SAC wasn't listening at the beginning he was surely listening now. Someone would have called him and told him to dial in. The SAC has a complete radio system in his home compliments of the DOJ. He can talk to Washington, D.C. if he wishes to.

We finally arrived in Springfield, got rooms at the Holiday Inn, and I went to bed. The boys were roaming and drinking and looking for stray broads for most of the night.

I awoke early, went to the hotel restaurant and had a nice

breakfast. The boys stumbled in as I was finishing. Jim Bob was on the telephone talking to his informant for the big buy-bust that was allegedly going down this afternoon.

"It's in the mix," Jim Bob assured us. "It's going down this afternoon, 500 pounds of weed."

After you do this job for a while you get a feel of a good deal compared to a bad deal. I got bad vibes from Jimmy's deal. I kind of knew it wasn't going to materialize. I wandered back to the room, watched TV and waited.

The morning turned into afternoon and Jimmy was still talking to his informant. Finally he said, "It's on, saddle up we're going to meet up on a country road out in the boonies."

By this time everyone was skeptical. We followed Jimmy to the parking lot and the convoy headed south of town to an old dirt road. There was a cleared area where cars can meet up or turn around. There was a car there with one occupant. Jimmy got out and went to the car and spoke to the driver. We all watched and waited.

Jimmy walked back to us. "The informant says he can't find the weed dealer. He wants us to give him some more time to set up the deal." Jimmy had a sick look on his face.

"So the deal is off?" I said.

"Yeah, for now anyway," Jimmy replied.

"Head for St. Louis," I advised Detective Horowitz. He turned the Buick around and we headed northeast.

Things were cool in the DEA Field Office. It was all over in the gossip filled halls about our racist skit on the way to Springfield.

Group Supervisor, Palance was looking forlorn. He called Jimmy and Detective Horowitz into his office and had a closed door meeting with them. They no doubt blamed the racist skit on someone else, probably me. We all waited it out and it went away.

Detective Horowitz had some big time ass kissing to do. He sent floral arrangement after floral arrangement to the bosses. They got tickets to the ball games, concerts, plays and any other kind of sporting event you could imagine. He was eventually forgiven for his racism. Money talks! Marijuana was playing big for the task force. Palance was big-time friends with the Sheriff of Ripley County, which is way south in Missouri, almost to Arkansas. The county is mostly made up of the Mark Twain National Forest. There are towns sprinkled throughout it with fitting names: Wilderness, Many Springs, Doniphan, and the Current River meanders through it.

It's the perfect place to grow marijuana. The federal government refers to the eradication of marijuana as "cash crop."

These days super strong weed is called "kush loud," or just "kush."

It's killer weed, real potent and expensive and the growers plant and cultivate it in the dense national forest. The sheriff and his deputies get tips as to where the patches of expensive weed are growing and we (DEA) are called to go there and eradicate it.

Of course the sheriff of the county we are eradicating in gets a piece of the pie from the fed. It's lucrative for the county sheriffs and the county government.

Palance put the word out that we, as a group, were heading for Ripley County, Missouri to eradicate weed in the Mark Twain National Forest.

We took off in a convoy, spent the night in Poplar Bluff, and headed out early in the morning to meet up with the sheriff and his deputies.

We were all dressed in Marine Corps cammies, had automatic rifles and sawed off shotguns as well as side arms.

It was like we were going into combat in some foreign land. To me Southeast Missouri was a foreign land.

The sheriff and his deputies were good old boys. Their lives evolved around turkey, deer, duck, and squirrel season. Summer was fishing and drinking beer on the Current River.

We all piled into the beds of four wheel drive pickup trucks and headed into the forest. The deputies were driving as we laid out and watched the trees go by, cracking jokes and relaxing. The pressure to excel was off of us for a couple of days. It was like being on vacation.

The trick was for us, as a group, to get close to a patch, then sneak up on the patch and try to arrest the guards and cultivators living in and around the weed patch.

The pickups would stop and we would climb out, form a line and invade the enemy camp with our weapons at the ready.

Most of the time the camp was deserted. We did make a couple of arrests. These poor slobs who lived in tents and ate canned food were interrogated on the spot as to who the owner of the patch was. They rarely talked.

The United States Attorney didn't wish to prosecute the weed patch guards. I always felt it was a skit being put on by the sheriff and his deputies.

The patches we raided were small by comparison to the large kush operations we had eradicated. But it was fun and entertaining and the TFD's and the special agents got along with each other for a couple of days.

Palance was a happy man. The Sheriff was a happy man. We were advised to count the marijuana plants in twos, meaning the count was doubled.

The Sheriff was paid by the fed for every plant we eradicated from his county. Palance had more fodder for his upcoming promotion.

The sheriff owned a big spread outside of Poplar Bluff. He had a large lake with a high diving platform, a pavilion for parties and huge bar-b-que pits. He threw a big party for us after the Mark Twain National Forest raids.

There was all of the beer we could drink, all kinds of grilled food, and places to shoot our guns if we chose to.

Palance tossed the keys to his Nissan Turbo to the boys and they raced it up and down the rural highways around the sheriff's compound, banging gears and pushing the turbo to its max.

As in any delicate sports car, the fun was abruptly stopped when the engine blew a spark plug out of the block. Palance called a tow truck and had it towed to a Nissan Dealer nearby.

It wasn't cheap to repair. The fed ate the bill, but the car was never the same after that episode. It had no power or pizzaz. It was just neat to look at.

After the fiasco in Ripley County we headed back to St. Louis with hangovers. We figured we'd have a little time to recoup, but it wasn't possible.

We staggered into our classy government offices in beautiful downtown Clayton the next morning and Palance was waiting for us checking his wristwatch as we stumbled into our chairs and sipped coffee.

He had our attention as we watched him through glossy eyes. "Today we are going to Pelican Island. Anybody know where that is?" he said with a wry smile.

I knew where Pelican Island was situated but I wasn't in the mood for question answer games so I kept my mouth shut.

"It's an uninhabited island on the Missouri River. Somebody's growing sensimilla there and we are going to try to catch the growers and eradicate the weed."

Palance was reading us and enjoying our pain. Little Stevie Wonder, Palance's nemesis, raised his hand like a fourth grade arithmetic student. Palance nodded to him with disdain.

"Where did this clue come from," Little Stevie Wonder asked.

"St. Louis County Police," Palance replied. "They were patrolling in their chopper and observed the patch from the air. It's a nice patch, grown and almost ready for harvest. In fact, St. Louis County is going to convey us to the island via their chopper. We'll land on the north side of the island and make our way toward the south side, that's where the weed is. If we're lucky we'll catch somebody there cultivating or guarding. Get your cammies on and head for the Spirit of St. Louis Airport. We'll all meet there and fly off to Pelican.

The group was grumbling and making moves toward the door to get to the trunks of their "G" cars to retrieve their cammies and boots.

We got our gear and moved back into the large office. We changed clothes in the open office, drank more coffee, filled our canteens with cold water and headed for the door again.

We drove to the airport in Chesterfield, Missouri in a convoy, parked and wandered into the giant hangar. The helicopter was state of the art gas turbo, quick and cool.

The lady cop pilot was friendly and acted like she was happy to have us as passengers. The chopper was wheeled out of the hangar and we all climbed aboard. We were up and heading north in an instant. I had Marine Corps flashbacks as the hot St. Louis air blasted me in the face.

I'd been in helicopters all over the world but none were as neat as this one. But in retrospect, I was again sitting next to an open door in a helicopter, wearing a Marine Corps uniform, armed with a semi-automatic weapon with a bunch of guys with hangovers. I wondered if this life/dream would continue to play over and over until I died.

We landed north of the patch, probably two football fields away from the target. Across from the patch area, on the south side of the Missouri River and up a hill about a quarter of a mile was a state park and a subdivision of expensive homes. Several of the homes had a view of wild and uninhabitable Pelican Island.

Palance figured that the owner of the patch of sensimilla sat on his deck drinking beer while he had his $300,000 patch of weed under surveillance. I agreed with his theory.

The special agents and TFD's clambered out of the chopper, about eight of us total. We stood in ten foot high milk weed trying to get our bearings.

The chopper pilot pointed south and then took off. Palance took the lead and we followed him. We chopped and crawled through the milkweed.

Mosquitoes were attacking us as we sweated out the booze from a two day binge in Ripley County. We had only gone about one hundred yards when one of the agents (Mike Schweig) went down.

"I am a United States of America federal agent with the Drug Enforcement Administration and I demand to be evacuated," he mumbled.

We picked him up and helped him as we walked and stumbled toward the patch of cash crop.

Little Stevie Wonder went down and couldn't stand on his own. I didn't think any of these special agents had ever been in the military. These guys were mostly good students who couldn't find a niche in the outside world. DEA was an easy job to get hired into. In most cases there wasn't even a written test. I grabbed onto Little Stevie and helped him the rest of the way.

We finally came to a clearing and then the patch of weed. It was a beautiful patch; bright green and obviously cared for daily. Marijuana has to be watered and preened and fertilized. This patch was someone's hobby.

I figured that the grower probably had the money he was going to make off of this patch earmarked for something special. Maybe he was going to invest in real estate, or buy an expensive sports car, or a yacht.

He was probably watching us as we approached his nest egg dope patch. He could tell that we weren't there to steal from him; we were there to destroy his dream.

A high powered rifle could kill us from the six or seven hundred yards which separated us from the back of the expensive houses. A rational man wouldn't kill cops and agents to save a weed patch. But I thought to myself, would a rational man spend the amount of time it took to grow this patch? I felt uncomfortable standing in the clearing looking at the beautiful cultivated sensimilla plants.

"Let's eradicate it," Palance shouted. We started chopping it with machetes, then found that it was easier to just pull it up by the roots. We laid it in a pile and Palance poured gasoline on it and ignited it.

The expensive weed burned for a while and then the fire went out. It was so green that it wouldn't stay lit. The weed seemed indestructible.

Palance got on the radio and contacted headquarters in Clayton. He asked the secretary there to contact the chopper pilot at Spirit of St. Louis airport and advise her we needed more gasoline. She was due to pick us up in an hour or so.

We sat in the heat and waited. The insects were attacking Little Stevie severely, and another agent barfed and had dry heaves. Finally the chopper arrived. It was being piloted by a man, the county had changed shifts and the lady pilot was off duty.

Palance removed a five gallon can of fuel from the open door of the chopper and again doused the green weed. We stood back as he lit the gas. It exploded in his face. He was engulfed in flame. We jumped on him and smothered the flames.

Palance was badly burned on his face, head and neck. His eyelashes and eyebrows were burned off. Part of his hair was gone. He laid on the ground and moaned as the unrelenting insects of Pelican Island feasted on his raw flesh.

We loaded him onto the chopper and took off for the nearest trauma center with a helipad, which happened to be De Paul Hospital in Maryland Heights, Missouri.

I watched as the chopper banked away from the island. The weed was burning brightly and would be destroyed in about fifteen minutes.

I wondered if the grower observed the drama that was displayed at his patch of dream weed. He would think it was fitting and justified.

The grower was denied his crop. It was probably his life dream to grow expensive weed and get rich from it. Palance was a ladies man. His life's work was DEA and being a ladies man. He will now be scarred forever. An eye for an eye!

My curiosity got the best of me. I asked the co-pilot, who in actuality is a spotter and not a pilot, where the five gallons of gas had come from. "The pump at the airport hangar," he proudly replied. Palance had doused the green weed with high octane jet fuel.

Palance was admitted. We hitched a ride back to the helicopter hangar, entered our "G" cars and headed for our homes.

We were now a group of privileged cop kids without a

leader. That was good in my opinion. Maybe things would calm down in the unit. But it was bad in other regards. What if we got a new boss who didn't give us carte blanche? Our freedom was at stake.

The irony of the cop business amazed me.

VIII.

THE MISSING SNITCH

As I suspected, the young cops stopped working. We lounged around the office, had long lunches, dabbled in paperwork and went home on time. I was starting to feel like a human being for a change. My wife even smiled at me on occasion.

Special Agent Braun, who was the poster child of the Drug Enforcement Administration, was the unofficial interim supervisor of the task force. He had studied all of us and had befriended a couple of the cop kids.

Since Reszler was marked as a candidate for the DEA academy, Mike globbed onto him. He also cultivated the friendship of Detective Sultan.

Most of the special agents, the federal proscecutors and even the defense attorneys treated Detective Sultan as a VIP because of his influential attorney dad. It was sad to watch.

Braun's desk was close to mine in the big open office. I overheard him talking to Detective Sultan about a cocaine delivery at a storage unit in Wood River, Illinois.

Wood River was at one time my home town. I lived there as a young child and my dad owned a Buick dealership there. We lived across the street from the gigantic Wood River swimming pool, built by Standard Oil for the citizens of that little oil refinery burg.

I dismissed the eavesdropped conversation and tried to concentrate on my own life. A day went by and Braun, Detective Sultan and Reszler (Conan) were conversing about the arrest they had made in Wood River. I tuned in again.

They had gotten a couple of kilos of cocaine from the

courier (George Fletcher). The arrestee immediately gave up his source. It was a small time businessman and hustler by the name of Rich Latchkey. As I previously stated in this writing, I knew him and I had investigated him occasionally when I was with the Intelligence Unit. One of the things we did there was to periodically initiate car checks/interviews of suspected criminals; people who seemed to have acquired wealth without having the legitimate cash flow to justify it.

Rich Latchkey seemed legitimate on the surface, but he was occasionally spotted with some professional criminals, the Robinson brothers, drug smugglers and organized criminals who I had introduced in the first chapter of this book.

Gus Torregrosa, a barber in downtown St. Louis allowed Rich Latchkey and a smuggler named Dan Robinson, Paul's younger brother, to hang out in his establishment. The Intelligence Unit had them under surveillance wondering what they were up to.

Dan Robinson was a known hustler in the downtown area. He had cop friends and he was well known as a big talker, a guy who was trying to be friendly when he wasn't trying to act like a tough guy.

Part of the rebuilding of the downtown riverfront in the mid-1960s, was the building of the Mansion House Complex. It was a series of three towers housing luxury apartments, a view of the eastside and the Mississippi River, and a gigantic garage.

There were fancy nightclubs in the complex with entrances off of the garage or the upper levels of the buildings.

Dan Robinson hung around the nightclubs. He didn't drink, or dance, or bring his gorgeous Italian, almost Mafia wife, to these clubs, he just hung around and glared at the patrons coming and going. He was almost a fixture there, and he was offensive.

I had seen him at a club named The Garage. His tough guy act had cracks in it. He tried too hard to be tough. I had just gotten out of the Marine Corps and I noted his physiognomy; it was false. He was living on his brother's (Paul) reputation.

Dan Robinson and Rich Latchkey were rolling in cash from weed sales and living the good life. The barber shop was a welcome diversion for them. It was comedy central for the stressed out drug smuggler.

Gus Torregrosa was a fence and he was not on good terms with some of the higher ranking city cops. Intelligence watched him and so did a police Detective Lieutenant named Greg Menenges.

Gus knew his shop was under surveillance and he would sometimes come outside and give the cops the finger. Gus was a funny guy who didn't much care about anything, except money.

There was a little guy who worked at the barbershop, Jimmy the Midget. Jimmy swaggered and talked like an old time gangster. He carried a fake badge and a fake gun and wore zoot suits with big fedoras. He was also a funny guy. I personally could understand why Dan Robinson and Rich Latchkey hung out there. The place was a laugh a minute for me and I was on the outside looking in through binoculars.

Paul Robinson, Dan's older brother the smuggler who lived in Hollywood, Florida in a big house with a pool that went in and outside of the house, was arrested in 1976 at his house by the Hollywood, Florida Police Department.

He and George Fletcher, his servant and partner in crime, were both convicted from the Hollywood, Florida search warrant, but Paul didn't report to prison until the mid-1980s.

Paul had lived like a millionaire and he wasn't about to

give up his lifestyle until he absolutely had to.

The house was always filled with young waifs from St. Louis who wanted to live on the wild side for a while. Paul would whore them out, for in reality, Paul was a super pimp.

Paul had so much money that there was no place to hide it in the house, but once a pimp always a pimp.

Paul's brother, Dan Robinson, was a slow witted sibling worshipper. He would do Paul's will without question. They were famous for smuggling marijuana in from south Florida in the sixties and seventies.

The Robinsons and Rich Latchkey were ho hum crooks to me. They weren't Mafiosi; they were low life scum sucking weed smugglers who spent most of their time in Florida.

I lost interest in the group, but I had heard that Paul had gotten out of the penitentiary and was back in the St. Louis area. I knew these guys well. I studied them at one time.

Braun, Reszler or Detective Sultan did not know the Robinson brothers group. Obviously, I did, and I conveyed that fact to Braun, who by that time had acquired the nickname of "double naught spy."

Braun wasn't interested in my knowledge of the group of dope smugglers, so I took my family to southwest Florida for our annual beach vacation. I was gone for a couple of weeks and returned to Florida tales of Braun, Detective Sultan and Reszler preparing for a meet and buy in the Fort Lauderdale area with one of the Colombian drug sources the Robinson gang had frequently used.

I patiently watched the dope game play out. It was super interesting to me now because I knew all of the players.

Rich Latchkey (who we took off after George Fletcher set him up for a delivery of cocaine) was their key informant and they treated him with kid gloves. Rich was allowed to get on with his life. He had a restaurant in the downtown area of the city and he went to work as if he had never been arrested.

But a problem arose; always does in the cop/crook game. Rich Latchkey disappeared. He was instructed to check in with Mike Braun daily. That was part of his agreement with the United Sates Attorney and his defense attorney.

The agreement was a long and drawn out legal document stating what Rich Latchkey could expect if he worked with the government to make a case on the Robinson brothers. It was kind of like a prenuptial agreement wealthy folks have drawn up by high priced lawyers.

Of course Rich would have to surrender some of his money, cash he had allegedly made during the smuggling and sales of marijuana and cocaine.

Rich had his money separated, some for his attorney. Some for his business, and some for himself. He gladly gave his money to the federal government. He had $30,000 stuffed in a hole in the wall behind his refrigerator in his modest home in Overland, Missouri.

The government loves to take flashy and expensive cars from their targets. Our impound lot was at Scott Airforce Base in southern Illinois. It was filled with super expensive German and American cars. Rich Latchkey drove a junker. He was a smart dope dealer.

The impound lot was outdoors and secured by a ten foot high chain link fence. There were probably thirty cars there. We drove the vehicles there and secured them. Every time we went back, a car had been broken into and a stereo or some other expensive damage would be done to them by the Air Force guys who had scaled the fence and done their dastardly deeds.

The asset forfeiture procedure is done by the United States Attorney's office and it usually takes a couple of

months for the process to be completed. These super
expensive cars would sit with broken windows and open
doors until we could duct tape tem back together. It was a
sad thing to watch for a car lover.

The federal government, the Drug Enforcement
Administration, Braun and I knew that Rich was holding
out. He'd been a smuggler and dope pusher for two decades,
at least. He was the one in the group who took control of the
drug proceeds. He would doll it out to Paul and Dan
Robinson. But there was no way to question Rich
Latchkey's financial accountability. So the government took
what it could and used Rich like a whore to get the
Robinson brothers.

Braun was frantically trying to locate Rich Latchkey. The
Robinson brother's case was a big one for him. It would be a
feather in his cap if he could get it prosecuted successfully.
It was the second rung in the ladder of success in DEA. The
first rung was graduating at the top of his academy class.
Headquarters DEA is impressed by intelligence and
initiative.

The Robinson brothers, especially Paul Robinson, were
class one violators. Paul had the killer reputation and an
affiliation with the East St. Louis, Illinois mob.

The eastside mob controlled all of the labor locals on the
west side of the river and was controlled by the Outfit in
Chicago run by Joey Doves Aiuppa. Those affiliations made
Paul Robinson a high profile candidate for any federal
agent.

Paul was so feared that when the local Italian Mafia came
calling on him to find out where he got his wealth, which
came from smuggling weed, (wanting their cut) he told them
to "fuck off" and they did. The Mafia was too dumb to
figure out the Robinson's were smuggling weed into St.

Louis.

Paul's killer, pimp, smuggler resume was reinforced by the fact that Rich Robinson, Erv Robinson and his little brother Dan were backing him and he had numerous organized crime contacts in south Florida and in the country of Colombia.

At one point in time, Paul had squandered all of the groups dope cash on hookers and high living. He lavished money on his house guests in Hollywood, Florida throwing huge cocaine parties and paying for everything.

The partiers would get bonked on drugs and Paul would order large meals (steak and lobster) from area restaurants and have them delivered by taxi. Paul would tip the taxi driver thousands of dollars.

The partiers were, by that time, so intoxicated that they couldn't eat the food. Paul would feed it to his German Shepherds. Stacks of cash were sitting on tables and in corners. Paul spent it all. Rich Latchkey advised me that Paul spent $700,000 in a four-year time span free basing cocaine.

The Robinson group needed product to ship to St. Louis. Paul ordered Rich to make contact with their Colombian contact and order up a ton of weed on consignment.

Rich was hesitant. He knew that Paul was out of control and that any funds the group made from the sale of the weed would be spent by Paul and their contact in Colombia would not be paid. That could mean death for everyone involved.

Rich expressed his desire to leave the group to Paul. Paul was nice and professional to Rich. "You want to leave the group? Okay, then I'll kill your ass. You want to leave that way?"

"No, Paul." Rich meekly replied.

"Now get on the phone, make your connections in Colombia and order up a ton of weed. They're your connections, not mine. They like you, they don't like me. Without you, I'm out of business."

"Yes, sir, Paul," Rich replied.

Rich made the connections and the weed was shipped to south Florida via the freighter Corn Island. The Corn Island could not come into port in south Florida so Paul and George Fletcher stole two large go fast boats in Miami and drove out to the Corn Island.

They off loaded as much weed as the boats could carry, and then the Corn Island headed for New Orleans to off load the rest of it. The freighter could enter the harbor in New Orleans without the possibility of being boarded and searched.

Paul had a driver in a U-Haul truck waiting for the Corn Island in New Orleans. He had an associate in Louisiana who recommended the driver. They off loaded the weed onto the U-Haul late at night and the driver was starting to pull away from the loading area heading for southern Illinois, to a farm owned by a distributor. This fellow was never identified by DEA.

The driver decided to light up a joint and a New Orleans cop on the beat noticed him. The cop pulled the U-Haul over, arrested the driver and seized the weed. Paul lost most of the load of consignment weed.

Half of the ton load went to St. Louis and was sold. Paul squandered the proceeds. The Colombian connection telephoned and wanted payment. Paul told him to fuck off, and he did.

Rich Latchkey was beside himself. The connection in Colombia was dangerous and he feared retribution, but it didn't happen.

Paul ordered Rich to make contact with the connection in Colombia and to order up another ton of weed on consignment. Rich balked! Paul told him he would kill him, so Rich made the call.

The Colombian connection invited Rich to come to Colombia to talk. Rich told Paul that if he went to Colombia the connection would probably hold him for ransom. Paul replied, "Ransom there or death here. Which do you want?" Rich headed for Colombia.

On the surface this sounded like a death trip, but Rich Latchkey was playing within himself. He was friends with the Colombian drug lords. All he had to do was to blame everything on Paul Robinson's ferocious appetite for drugs and cash. The Colombians knew Paul, and being businessmen, they knew Rich was just a pawn in the smuggling game.

The Colombian's business was to smuggle drugs into America. Paul Robinson's game was to distribute smuggled drugs inside of America, preferably the St. Louis regional area.

The Colombian connection held Rich for ransom, but it was only a game. They were on Rich's side. They figured that somewhere down the line Paul would either be incarcerated or killed and they would still have Rich Latchkey to do business with.

Paul spoke to the connection by phone and it appeared they ironed out their differences. The agreement was that 25,000 pounds of weed would be loaded onto the Corn Island and delivered to Paul Robinson and Rich Latchkey off the coast of Galveston, Texas.

Someone in the Robinson group obtained another large vessel (The Mister Joe M) and they went out to off load the weed from the Corn Island.

A storm struck the area and the other ship, The Mister Joe M. crashed into Corn Island as they were moored together. The Corn Island sunk and the Mister Joe M.

headed toward shore with heavy damage.

A Coast Guard airplane circled the distressed vessel as it tried to get to shore. The occupants of the Mister Joe M. started throwing bales of marijuana overboard to lighten the load . The Mister Joe M. was eventually beached and the boat was set on fire.

Before the fire, approximately 4000 pounds of weed was salvaged from the Mister Joe M. without any cops or Coast Guard officials interfering, and was placed into U-Haul trucks and shipped to St. Louis.

Paul, desperate for cash, went to Miami to rob one of their coconspirators who Paul felt had large amounts of cash on hand. The guy was terrified of Paul Robinson and would have given him anything. He eventually gave Paul a kilo of cocaine to leave him alone.

The place in Hollywood was an open door for almost anyone from St. Louis. Cute girls and weirdos from the lower rungs of the eastside and higher rungs of west St. Louis County showed up. Paul would allow them to stay for a while then he would intimidate the male guests to leave.

Everyone was afraid of Paul. He was big and thick with dark eyes and hair, kind of like Sicilians, but they weren't of that breed, and the Robinson clan had deep voices which intimidated average males.

Paul was giving large amounts of cash to an ex-wife living nearby and he had a new wife that he was lavishing money on.

Rich Latchkey was a businessman and he hated losing money. He would glob onto every dollar he could get his hands on and sock it away. Paul and Dan figured Rich was stealing from them but they weren't smart enough to prove it.

A big and tough labor organizer from St. Louis, Don Grosse, came to the house. He lived there with the hookers and dopers, partying as much as humanly possible.

As in any dwelling, there can only be one man of the house. That was Paul. Paul and the tough guy, Don Grosse, had words about one of the female house guests.

In Paul's mind, he owned the girls. Actually, in his mind, he owned everyone in the house. Paul beat Don Grosse with his fists and feet and Don vacated Paul's Hollywood house. He went to another St. Louis dope dealer's house in Miami and took up residence there.

Don Grosse turned up dead in the bedroom of the Miami dope dealer. He had apparently shot himself in the head. The bullet entered the back of his head. The Miami medical examiner declared the death a homicide.

The word amongst the smugglers was that Paul murdered Don Grosse. Drugs, money and young girls were the things Paul worshipped. If anyone crossed him on any of these fetishes, he would kill them.

All of the smugglers knew the creed of Paul Robinson. The group had been organized to make tons of cash, not kill for the sake of a young wayward waif, or a super pimp's desires.

Now, among the smugglers, Paul Robinson was a pox. Personal desires were supposed to be laid aside while the smugglers were amassing huge amounts of cash.

Rich Latchkey came to the forefront of the organization. The smugglers, in Florida and in Colombia, would only deal with him.

South Florida was awash with St. Louis dope smugglers. A St. Louis boy, Eddie Vaughn, had worked his way up in the large scale marijuana business based in Fort Lauderdale. He was not a member of any large smuggling group but worked for some of the mid-west distributors.

Eddie was in charge of the many stash houses and distribution points between St. Louis and South Florida. Eddie saw a chance to steal some of the weed money from his partners and he did it. He stole $350,000 and fled, out of desperation, to Hollywood to Paul Robinsons' house. He gave Paul $25,000 in cash to protect him.

Paul gladly took the money. Paul convinced Eddie to invest some of the cash in cocaine and smuggle it into St. Louis. He did! He had his brother, Phil Vaughn, deliver a large amount of cocaine to Dan Robinson in St. Louis.

But Paul wasn't satisfied with being a partner in the cocaine business with Eddie Vaughn. Paul instructed Dan Robinson to kidnap Phil Vaughn and to hold him for ransom until Eddie gave Paul the remainder of the $350,000 he had stolen.

Dan did as he was told. Nobody went against Paul Robinson. But Dan was upset about the kidnapping. Eddie refused to give Paul Robinson anymore of the stolen money so Dan Released Phil Vaughn.

A cop detective in Hollywood declared war on Paul Robinson. In 1976 he eventually did a search warrant on Paul's house and Paul and his trusted companion George Fletcher from Alton, Illinois (the courier who was taken off in Wood River and snitched on everyone) and Paul and George went for a vacation in the Florida State Penitentiary. Paul delayed his sentence with appeals, but he eventually turned himself in to the Florida penal system.

Paul did about ten years and then he came back to St. Louis. George didn't do as much time as Paul and he came back years earlier and worked for Rich Latchkey selling Rich's food from a cart in and around the downtown area during lunch.

Rich was always in the restaurant business and he owned a restaurant and bar in the old Union Market building. He was at one time a waiter at Tony's in downtown St. Louis, the only five-star-restaurant in the state of Missouri. George. Fletcher had been Paul Robinson's servant, now he was Rich Latchkey's servant.

Rich Latchkey, Dan Robinson and George Fletcher went into the cocaine business. Rich still had contacts in Colombia and south Florida. He made the connections and George would rent a car at the airport and drive to Florida and bring the dope back in the trunk.

Dan basically did nothing but collect cash from Rich Latchkey. He was a guy who was always looking for a place to hang out. Besides Gus Torregrossa's barbershop, he chose to hang out at the law offices of Norm London, a prestigious St. Louis defense attorney.

Dan had an open door at the lawyer's offices. Norm London also represented Paul Robinson when he was prosecuted for cocaine possession in south Florida and was sent to the Florida State Penitentiary. His fee was $250,000. Paul reluctantly paid him.

Dan Robinson also frequented a dentist's office and hideaway in South St. Louis County , Missouri. The dentist had an apartment near his office and Dan entertained a lady friend there. A team of detectives from the St. Louis Intelligence Unit had Dan under surveillance for years.

Dan Robinson would give the dentist cash from his drug business and the dentist would in turn give Dan a paycheck; another scam so that Dan could show the government how he obtained money and to maybe someday get forty hours in social security and gain benefits.

The average person the Robinson brothers associated with were impressed with them. In their minds Dan was a friendly guy who just happened to be a gangster who smuggled weed. They didn't take into consideration that Paul was a super pimp and murderer who had spent most of his life behind bars.

Paul came into town with a vengeance after being released from the penitentiary in Florida. He had no cash and to Paul that was like a starving man not having any food. He ravished cash; it was his reason for living.

A notorious gangster, Tommy Venezia, owned a horse farm near Creve Coeur Park in St. Louis County. There was a small trailer there and Paul and his then wife took up residence there.

Paul was under surveillance by St. Louis Intelligence. Paul went to Rich Latchkey and Dan Robinson and advised them that he was owed part of the money they had accrued from the cocaine business while he was in prison.

Paul was still a scary guy and Rich Latchkey felt Paul was going to eventually murder him for skimming drug proceeds in the past.

Paul reinforced Rich's suspicions when Paul told Rich and Dan that if he didn't get his cut he would kill them, and their children. They ponied up some cash for Paul and he and his wife moved out of Tommy Venezia's trailer.

Rich Latchkey was MIA. He hadn't been checking in with Braun and when Braun paged him he didn't call him. Braun assumed the worst; someone from the Robinson group had killed Rich Latchkey. I sat at my desk and smiled about the Robinson/Latchkey group. It was a lot like DEA; a comedy of errors.

As Braun was contemplating his next move in locating Rich Latchkey, Group Supervisor Palance walked in the door. He was wearing a ball cap and sporting large Ray

Bans to hide his face.

Palance saw this as an opportunity to again motivate the boys. He stood in front of the group, removed his Ray Bans and ball cap and allowed everyone to look at his scorched face and head.

"I'm one hundred percent DEA," Palance began. We all stared at him. He had snake eyes, no eyebrows or eyelashes. His head and face were raw meat with medicine covering it.

He probably could have gotten some sort of federal disability pension if he wanted one, but Palance loved his life as group supervisor with a future.

His life was being a federal bureaucrat, driving someone else's sports car, leading his brainwashed group of entitled cops, and having as many girlfriends as humanly possible. He wasn't about to give all of that up because of a little accident.

Palance went into his office. Braun was summoned by Palance's secretary. I watched the continuing saga of the disappeared Rich Latchkey play out. It was still act one of a three act play.

Basic police work is always in play for every cop and investigator. Whenever someone is missing the cop usually checks hospitals and morgues.

Braun started calling area hospitals; he finally checked Alexian Brothers Hospital on South Jefferson. The hospital was known for being discreet in their patient's identity.

It was a hospital for ill gangsters. Several of the area organized crime barons were treated there. The notorious eastside gangster, Frank (Buster) Wortman died there. Rich Latchkey was there, admitted into the psych unit, being treated for an overdose.

"You want to go with me to interview a suspect?" Braun asked me.

"Sure," I replied.

We took off in Braun's "G" car, which was a new Oldsmobile, much better than what the TFD's got to drive. I directed him to Alexian Brothers.

We parked and walked in like we owned the place. I asked a security guard where the psych unit was located and he directed us to an upper floor. He probably made us as cops because he didn't question us about anything.

We got off the elevator and walked right into the unit. We went from room to room looking for Rich without ever being challenged. We finally found him.

He was in a private room, lying on his side with a pile of vomit next to his mouth. He had soiled his bed in every way imaginable and the stench was unbearable.

He was green around the gills and unconscious. We stared not knowing exactly what to do with this dope creature.

Braun wasn't stumped for long. He knew that Rich Latchkey was his first ticket to stardom in the Drug Enforcement Administration and he wasn't about to allow this creep to stop his upward momentum in the federal drug game. He kicked the bed; "Wake Up!" he sternly said to Rich.

Rich moaned and started to move. He looked up at us and instinctively pulled down on his hospital gown. He looked at us through glassy eyes and tried to speak with his green mouth but the words didn't come out. He grabbed a glass of water sitting next to his bed and gulped it.

"How did you fuckers find me?" he moaned and put his head back down on his pillow and closed his eyes.

"Hey, Braun sternly said, "Wake the fuck up. You've got an obligation to fulfill." Braun shook the bed and then kicked it again. Rich raised his head and stared at us.

"Act two," I mumbled to myself.

I played the part of the casual observer. I had just gotten back from Florida and I was tanned and relaxed and away from the police department playing federal agent. I felt like I was winning.

I knew Rich Latchkey so well that this skit he and Braun were playing was continuing to amuse me. Rich, the successful businessman in this big-little-city, playing the role of an honest law abiding citizen while in reality, Rich was a successful drug smuggler living amongst the masses and getting away with it. Now he was just another wildebeest caught by a crock and he was trying to escape the jaws of the fed.

But he was a slick wildebeest and he knew the crock only had him by the hoof and that if he was as smart as he thought he was he would be able to kick free and escape.

"Get your ass out that fucking bed," Braun ordered him. "Go in the fucking bathroom and clean yourself up."

Rich Latchkey rolled out of bed and headed for the bathroom. He looked at me as he rolled out and said, "You hate me, don't you?"

That prick doesn't remember me, I thought to myself. He thinks I'm a DEA agent from Miami. He read me and figured since I was tan and casually observant I was from south Florida.

He stumbled into the bathroom and made himself presentable. "I hate you fucking guys," he mumbled at us from the bathroom. "You fuckers have ruined my life."

He came back out and sat on the bed like a scolded little boy. "I overdosed," he explained. "I'd been on the wagon for years but I relapsed. The pressure got to me. What do you want from me?"

"It's time for you to go to work," Braun said. "Come with us." We walked into the hall and Rich followed us. There was a pay phone on the wall. "You're going to make some calls," Braun said.

"I'm fucking sick, man, Rich replied. "I'm in no shape to play any fucking DEA games now. I'll make your fucking calls some other time."

We all had telephone codes we could use in pay phones. Braun typed in his code, hooked up a Pearl recorder to the phone and handed the receiver to Rich. Call Eddie Alvarez, the race car driver in Fort Lauderdale. Engage him in conversation."

"This guy's a family friend, he's my best friend in the world; he would do anything for me. I can't do it," Rich whined.

"Do it, or you go directly to prison for twenty years," Braun replied.

Rich suddenly found his motivation, cleared his throat and dialed the telephone.

Rich talked with Eddie Alvarez while we listened, standing in the hallway of a gangster insane asylum in south St. Louis.

Rich and Eddie talked like brothers. They talked about their families, their children, about Eddie Alvarez's last race, and then they finally talked about dope. Rich ordered up five kilos of cocaine. Eddie agreed to give Rich the cocaine on consignment.

The deal was to go down in Fort Lauderdale in a week. The call was terminated. Rich stood in the hallway and stared at us, as if to say, "What now?"

Braun typed in his code again and hooked up the Pearl recorder. "Call Paul Robinson's wife," Braun ordered.

"Paul's wife, no I won't do it. She's got nothing to do with the dope business. She's just a wife, nothing more. I won't do it!"

"Then you leave me with no choice," Braun continued

with his DEA spiel. "I will go to the United States Attorney this afternoon and advise him to withdraw your agreement with the federal government in the investigation and prosecution of Dan and Paul Robinson. Is that what you want?"

Rich dialed Paul's wife and they talked like brother and sister. Nothing was learned from this conversation. Paul's wife was slicker than all of us.

Rich stumbled back into his hospital room and sat on the bed. "You see what you motherfuckers are making me do? I love these people. They are my friends. I've been the best of friends with them for years. I hate you motherfuckers."

Braun stared at Rich with hatred. "You think you were going to get into the dope business without having any repercussions? It's time for you and all of your doper friends to pay the piper. The game is over for all of you. You are the only one who isn't going to prison for a lifetime, and that's just because you are the snitch. So don't get self-righteous with us. You are a dope smuggler and a snitch. Accept it, it's the real world."

"I hate you fucking guys," Rich tearfully replied.

"You're going to be here for observation for three days," Braun replied. "On the fourth day you be in my office bright and early. It's time we had a sit down meeting and hash this shit out."

Braun and I walked out as Rich spewed insults at us. It was a fun interview but I wondered what part in this investigation I would have a play in.

The Crew in the Parking Garage of the Chromalloy
Building, Clayton, Mo., circa 1986. Courtesy of T. Sloan

AUSA Clifford J. Proud, Special Agent Mike Braun &
author TFD Tim Richards. (Photo courtesy of Cliff Proud
circa 1988)

Intelligence Unit Detective Tom Rangel on surveillance in
Lincoln County, Missouri. DEA surveillance van in
background. (Photo courtesy of Tom Rangel) circa 1987.

Author with TFD's in Grafton, Illinois. Circa 1988

Author with St. Louis County TFD Chuck Boschert before going to court. Circa 1989.

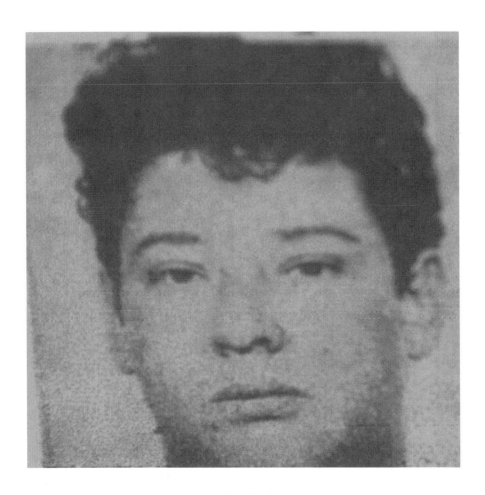

Street hustler, drug smuggler, gangster Danny Robinson.

Happy TFDs, circa 1985.

Customs agents working at my bugged desk in Clayton,
Missouri. Circa 1988.

Interrogating a drug suspect arrested in a marijuana camp in southeast, Missouri. (Photo courtesy of T. Sloan) circa 1984.

Fishing in Key West with a broken hand. Circa 1988.

Photo of gangster and drug smuggler Paul Robinson.

Photo of author working at his "bugged" desk. Circa 1989.

Photo of Police Department surgeon Dr. James F. Cooper,
A friend to all St. Louis cops.

Tim Richards

Photos of the house in Fosterburg, Illinois. Note guard dog.

Photo of Steve (Johnny) Reszler and his girlfriend.

Photo of Reszler shooting pool, undercover.

Burning weed in southeast, Missouri. Circa 1989.

Little Stevie Wonder pulling marijuana plants in the Mark
Twain. Circa 1989.

TFD's in a pickup truck in Mark Twain (author on right)
Little Stevie Wonder (S/A Steve Stoddard) left of the photo.
Circa 1989.

Tim Richards

Weed in a pickup. Mark Twain National Forest. Circa 1989.

A TFD expressing his desire to die rather be sent back to the police department. (Photo courtesy of T. Sloan circa 1985)

Weed grower tents in the Mark Twain. Circa 1989. Courtesy of T. Sloan.

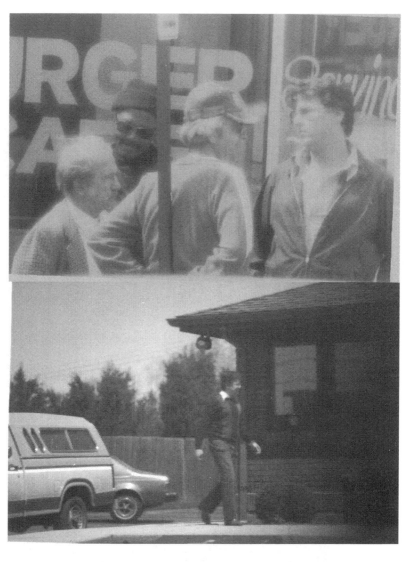

Surveillance photos of Dan Robinson, standing in front of
Gus Torregrossa's barber shop, and at his dentist's hideaway
apartment in South St. Louis County, Mo. (Photo courtesy
of G. Venegoni) circa 1985.

Surveillance photo of Dan Robinson at his dentist's friend's
condo in south St. Louis County on Tesson Ferry Road.
Circa 1985. Courtesy of G. Venegoni (circa 1985)

Farm in Grafton near Pere Marquette State Park, with the weed confiscated there. Circa 1987.

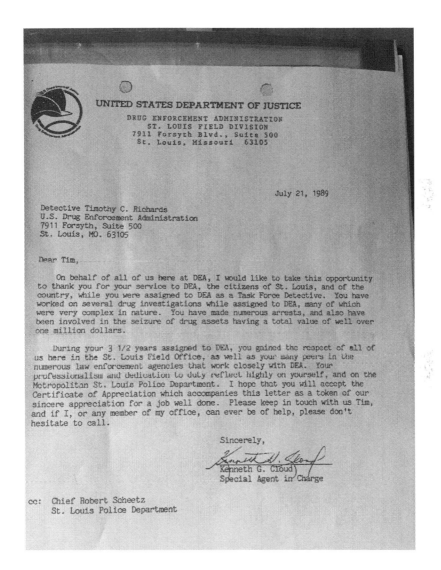

UNITED STATES DEPARTMENT OF JUSTICE

DRUG ENFORCEMENT ADMINISTRATION
ST. LOUIS FIELD DIVISION
7911 Forsyth Blvd., Suite 500
St. Louis, Missouri 63105

July 21, 1989

Detective Timothy C. Richards
U.S. Drug Enforcement Administration
7911 Forsyth, Suite 500
St. Louis, MO. 63105

Dear Tim,

On behalf of all of us here at DEA, I would like to take this opportunity to thank you for your service to DEA, the citizens of St. Louis, and of the country, while you were assigned to DEA. You have worked on several drug investigations while assigned to DEA, many of which were very complex in nature. You have made numerous arrests, and also have been involved in the seizure of drug assets having a total value of well over one million dollars.

During your 3 1/2 years assigned to DEA, you gained the respect of all of us here in the St. Louis Field Office, as well as your many peers in the numerous law enforcement agencies that work closely with DEA. Your professionalism and dedication to duty reflect highly on yourself, and on the Metropolitan St. Louis Police Department. I hope that you will accept the Certificate of Appreciation which accompanies this letter as a token of our sincere appreciation for a job well done. Please keep in touch with us Tim, and if I, or any member of my office, can ever be of help, please don't hesitate to call.

Sincerely,

Kenneth G. Cloud
Special Agent in Charge

cc: Chief Robert Scheetz
St. Louis Police Department

Letter written by the Special Agent In charge (SAC) commending my work while assigned to the Drug Enforcement Administration.

Photo of Attorney Norm London, Dan Robinson's best friend. He laid down with dogs and came up with fleas.

Photo of Defense Attorney Frank (Tony) Fabbri. He trusted
a defendant and was imprisoned and disbarred.

Photo of Federal Judge William Stiehl Southern District of Il. (Hanging judge)

Photo of 1938 Chevy (snub 38) Bad luck car. Seized by DEA. Purchased by Attorney Frank (Tony) Fabbri. Both owners ended up in a federal penitentiary.

Photo of Dan Robinson shortly after doing 20 years of
federal incarceration. Circa 2007. He decided to take his
brother Paul's advice and play hardball with AUSA Cliff
Proud and Judge William Stiehl. He could have gotten 10
years, and lived much of his life a free man.

XIV.

SUPER SNITCH REAPPEARS

It was a new week and I thought about what was going to transpire. Rich Latchkey was supposed to be in the office bright and early. He hadn't shown.

The boys still weren't working like they once were. Their trust of the system was waning. They trusted Palance but not DEA, or the federal justice system.

Steve's secretary, Liz Bates answered her phone and quickly said "okay, let him come to the task force offices." We all waited for who might be appearing. Rich Latchkey walked through the door. My interest peaked immediately. It was act three.

Braun got up from his desk and walked toward Rich. They both stood outside of Palance's office waiting for the command to enter.

Rich wasn't as surly as he was in the hospital. He was like a kid waiting to go into the principal's office for a scolding, nervous, weight going from one foot to the other. He was pulling on his face, running his hands through his hair.

"Enter," Palance said. Braun and Rich Latchkey slowly walked into the office. "Close the door, please," Palance said to Braun. The door closed and I quickly walked up to the door and eavesdropped.

I figured Palance had his Ray Bans and ball cap off. He seldom wore them in the office. I wondered what Rich Latchkey thought while he was staring at those snake eyes and burned head.

"I understand you had a little breakdown," Palance began the interrogation. "Are you going to be able to continue with this assignment?"

"Yeah," Rich replied. He was again acting surly.

"I have the authority to stop this agreement Mister Latchkey. Are you aware of that?"

"No, my lawyer hasn't told me that," Rich replied.

"Your lawyer is no longer in this deal, Mister Latchkey. What happens from here on out depends upon your performance as a confidential informant. I will not allow my agents to accompany you to south Florida for an undercover drug deal if your attitude is not 100 percent positive. If you show any signs of not being able to fulfill your obligation to the federal government, I will instruct my agents to arrest you and house you in the federal jail in Fort Lauderdale awaiting transport back to St. Louis. Got it?"

Rich changed his tune. "Yes, sir," he replied. I walked away from the door and sat back down at my desk. Rich and Braun came out into the large office and walked to Braun's desk. Braun grabbed a Pearl recorder out his desk drawer and motioned for Rich to follow him.

Braun and Rich walked into the soundproof undercover telephone room and closed the door. They came out in approximately fifteen minutes and returned to Braun's desk. Braun left Rich at his desk and went to Palance's office.

I could feel Rich's eyes burning a hole in the back of my head. I turned around and smiled at him. "How's it going? I asked.

"Fine, I mean okay, I guess. Better than the last time we met," he laughed.

"I can see that," I replied with another laugh.

"You know," Rich continued. "After you guys left the

hospital room I kept wondering where we had met before. I still haven't put it together. Can you enlighten me?"

"Yeah," I replied. I'm a city cop detached to DEA. I was in the Intelligence Unit when you and the Robinson brothers were smuggling big-time weed and cocaine into St. Louis. I did a car stop downtown with you and George Fletcher. It was in the early eighties." I stared at him. His wheels were turning.

"I remember you," he loudly said. "You said something smart and funny to me, but I don't remember what it was. I remember now. That's been a long time ago, yeah a lot of water's been under the bridge since then."

"A lot of dope, too," I replied. Braun came back to his desk. He was accompanied by Detective Sultan and Reszler.

"We're leaving tomorrow for Fort Lauderdale," Braun began. "Rich, you fly down tonight, get set up in a motel down there and don't make contact with the target until we get there. We will contact you at your room."

Rich left the office, Braun and Detective Sultan had a private conference. I was out of the case, but I still had fish to fry. I had my own little investigations to play with and my street informants who telephoned me daily.

Little Stevie Wonder came to my desk and advised me that he and I were going to be driving to Burlington, Iowa for a dope deal. I was cool with it and we left the next day. Travelling with DEA wasn't so bad as long as we weren't going to Southeast Missouri.

Little Stevie and I had a good and profitable trip. We took two cars and drank beer on the way north, communicating by DEA closed circuit radio telling each other tales.

In the boondocks the Fed has lawyers who are on contract with the Justice Department to act as Federal Magistrates. We did surveillance on a hotel room and Little

Stevie drew up an affidavit. We checked a list and found an attorney nearby on it and strolled into his office. The guy was surprised to see us; we were the first agents he had ever had to assist. "I can't believe someone would come to Burlington, Iowa to deal drugs," he commented.

But it was the way of the drug trade. Burlington, Iowa has a commuter airport. It is a fifteen minute flight to Chicago, Illinois. Law enforcement was lacking and untrained in the art of drug enforcement. It was a perfect place to chill out and distribute large amounts of drugs.

We returned to Clayton, Missouri and Braun, Reszler and Detective Sultan were back from Fort Lauderdale. Their trip was successful. Rich Latchkey took possession of five kilos of cocaine on consignment from Eddie Alvarez.

Braun's big dope case was going to be successful. But there was a problem. Detective Sultan and Reszler lost interest in the case. They were accustomed to quick cases, buy-busts that were culminated and terminated in the same day. They distanced themselves from Braun.

Part of Braun's mystic was that he was on the super fast-track with DEA. He was being examined under a high power microscope by headquarters DEA and being groomed for greatness.

Braun was still being sent out of country for some sort of DEA operation. DEA wanted to load his resume with as much positive fodder as possible. The Rich Latchkey, Et al case needed constant attention.

Rich Latchkey continued on with his business dealings. He went to his restaurant daily and acted normally. Braun had a video camera installed just over the head of Rich which was motion activated by anyone coming into the doorway and stayed on until the person entering exited.

Dan Robinson showed up first. Dan appeared at the open door and stared at Rich as he sat and crunched numbers. Rich looked surprised as he looked up and observed Dan. "Dan," he said, "How are you, come on in and have a seat."

Dan was carrying a legal pad. He shook his head and scrawled on the pad. "You get taken off?" He turned the pad around and showed it to Rich.

"No," Rich replied. "Why do you ask?"

Dan shook his head in the negative and then wrote, "Where have you been?" He showed Rich the scrawling.

"I fell off the wagon. I was in the hospital. You can check, Dan, I'm not lying."

"You okay, now?" Dan scrawled and turned the pad.

"Yeah, I'm fine, you don't have to worry. Everything's going to be fine."

"I'm going to have lunch, "he scrawled and showed Rich.

"I'm buying," Rich replied and they both left the office and headed for the restaurant which was upstairs in the station.

Rich telephoned our office and Braun went to the restaurant and collected the video tape and reloaded the camera.

Approximately one week went by. Rich called the office and told Braun that Paul Robinson was coming to his restaurant to collect some cash he felt he was owed. Rich was almost in panic mode. He was at this time in his life terrified of Paul. Paul had the physical ability to kill Rich in an instant.

Placing Rich's restaurant office under physical surveillance was not possible. It was in the basement of Union Market. There was no place to hide. If Paul murdered Rich Latchkey it would be on camera. Rich was on his own, and Braun advised him of such.

But Braun asked me to go to the restaurant and act like I was a customer. I was being brought back into the case and I was happy about it. Long term investigations were my forte.

I actually enjoyed documenting information, identifying individuals and reporting my findings. Intelligence investigation was what I had been trained for.

I headed to Rich's restaurant and wandered up to the mezzanine. It was a fancy place, decorated with palm trees and tropical paintings and packed with baseball fans going to a Cardinal's game.

I glanced around the room as I looked for a place to sit and observed Paul Robinson with two beautiful women. I later found out that they were his wife, Jo Ellen and her sister, Gina Lapicca. I ordered a soft drink and had a difficult time not staring at these two beautiful ladies. Paul observed me staring at them and he gave me an inquisitive look.

"Get a grip on yourself," I mumbled to myself. Rich came into the room and observed Paul and his women. He went to their table and then Rich and Paul exited the restaurant and headed downstairs. I sat and waited. I observed the two women staring my way through the bar mirror. They thought I was a trick.

Paul did his routine on Rich, (on camera) threatening and intimidating him. He called Rich a pipsqueak and told him he would choke him to death. He ordered Rich to give him some cash, and Rich did. Rich even counted it out for Paul and the camera. It was the first payment of a two payment venture. It was crime drama at its finest.

Paul would start talking about the dope game and then he would switch gears and instead of mentioning dope, he would place the restaurant business in its place. It was typical prison yard double talk.

Whenever Paul would switch to his brother Dan, he
would refer to him as Dan'l Boone, or Boone. Paul pocketed
the thousands of dollars Rich gave him, and he and Rich left
the office and headed back to the mezzanine.

They walked in and I was relieved that Rich was still
alive. The video tape of Paul threatening and demanding
money from Rich was the damning piece of evidence
against the notorious and infamous Paul Robinson. The
predator pimp/smuggler towered over the frightened little
Rich and bullied him into panic mode.

Anyone who has ever been bullied, and that means all of
us, would be incensed by the video. Jurors have been
bullied, also. It was the last nail in the coffin of Paul
Robinson.

Paul and his women exited the restaurant and I couldn't
resist giving them one more look. Paul gave me another
look. I'd seen similar looks. It was the look of a super pimp
with a commodity that most men were weak for. He too
thought I was a trick.

I called Braun on Rich's restaurant telephone and advised
him that the meeting was over and he could respond and
collect the evidence (video tape).

Braun and Palance had several closed door meetings
concerning the Paul Robinson taping. Palance advised
Braun that he thought it was time to "take off" Paul
Robinson.

Braun advised Rich Latchkey that he should come to the
DEA offices for a meeting. Rich strolled in a couple of
hours later and he and Braun went into the undercover
telephone room. They came out in five minutes and Rich
looked scared.

"Want to come along?" Braun asked me.

"What's up?" I replied, although I figured it was Paul

Robinson's time to return to incarceration.

"Paul thinks he's going to get some more cash. We're taking him off," Braun replied.

We left Clayton in a convoy. Rich was in the lead. The meet was going to be in a fancy strip mall in west St. Louis County on Olive Street Road.

We set up on the scene and watched as Paul came into view. His wife was driving and they observed Rich's junker Oldsmobile parked in a line of expensive cars.

Paul got out and walked to Rich's car. He got in and Rich gave him a bag of cash and then Paul exited the vehicle and returned to his wife's car.

Larry Wheeler (Mad Dog) saw his chance to terrorize a deserving white guy. He had been riding with me. He jumped out and ran toward Paul with his automatic pistol pointing at Paul's big head and face.

Paul wasn't terrorized. It was as if he knew that he was going to be taken off. He was an animal and he had those instincts. He raised his hands and wryly smiled. I grabbed the sack of cash and handcuffed him behind his back.

Mad Dog and I conveyed Paul Robinson to the federal courthouse, booked him and turned him over to the United States Marshall's Service.

It's a long process to federally book someone. I subsequently had to sit with Paul while the process was in motion. Paul had been through it before and he wasn't concerned about his future.

Paul looked at me as we sat and waited. He studied me and I studied him. It's what the captor and the captured do. "I saw you last week in Rich's restaurant," he began. You were sitting at the bar." He paused and stared at me again.

"Did you make me for a cop?" I asked.

"No," he replied. "I thought you were interested in my

women, or a guy going to the ballgame."

"They were quite lovely," I replied with a smile. He smiled back with a pimp's aggressive attitude. There is always a pause between comments when the captured is speaking. It is as if they are attempting to sense the effect of their words after they speak them. They watch the captor and attempt to gauge his demeanor.

"I know what you're thinking," he continued. "You think it's over for me don't you? You think I'm going to prison for a long time, right?"

"Yeah, Paul," I replied.

The pause kicked in.

"I've been through it before, I know the game, and I'll do some time and then I'll get out. I always get out."

"This might be a long sentence," I said.

Another long pause.

"Oh, yeah," he replied. "Everybody's got to be somewhere."

I had watched Paul in the rearview mirror as I drove toward downtown St. Louis. I took the long route, through beautiful and lush Forest Park. People were out enjoying the beautiful day. The sun was bright and there were young Washington University coeds jogging and scantily clad.

I wondered what was going through his mind. I wouldn't ever gamble with my freedom. The stakes are too high. I had been in federal penitentiaries interviewing prisoners. The thought of not being able to walk out after the interview terrorized me.

But people take chances in life every day; doctors, lawyers, cops, and most of the time it's for money.
It was over for Paul Robinson.

The cat was out of the bag: everyone associated with Rich Latchkey knew that he was a government informer. Dan Robinson disappeared. He was now considered a wanted federal fugitive from justice.

Eddie Alvarez, the dope smuggler in Fort Lauderdale, fled the country. He left his wife and children in south Florida. She sold their house and his sports car business and then she left the United States.

The dope associates from drug sales in the past conveniently took long vacations. Smugglers don't like being interviewed by DEA. It's the way of the federal government, the long list of St. Louis drug smugglers were now on a hit list for the St. Louis Field Office to investigate.

But there was a problem with that scenario. There were too many St. Louis smugglers. Braun was preparing to leave the country himself for parts unknown for DEA Headquarters.

DEA is small in comparison to the FBI. There aren't many special agents available to do some other agent's follow up investigations. It was kind of like the smugglers knew this fact. So they laid low until the dust settled and then they began smuggling again. It was business as usual in no time, but without Rich Latchkey and the Robinson brothers. St. Louis was still awash with weed, cocaine and heroin.

Rich Latchkey's life wasn't worth a plug nickel at this point. He stopped going to his restaurant and he had to leave his little house.

He let his manager run the restaurant for him but she was terrorized by organized criminals who barged into the restaurant looking for Rich. He eventually closed the doors.

The Robinson case was being prosecuted through the United States Attorney's office in Fairview Heights, Illinois (the same office where my cop cousin skated on a drug charge).

Our friend, the lead Assistant United States Attorney, Clifford J. Proud, who was a St. Louis cop for a while and was close friends with the police department surgeon, Dr. Jim Cooper. In St. Louis everyone is connected in some manner.

Cliff Proud drank beer with us, hung out with us and even went on federal search warrants with Braun and me. He was concerned about the safety of Rich Latchkey. Rich was also the ticket to Cliff Proud being moved up the federal ladder of success.

Cliff spoke to the Special Agent in charge of the St. Louis Field office and they agreed that Rich should be given funds to hide himself until he was able to testify against Paul and Dan Robinson. With Braun's absence, that left me with the responsibility of tending to Rich Latchkey.

The problem which arose was that Cliff desired to prosecute Paul and Dan Robinson together. Dan was a federal fugitive. Informants advised DEA and the FBI that Dan was touring the country with one of his lackey's and that he had been sighted in California.

It was only a matter of time until Dan Robinson would do something stupid and be arrested, but until that happened, the case was on hold.

Rich had my pager number and he would page me once a week stating that he needed more cash. I would go to the SAC's office and sign for the funds and then I would wait for Rich to page me again with his location. It was cloak and dagger stuff and I loved it. I think Rich enjoyed being able to hide, he was always in a good mood when I met up with him.

Rich, at this point in time, was a lonely man. I usually met him in hotel lobbies. I would walk in and sit down and just wait for him to appear. It was a game for him to sneak up behind me and tap me on the shoulder. I figured he was watching me as I entered the lobby and he could have just walked up to me and engaged me in conversation, but he insisted on playing spy games.

He wanted to talk to someone. He would have much rather dealt with Detective Sultan but Detective Sultan had bigger fish to fry. Rich was impressed with Detective Sultan's future. Having influential relatives in the political scene in the little city of St. Louis, especially with cops, was impressive. Rich was always thinking of the future.

In Rich's mind, when this little federal setback gets settled and when Paul and Dan go away for a long vacation, he'll be able to do what he wants in St. Louis.

Rich had funds, mostly ill-gotten and not reported to the IRS. Cash money is real money in America, and everywhere else. His cash was hidden and invested and he had long range plans. But he was saddled with me, not Detective Sultan.

In a way I felt sorry for Rich. Going from hotel to hotel and always looking over his shoulder couldn't be fun. So I sometimes had brief conversations with him.

Most of the time Rich talked about Paul Robinson; a guy who he had known for a decades, gotten wealthy with, but feared like Satan himself.

Rich told me story after story about the house in Hollywood, Florida. The girls from St. Louis who migrated there for short stays were mostly gorgeous. Rich was smitten with one of them.

These girls had been out of Rich's comfort zone for his entire life. They were upper middle class girls from good families in West St. Louis County. Their dads were professional people, doctors, lawyers, business executives.

Rich felt this girl was maybe smitten with him. They both had things in common: Paul Robinson and dope.

To a super pimp like Paul Robinson, paranoia is a way of life. Guys like him are fearful of losing control of their domain. Paul also was smitten with the gorgeous St. Louis girl, and he in fact felt that he owned her. In his pimp mind, she was his property.

Rich and the girl were talking at the pool one morning, drinking coffee and coming down from a late night binge of weed, coke, and wine.

Paul came to the pool deck, nude under his house robe that he always wore. He quickly sized things up, loosened his robe and ordered the girl to perform a sex act on him. She did as Paul stared at the puny but intelligent Rich Latchkey.

The girl finished her task, spat in the pool, went to her room and packed her bags. Paul continued to stare at Rich, terrorizing him. "I own everything and everybody in this house, pipsqueak, including you. Don't you ever flirt with any of my girls."

Rich quizzed me about how cops and DEA agents actually feel about drug dealers. I gave him my opinion and I wondered where this conversation was going.

I advised him that I got beat up by a drug dealer on a hotel room raid and the beating didn't endear me to DEA or drug dealers in general.

He questioned me about the drug raid. I gave him the name of the drug dealer and the whereabouts of the raid. He became excited, "That was my dope," he said. "I gave that guy the dope on consignment and I never got paid for it. You got beat up and I lost $10,000. That's karma! We're connected by that event." He wanted to shake my hand so I shook hands with him. The dope, the fight, the swollen face and sore muscles, it had gone full circle for me and I was able to put it to bed.

The irony of the cops and robbers game and the closeness of white society in St. Louis haunted me. Everything was connected by someone or something, and the FBI controlled most of what every cop did.

I worked Italians and Syrians. I was a specialist, I thought. But in reality, I was just a guy who someone, somewhere, wanted to give a break to.

The Intelligence Unit went straight to my head. I was certain I was a special guy, not lucky; smart and special. In reality I was a puppet following a script written by the gangsters and drug dealers and edited by the feds.

After the organized crime guys all went to prison, or the grave, I felt like I had played into the grand scheme of things by being transferred to DEA. It was just weird!

There were times that when I met Rich Latchkey I felt that he was grooming me for a long term friendship after he got out of prison. I didn't feel good about it. He was a user of people and he had gobs of cash. I planned to keep him at arm's length.

Rich paged me at one point in time and asked me to meet him at an Irish restaurant in Soulard (Norton's Pub) with some cash. Soulard is St. Louis' version of the French Quarter but not as large or opulent. It's a neighborhood where for some unknown reason, entrepreneurs purchased old turn of the century brick buildings and turned them into neat little pubs and nightclubs.

Rich told me he was buying lunch and he even recommended the Reuben. These meetings had been going on for months and Rich and I had become business friends.

Rich knew me now. He knew that I had a family, mortgage and car payments and a wife who worked. We were relaxed around each other.

I figured that Dan Robinson would be arrested soon. He was probably running out of cash and he would eventually over extend himself by reaching out to friends and relatives. It was only a matter of time before he got arrested.

Besides that fact, I had an informant who was a friend of one of Dan's girlfriends. This guy was also an informant for the FBI. He would weigh information and then decide who to give it to. The FBI always paid more for informant information, so he would give me the small stuff.

Dan was telephoning the gal often and she would vent to her friend and the friend would get federal money for the information.

At the Irish Pub, Rich got serious with me, "When this is all over and when I get out of prison, if you ever want to find me you can come in here. I own this place."

I was impressed; it was a busy and thriving restaurant. But I also knew that the federal government didn't know Rich Latchkey owned another business. And that AUSA Cliff Proud and Special Agent Mike Braun didn't know either. But I wasn't going to snitch Rich Latchkey off to the feds. And I didn't!

Snitches are the life blood of any federal investigation. Every agent depends on them, but mostly they are products of the federal government. Local police departments don't have the money to pay informants. But the bottom line with informants is: cops and agents hate them. Even prosecutors and judges hate them. Everybody hates a tattletale and I wasn't going to be one.

I thought hard about the information Rich Latchkey gave me. He was doing everything in his power to draw me into his friendship trap. He'd been trained by the best, Paul Robinson.

I rationalized his overt act of giving me information on

himself. He was baiting me to see if I would snitch on him. But in retrospect every cop and agent is a snitch in his or her own way.

A snitch gives us information, we verify it, go to a prosecutor and tell him what we have, we then go to a federal magistrate and snitch to him, and then we all get together and arrest and beat the guy up. Without snitching there wouldn't be any cases. But we all hate snitches!

AUSA Cliff Proud knew about Dan Robinson's girlfriend. There were surveillance photos taken by city Intelligence showing them together at the dentist's hideaway in south St. Louis County, Missouri. And I told him that I had been in contact with her and had rapport with her.

This girlfriend and I lived in the same neighborhood in beautiful north St. Louis County. She walked with her mother and their dog by my house. She was in fear of her life for being Dan's paramour and she felt I could protect her.

But she was playing both sides. Every time Dan telephoned her she would vent to her friend and the friend would inform us, either me or the FBI.

I would contact the girl and she would deny that she had contact with him. Cliff Proud wanted to bring her before a federal grand jury. He gave me the subpoena and I searched for her to serve her. She was avoiding me.

This gal had a heroin habit and she mainlined whenever she could, but she still had a secretarial job and she was able to do what it took to keep it.

During my interview of her concerning Dan Robinson, she freely spoke about the dentist's office on Tesson Ferry Road where she and Dan would meet.

The dentist had a condo and a hot tub. She would leave work early and meet Dan there. They would frolic and eventually end up in the hot tub. She purchased waterproof makeup to hide her heroin injection tracks on her arms. She felt empowered being the paramour of a famous gangster and she didn't know how Dan would feel if he knew she was an addict.

I had seen Dan Robinson's wife several times. She was gorgeous. I couldn't figure why he would want to bed down with this little hard scrabble north county junkie. I came to the conclusion that Dan, like his brother Paul, was a congenital low life.

It seemed like I was bumping into low life's on both sides of the fence; some of the cops I worked with, drank beer with and traveled with were scum, and it was the same way in the police department. I was feeling out of place again.

I eventually made contact with the friend who was snitching on the heroin addict girlfriend and I befriended him. He too thought I could protect him from the Robinsons, if they ever figured out who was snitching on them. I told him I would protect him, basically, I lied.

The grand jury subpoena for the junky girl was burning a hole in my pocket. As luck would have it, the friend paged me and I called him back. "She'll be leaving our offices in fifteen minutes and walking to her car in the parking lot. You can serve her there," he advised.

I drove like a madman to get to her place of employment, a large hotel near the airport. Sure enough there she was, walking to her car. "Hey," I said to her without exiting the "G" car. "This is a coincidence. I was just coming to see you. I have a subpoena for you." I handed it to her and she had a sick look on her face. I figured she was on her way to score some heroin.

"Thanks," she replied. I could tell that she was terrified, besides starting withdrawal. You can't stop shooting heroin

without going into convulsions. She read the subpoena as I
sat and watched her.

"This is in Illinois," she said. "I don't know my way
around there, I'll get lost. Can you take me?"

"Yeah," I replied. "I'll give you a ride."

There were other people associated with the Robinson
brothers who Cliff Proud wanted before a grand jury. I had
the subpoenas and I served them.

There was an old man in south St. Louis who allowed
them to stash multi kilos of cocaine at his apartment,
whenever they desired. He never asked any questions, he
just did what Paul and Dan and Rich told him to do.

This old guy could hardly walk and he was feeble
minded. I didn't give him a ride over to the eastside but his
grand jury date was the same as the junky girlfriend. In fact
he went in first.

He came out crying and sobbing and plopped down on a
bench in the courthouse and cried. I felt sorry for him. I
asked him how he got to the courthouse and he told me he
had taken a bus. He was afraid of the streets on the eastside
and he didn't know how he was going to get back. I advised
him that I would take him back and to just sit and relax.

The junky girlfriend was watching the turn of events and
she was completely spooked. Her eyes were darting around
and her face was contorted, her hands were shaking and she
was pale. I wondered if she was going to take a dive. She
held onto my arm and stared at me as if I could somehow
help her, since we lived in the same neighborhood.

"Your federal uncle doesn't care if you are sick or not.
He wants information so when they call your name go in
there and tell them what they want to hear. Understand?"

She nodded and the Marshall came out and called her
name and she slowly walked into the jury room. Cliff Proud,

Braun, and a couple of FBI agents who I had worked with
before watched this show, and they particularly watched me.
I wondered what was up.

Cliff called me into his office and closed the door. One of
my FBI associates, as well as Braun, were sitting in
overstuffed government chairs and looking as serious a heart
attack.

"The FBI agent has something to ask you," Cliff said.

"The FBI agent?" I lowly said to myself. I knew the guy,
we'd worked together and I was on a first name basis with
him.

"Okay," I replied while looking at my associate as if to
say, "What's up?"

"We've gotten word that you've been screwing the
blonde informant/grand jury witness. That's against federal
regulations and guidelines and you can be prosecuted for
your indiscretion," the agent said in a low tone.

I looked at Cliff, my beer drinking buddy, for assistance,
but he was stone faced. "I'm married," I began. "I'm not
screwing anybody but my wife."

Finally the FBI agent started laughing, "I can't do this
anymore," he said with a laugh. It was a prank initiated by
Braun and AUSA Cliff Proud. I laughed with them,
hesitantly.

I gave the two witnesses a ride back to civilization on the
Missouri side of the river and headed for home.

About a week went by and a beer drinking AUSA buddy
telephoned me at my DEA office. He wanted me to pick him
up in my "G" car and convey him to Benton, Illinois. The
East St. Louis United States Attorney's office had an office
in Benton.

I asked him what was up. He advised me that he wanted
me to testify before a grand jury there. I was accustomed to
grand juries and had testified before many. It was a casual

affair and the jurors were friendly and respectful. In most cases the witness giving testimony just waited for the AUSA to ask a question and you answered "yes" or "no". It had never been a big deal.

I looked forward to a road trip with my new buddy. It was always a good time being around AUSA's. I knew I didn't have to clear the trip with my DEA supervisors because I figured they already were aware of my plans. They listened to every phone call I received or made.

It was common knowledge that I had enemies back at the police department and that they had made rank and were in positions to do me harm if and when I returned. It was an ideology conflict between me and the lead dog and the little pedigree dog. They were now powerful within the police department.

I thought maybe I could finagle a "step and fetch" government job with the United States Attorney's office. They hire cops with investigative skills, and I was looking for a new home. I would have twenty years as a cop by the time I returned to the world of mediocrity and would be eligible for a meager pension.

I picked my AUSA friend up at his office and we were off. It was relaxing and we mostly talked about the Robinson case. Dan Robinson, still being a fugitive was holding up the judicial process and the United States Attorney (Rick Hess) was about to throw in the towel and put Paul on trial by himself.

The saving grace for a double defendant trial was the heroin junky girlfriend of Dan's, and her venting to her friend. Dan still telephoned her and eventually he would tell her where he was. Then he would be arrested.

We arrived in Benton and I waited outside of the grand jury room. The AUSA came out and said it was time for me to come in.

"Give me some info on my testimony," I said to him. "Is this a Paul and Dan thing or a Latchkey thing?"

"Neither," he replied. "We're having trouble with our grand jury in East St. Louis, there's a leak and we don't know which juror it is so we're trying for an indictment down here. I'll ask the questions and all you have to say is "yes" or "no". Got it?"

"Yeah," I reluctantly replied.

I walked in and the scene was casual. I was introduced and sworn in and took a chair. The AUSA started asking me questions about something I knew nothing about. I didn't know how to respond, so I stalled a couple of times. I must have had a strange look on my face and I was embarrassed.

The AUSA was finished. A guy on the jury intervened and started asking me detailed questions about what had transpired. He eventually said, "You really don't know anything about this case, do you?"

I didn't answer the guy. I looked at the AUSA and he called the testimony off. I was excused. I figured it was another federal prank. I quickly exited the room and the AUSA came out after me. I figured my chances for a government job with the United States Attorney's office in the Southern District of Illinois were dead after that court testimony.

There was never any conversation about the grand jury. I never asked any questions and the AUSA never offered any explanation.

I reverted to my first days at DEA. I was told, "You are not here to ask questions. You are here to do what you are told and to be one of the boys." It was a Palance moment. I had being one of the boys down pat. It was a quiet ride back to East St. Louis.

I thought deeply about grand juries. They're secret and

leaked information can be prosecuted. I realized that given the right set of circumstances, anybody can be federally indicted. And if a person is indicted, federally, the United States Attorney has the indicted person's balls in his hand. It was a scary thought.

There's a saying in the legal profession: "You can indict a ham sandwich." It didn't happen this time. I was being used as a pawn to railroad someone in East St. Louis, Illinois. The system is flawed from the top to the bottom.

XV.

HELL'S ANGELS METH LAB IN HELL

Besides the Rich Latchkey/Robinson brother's case, for some strange reason, I lucked into cases in the eastside, so I mainly worked out of the United States Attorney's office in the Southern District of Illinois. But I strolled into the task force offices in Clayton periodically.

The boys were drinking every night and Reszler was drinking a lot. Detective Sultan nicknamed him "weeble wobble" because he got so intoxicated. Reszler would get drunk, weeble wobble, and tell funny stories.

I walked in one evening and Reszler was telling a story about how he got blitzed in Soulard and had spent all of his cash on booze.

He knew he needed some greasy Mexican food to soak up the booze, so he drove through a Taco Bell and ordered a Grande Burrito. He got the food and didn't have any money to pay for it. He bartered his pocket knife and his handcuffs for the meal and drove to the lot to eat.

As he was devouring the meal a cop car cruised in and went up to the window. The attendant handed the cop something and the cop walked to Reszler's DEA "G" car.

"Rough night?" the cop asked.

Reszler was so drunk he could hardly speak, but he made enough sense that the cop knew who he was and that he was assigned to the DEA Task Force.

"I paid your tab," the cop said as he handed Reszler his knife and handcuffs. "You might need these tomorrow." The cop walked away.

It was another great story and we all enjoyed it. But

Reszler was on his way to being super intoxicated again, and he was weebling and wobbling and drinking and laughing. I felt he was approaching the danger zone, but who was I to judge? I was intoxicated most of the time.

The next day I got a call at home that five of us Task Force guys were supposed to meet up at a parking lot on Interstate "44" for a trip to Lebanon, Missouri. I quickly packed a bag, said goodbye to my wife and kids and my dogs and headed out into the unknown.

I had been advised to keep radio silence and that the group would be briefed to the nature of the assignment after we met up.

I pulled up and I was sober for a change. I had again been fighting the urge to drink beer; it was a difficult battle. First off, St. Louis was a beer town. Everything revolved around beer, and I, for most of my life, didn't think anything was wrong with drinking beer, lots of it. St. Louis is no longer a beer town; it is now a kush (weed) town. A large percentage of the population is addicted to it.

It was me, Jim Bob the country St. Louis County cop, Detective Horowitz, the city cop with influential friends, T Anderson and Reszler.

Jim Bob had all of the information and he advised us that the Missouri State Patrol, who has undercover narcotics cops, had taken off a large meth lab at a dairy farm near Lebanon and that we were supposed to go there and dismantle it.

"Shouldn't we have space suits or something to do that?" Detective Horowitz asked.

"Maybe," Jimmy replied, but we don't. We've got rubber gloves." He held up a box of thin surgical gloves. "That's it!"

"Somewhere down the line I'm going to sue the federal

government and DEA for damages for this shit," Detective Horowitz exclaimed.

"Fuck it man," I loudly said. "Let's get there, dismantle the damn lab, and get back to St. Louis. I don't want to spend any more time in sticksville than I have to."

We took off in a convoy, Jimmy in the lead because he said he had been briefed by Palance and he knew where the dairy farm was. We drove in the darkness for a couple of hours and then we poked around on some country roads until we came upon the dairy farm.

The farmhouse was a shack from the outside and I didn't wish to stay in it. There was an expensive motorhome toward the back of the house and I claimed it for sleeping. Nobody challenged me so I was feeling better about having a place to sleep when the time came.

Jimmy told us that Palance advised him that we should start the dismantling of the meth lab as soon as we get on scene, so we began.

We meticulously removed all of the meth, packaged it and placed it in a machine shed near the lab. We took the glassware and lab equipment out of the area and placed it on the ground to the rear of the farm shed.

The lab was situated in the part of the dairy farm where the cows were once milked. It was meticulous, as all labs should be, but meth labs seldom were. I could tell this was a first class operation so I asked Jimmy what the particulars were on the lab.

"Hells Angels from California own the lab. They had two or three chemists living here and cooking, twenty-four-hours-a-day. The chemists are incarcerated in the jail in Lebanon awaiting transfer to a federal facility. They aren't talking."

"So," I continued, "we get the lab torn down and then we head back to St. Louis?"

"Palance told me to call him when we get the lab down and then he'll advise us what's next," Jimmy explained.

We worked into the night dismantling the lab and eventually stopped at about 0400. I headed for the motorhome and got some sleep, woke up and was wondering about breakfast.

The house was stocked with food, so we cooked the morning meal and explored the farm. It was a beautiful farm, Ozarks hill country, pristine and wild.

There was a phone in the house so Jimmy called Palance and told him of our progress. "Stay at the farm," Palance advised him, so we stayed with nothing to do.

I drove into Lebanon and attempted to interview the chemists. The jail was like an ancient dungeon. The chemists looked like surfers who had been pulled over on the intestate for possessing a joint of marijuana.

They had been briefed not to talk, and they wouldn't even give me their names. They would be released on bond eventually and would be given expensive lawyers to defend them in court.

But the problem the chemists had was that they would be indebted to the murderous Hells Angels for life. They weren't bikers. They didn't have long hair and tattoos. They were Ivy League schools types, with horned rim glasses, trying to make some quick and easy money.

Spending time in the Lebanon City Jail would be a sobering experience. I told them that I hoped the amount of money they were being paid by the Hells Angels was going to be worth the misery they had in store for them. They just stared at me like I wasn't there.

A couple of days went by and Jimmy called Palance to get the lay of the land. We all wanted to go home. There was nothing left to do in Lebanon. Palance told us to stay at the farm. Jimmy asked him what our mission was. Palance advised him that he had information that the Hells Angels were coming there to pick up a load of meth. Jimmy advised the group.

"So what are we going to do if and when the Hells Angels show up?" Detective Horowitz asked.

"Arrest them," Jimmy replied. "That's what Palance said to do.

"We've only got pistols," I said. "They've probably got automatic weapons. This doesn't look cool to me."

"Well the county guys have semi-automatic pistols," T. Anderson said. "Us city guys have revolvers."

"Let's get some beer," Reszler said, "Fuck this shit. I'll shoot it out with those fucking bikers, I ain't afraid of them."

The group was mumbling and it was drawing toward afternoon of the third day, so a couple of guys went to a liquor store in Lebanon and came back with three cases of cold beer.

We grilled some steaks and made a salad and ate the Hells Angels food as we listened for the sound of rolling thunder. My gun was a five shot snub nosed pistol. It was a belly gun and I was feeling inadequate. Besides that, I only had ten bullets, five in the gun and five in my pocket in a container.

So we drank beer and the county guys brought out their multi shot semi-automatic nine millimeter pistols and we started shooting them. They had loads of county ammo because the county took care of their cops; the county had money. The city was broke, except for the assets the guys at the task force sent to the city.

I had carried a forty-five automatic in the Marine Corps and had qualified with it, since I was a machine gunner. I was familiar with semi-automatic pistols.

Detective Horowitz had a federal firearms dealer permit

and he carried a Glock forty caliber sidearm, even though he was a city cop and not authorized to carry automatic firearms. He had ammo, too.

We started out by plinking at the glassware we had removed from the lab. It was innocent enough, some experimenting with other cops automatics. We drank beer and plinked.

Finally the glassware was all shot up. There was a pile of glass where the expensive tubes and vessels once were. Somebody aimed at the massive glass windows in the milking facility where the lab was situated. It was just one shot, and then another and then we were firing in rapid succession and quickly reloading with another clip and shooting again. By the time the evening was over and we were ready for bed, the milking facility was destroyed.

"I smell cash," Detective Horowitz exclaimed. He was drunk and was walking around in circles, like a water diviner. He placed both arms straight in front of him (one holding a cold beer) and began walking toward the farm house.

The crew followed him and we all went into the house. Horrowitz scrunched his nose and pointed to the floor in front of the television, "Here, here there is money" he said as he pointed to the floor.

Jim Bob ran out to the shed and came back with a crowbar and a hammer. He began removing the floor boards to the house. There was nothing but cobwebs under the floor.

"Over here," Horowitz exclaimed pointing with his beer. Jim Bob destroyed the floor. No money!

"It's in the walls," Horowitz exclaimed.

Jimmy hit the plastered wall with the hammer. "Fuck Horowitz," Jimmy said in exasperation, "You certain about this? Is your smeller off?"

"Fuck this," I said as I headed for my motorhome. I slept good and awoke to the carnage we had caused the night before.

I heard Jimmy tell the guys that we could blame the destruction of the milking facility and the house on the Hells Angels chemists.

The sheriff's department showed up and inspected the farm for the owner. The farm had been rented like the farm in Paris, Missouri, through a farm newspaper, sight unseen.

The sheriff and his crew went directly to the owner of the farm and advised him of the destruction. The owner called his lawyer and the lawyer called DEA field office in Clayton and spoke to the Special Agent in Charge (SAC) who had Palance on the carpet for allowing us to go on an assignment without a special agent to keep us out of trouble.

Palance called the farmhouse and we let the phone ring. We figured it was him. It rang again and Jimmy finally answered it. Palance was furious. Jimmy lied to him and told him that the chemists did it. That didn't wash because when the chemists were arrested the milking facility was in good shape.

"Secure the farmhouse and report to the office," Palance advised Jimmy. Finally we were allowed to head for home. The boys were quiet on the ride home. We strolled into the office and expected to be shipped back to our police departments.

I was about ready for the demotion. I knew I needed to dry out and get back into good graces with my wife. My kids hardly even knew me. But my dogs remembered me.

I had gotten so tired of living in motel rooms that when we travelled, did deals, drank after the deals and retired to our motel rooms, I wouldn't even go to bed. I would quietly pack my bag and head for my "G" car in the parking lot. I drove home drunk from Iowa or southeast Missouri many times.

My Chrysler LeBaron turbo "G" car had a distinct sound and my wife told me that our Schnauzer would perk up and go to the door to greet me when I made the turn into our subdivision, which was three blocks from our house.

Palance shouted at us and told us we were childish and all kinds of other disgraceful things. But the bottom line was: DEA got the statistics for the arrests of the chemists. They also got the glory for the meth lab dismantling, the seizure of the motorhome and some cash that was at the scene.

DEA made some kind of a deal with the owner of the property. There was an active meth lab on his property. He can say that he wasn't aware of that fact, but that might not wash with the United States Attorney in the Western District of Missouri. The owner wasn't willing to take that chance, so the destruction went away.

I had feelings on the shooting up of the farm. If you leave five puppies alone in your house you are going to have poop, pee, and things chewed up. It's just a fact of life.

One of my duties as the elder statesman of kiddie cop heaven was to convey the seized assets to the Federal Reserve Bank in downtown St. Louis.

Every case had some kind of seized asset. Some just consisted of jewelry, Rolex's, diamonds, gold bracelets and necklaces. Other seizures consisted of thousands of dollars in cash, houses, farms, airplanes and boats.

Every group has a drop box for late night cash and jewelry seizures, and a larger safe for storage when the lock box gets filled, which was often.

Every seizure was documented with a case number. The seized items were noted on a clear plastic DEA bag with

dates and information when, where, and who, how much
cash, sealed with a hot machine and then placed in the drop
box.

Whenever the safe and the drop box were full, Palance
would instruct me to gather up everything in the two safes
and convey them to the Federal Reserve Bank in downtown
St. Louis.

I didn't mind the task. It was sort of like a day off, and
Palance appreciated me doing this job. The other guys felt
too important to run errands for DEA.

I used a large Marine Corps sea bag to tote the seized
assets, and I usually had to drag it to my little Chrysler
LeBaron parked in the DEA garage.

I usually had approximately a quarter of a million dollars
in cash, as well as gold and diamonds, watches and gold
coins. Drug dealers only purchased the finest of everything.

I would telephone the Federal Reserve Bank and advise
them that I was coming with seized assets and they would
have someone waiting for me at the loading dock in the rear
of the bank. I'd park the Chrysler and pop the trunk, then
someone would help me hoist the sea bag onto a four
wheeled cart and together we would roll it into the bank.

Together we would remove every plastic evidence bag
and open it while being videotaped. The cash would be
electronically counted and checked with the amount on the
bag.

The jewelry and other items of intrinsic value were
placed on a table and then locked in a lockbox. Every item
was documented and then the plastic bag was destroyed. It
was a day's job, interesting, and it got me out of the lineup
for kicking in doors or chasing crazed dopers down country
roads.

I had wealthy friends in the city. Most cops somehow
become close friends with businessmen. Many of these guys

were born into money and they were interested in the lives of the underclass. They wanted to be friends with city cops.

Two of my best friends owned Crystal Water Company on South Boyle in the city. I had fished with these guys, drank beer with them and I had lunch with them on a regular basis. We had fun together.

But these guys worshipped the dollar. Their lives revolved around making a profit. They were so cheap that when we went to lunch I had to tip the waitress. They put off going to church because they didn't wish to place any money in the collection basket, but they deemed themselves religious.

On one occasion I had a smaller duffel bag stuffed with cash and gold and diamonds. I carried it into their office and emptied it on one of the brother's desk. He looked at it like a starving man would look at a steak dinner. But he didn't touch it. It was a big laugh for all of us.

I got lackadaisical in my DEA duties and hardly ever knew where my little thirty eight caliber revolver was. We all carried leather briefcases (confiscated from drug dealers) which we used to transport our guns, recorders, cameras, handcuffs and binoculars.

Having to go to the United States Attorney's office in Fairview Heights, Illinois so often to kibitz with my beer drinking and golfing buddy, AUSA Cliff Proud about the Robinson brothers drug conspiracy case, I sometimes locked the little belly gun in my glove compartment or in the trunk of the LeBaron.

A civilian employee who was the DEA wire man (installed wire taps) called me at home one evening and asked me to go to Kansas City, Missouri with him to install a wiretap. He advised me he had it cleared with Palance. I told him I would go.

The next morning I met up with him at the DEA offices and we took off in his Ford van. I had my briefcase with my goodies in it.

We were in a rough neighborhood, in an alley and he was up on a pole installing the wiretap. He called out to me that he hoped I had my gun because he observed some folks from his high vantage point that he was concerned about.

I dug into my briefcase and there was no gun. I had left it in the Lebaron glovebox. I didn't want to tell him so I just didn't answer him. I was mentally preparing myself to go into hand to hand combat with, whomever.

I frantically searched the van and came up with a large folding knife and a hammer. I wasn't going to increase my vulnerability by staying inside of the van. I opened the pocket knife and stuck it in my waistband and stuck the hammer at the small of my back so that I could get to it quickly and surprise the bad guy.

I stood around outside of the van for an hour feeling stupid and finally George, the wire guy, came down the pole. "Let's get out of here," he said as he loaded his tools into the van. "There's a group of guys eyeballing us. You have your gun, don't you?"

"Actually, no," I replied.

"What?" he sternly replied. "Where's your fucking gun?"

"I think it's in my glovebox," I quietly said.

"Get in quick," he said. We tore out of the alley as a group of neighborhood toughs were closing in on us. "I don't fucking believe it," he said as we drove toward safety.

"Hey," I began. "It worked, right? You got the wire up and we got out of there. There wasn't any trouble, we're home free."

What I wanted to say was, "Hey, you're the jerkoff who placed the bug in my desk phone, my home phone, my car and probably my bedroom. Now you want to act self-righteous with me? Fuck you!"

But I didn't. This guy was just doing what he was told by some DEA bureaucrat. The wire guy would have gone to the SAC and told him I was aware of the listening devices. I would have been considered as a guy with a bad attitude, and shipped back to mediocrity before my time, although, my time with the feds was quickly dwindling.

I was like an old man lying in bed wondering when the grim reaper was going to tap him on his shoulder and say, "Get up fool, it's time for you to meet your maker."

All it took was a telephone call from the Chief's office and I would be back with my enemies, all of whom had gained rank and power. I didn't want to rush the process. I wanted to hang on as long as possible.

Several milestones happened simultaneously: Group supervisor Palance was promoted to GS-15 and was sent to DEA Headquarters in Washington, D.C. It happened fast. He got the call and he quickly cleaned out his office and was gone. No fanfare, just a charismatic leader deserting his followers.

The gossip in the office was that he also got his United States Attorney girlfriend transferred from the St. Louis office to another off ice in the D.C. vicinity. The fed continued to be one big happy family.

TFD T. Anderson rotated back to the city police department. TFD Larry (mad dog) Wheeler rotated back to the St. Louis County Police Department. Both were promoted to sergeant shortly after their return. All of this was without much fanfare. They were here and then they were gone.

TFD Steve Johnny (Conan) Reszler was hired by the Drug Enforcement Administration. He was to report to the

DEA academy in Quantico, Virginia in one month.

This was treated as a big deal in the annals of task force history. Reszler didn't have to return to mediocrity. He was the one who was going to succeed in the career of law enforcement, live in a good climate, make a decent wage, and do exciting things for the rest of his working life. We were excited for him.

But as I watched and observed I could still see that Reszler wasn't all that thrilled about his new venture. I figured he didn't want to leave his pin-up model girlfriend, and I didn't blame him for that. He would be gone for six months. That's a long time for a new relationship, even for an old one.

There was a huge party for Reszler, a kind of congratulatory/going away type of a party. The booze flowed like water and Reszler was the center of attraction.

All of his friends and a bunch of federal agents showed up to wish him well. I didn't attend, and I felt like there was a pall over the entire event. I couldn't place it, but the feeling had me concerned about Reszler.

We all felt so worldly and confident about our lives, but that was a false feeling. Our confidence came from the fact that we were city and county cops and we would always be cops with secure jobs for as long as we wished. Reszler was tossing the security away and for the casual observer, like me, he was childish in nature, spoiled and entitled as I've said many times in this writing.

I think Reszler was feeling the pain of cutting the apron strings with the P.D. It had been his bread and butter for his entire life. Every meal he had ever consumed, or every beer he had ever drunk, came from the St. Louis Metropolitan Police Department. He was born into it and he was accustomed to it. It wasn't perfect, but it was more stable (for guys like us) than the federal government.

The day before Reszler was scheduled to leave for Quantico he stopped by my desk. I was kind of expecting to get some kind of message from him before he left. The conversation was comical as usual and we both laughed at some of his stories.

He opened his briefcase and retrieved an antique pump pellet pistol. "I want you to have this," he somberly said. "I've had it since I was a kid. It's the first weapon my dad ever bought for me. And here," he continued as he reached back into his briefcase, "here's a bunch of twenty two's I'll never use. You've got a twenty two, right?"

"Thanks, Conan," I muttered, "but why are you giving me your toys? You might have a kid with the pin-up queen, don't you think you should hang onto the pellet gun?"

"Maybe, but I want you to have it," he sternly said.

"Okay, man, and thanks again," I replied. We stared and I was trying to read him. I thought he was depressed, but this was the first time he had ever left St. Louis for any amount of time. I chalked it up to that. And he was probably stressed to the max.

"You know if I can graduate at the top of my class at Quantico I'll be able to choose my own duty station," Reszler continued.

"Yeah, man," I replied.

"I don't trust that fucking Palance, do you?"

"Fuck, no," I replied.

"He told me that he could get me my choice of a duty assignment when I graduated. I think he's bullshitting me. What do you think?"

"I think so, too," I replied.

"So, I'm going to have to graduate at the top," Reszler continued. He stared for effect and I nodded in compliance.

"I talked to Doc Cooper about it and he agrees with me,"

Reszler continued. "He said that I have to get myself prepared to study into the night and make A's on every test, and to ace every physical test. Then I can name my own duty assignment. I'm thinking maybe Phoenix, or San Diego. I liked it there when me and T. Anderson went out there to seize that Canadian's drug assets."

"Sounds cool," I replied.

Reszler showed me a bottle of pills. "Doc Cooper gave me these," he said as he held them up for me to see. "They're uppers. Doc says to take one of these when I need a boost in studying or physical testing. You ever take these?"

"No," I replied. "Are those prescription drugs?"

Reszler laughed. "I'm sure they were prescribed to someone but not to me. He just gave me a bottle of them to use. He's a fucking doctor, he can do that, right?"

"Yeah, man," I replied. "But those are scheduled drugs, probably methamphetamine. You'll never pass a piss test with those in your system."

"Doc Cooper knows what he's doing," Reszler replied. "He would never give me something that would harm me. I need Doc Cooper for his pills and his political pull, and I need him for my career. My financial status rests on Doc Cooper's influence."

"You're right about that," I replied. I had an instant flashback to Main, the cocaine street dealer dealing for the Voodoo priest. He made almost the same statement to me about how he needed the Voodoo man and his drugs to sell.

I took a long look at Reszler. He was puffy again and red faced. He wasn't smiling much and he walked with his head down. I felt he was on the fast track to destruction.

But who does a guy like me confide in about one of my friends on the Task Force? I mentioned it to Liz Bates, the group secretary. She said I was nuts!

Reszler left for the academy and was soon forgotten in the Task Force. It's the way the job is. New guys get transferred in and old guys get transferred out. You go from important family member to the guy that nobody remembers.

Several days later I thought about the listening device in my desk phone. The SAC or anyone in power would get transcripts of my conversation with Reszler.

The SAC did not have positive feelings about any white cop in the task force. As far as he was concerned we were Ku Klux Clan night riders.

I thought about the day that four of us conveyed seized cars to the impound lot at Scott Air Force Base. Reszler followed us over in Little Stevie Wonder's "G" car Oldsmobile to convey us back. Having that many TFD's in one car was not a good idea.

First we had to make a stop for lunch, beer included, which I declined, and then we girl gawked in the downtown Clayton area and finally got within a block of the Missouri State Bank Building where our plush DEA offices were housed.

We were stopped in traffic when the DEA SAC, our boss, walked by us and looked in at us wondering what we were up to. The SAC looked out of place. He was a large man and he dressed in expensive suits, but his gait was off and he projected negative body language. He was out of place on the streets of Clayton, Missouri. His position of power consisted of sitting behind a desk playing the game of government bureaucrat and eavesdropping on little policemen playing federal agent. He acted like he was embarrassed to see us in traffic. He was probably suffering from Jim Crow fever. He stared for intimidation which caused a response from Reszler.

"I BE THE HEAD MOTHERFUCKER IN CHARGE,
THE NIC. YOU MOTHERFUCKERS UNDERSTAND?
UHUH, UHUH," Reszler began with his black shtick He
kept going on and on and the skit was funny, so we all
laughed.

The SAC wasn't laughing and I could tell that he took
stock of all of us. He was certain we as a group of underling,
white, racist cops were having a racial joke at his expense.

I was embarrassed by my reaction (laughing) as the SAC
was walking and I regretted the entire incident. I partially
blamed my behavior on Palance. He demanded that I
become one of the boys. My fate for noncompliance would
have been mediocrity.

But we were all doomed souls racing toward the
inevitable. We were all going back to the P.D. and probably
sooner than we wished.

The DEA lifestyle was a dream game and when we
awoke, or sobered up, we would be back in Kansas again
stroking Toto's boney little head.

In retrospect, I liked the SAC. He was articulate and
professional and he was a man's man, although I was told he
did accept gifts from Detective Horowitz. But that was an
entitlement fetish everyone in law enforcement, federal or
state or local had, including me.

It's amazing how we forget about the little things in life,
like listening devices in our work space, our homes, and our
cars. As soon as Reszler pulled that bottle of pills out of his
pocket I should have raised my hand and motioned for him
to stop. I should have taken him by his arm and marched
him into the hall and resumed our conversation.

Wherever Reszler is transferred after the academy you
can bet that they will be waiting for him with a piss test. It's
the way of big business.

XVI.

ZIPPITY DUDA

The group was anxiously awaiting the appointment of our new charismatic leader. In the interim, Special Agent Mike Duda (the guy who I did the favor of transporting his personal property back from Miami in the motorhome) assumed the post of Group Supervisor, Task Force, St. Louis Field Office.

Mike was well received by the haphazard cops. I vouched for him since I had traveled with him and had catalogued his personality.

Mike Duda had a strong reputation. He had been sent to the Golden Triangle overseas and had documented heroin traffickers for the government for several years. He was smart and personable and the cops respected him. We worked for Mike Duda and he rewarded us with a friendly attitude and mutual respect.

My desk and the desk of Detective Horowitz were so close that I could reach over and retrieve a report. Horowitz was a deep thinker and he was trying to figure out a way to get on the good side of Group Supervisor Mike Duda.

Mike Duda wasn't married, so Detective Horowitz couldn't exactly send floral arrangements to his house. He wasn't a sports fanatic so Detective Horowitz crossed ball game tickets off of his list. But Mike loved food. He was a big man. He was a gourmand.

While he and I were in Miami we joined some other agents at a Nicaraguan steak house. The food was excellent and the place was filled with South American dope dealers. I was in heaven watching them. These macho guys would walk into the restaurant with their jewelry and shirts unbuttoned with, "I will kill you", looks on their faces. They always had gorgeous Latino beauties in tow that walked with their heads down.

When you ordered a steak they always brought you two steaks, and they were big steaks. I could hardly get through mine; Mike polished both of his off and was eying my plate. "Could you finish mine?" I asked. Mike speared my steak and dragged it over to his plate. He devoured it.

As Detective Horowitz and I sat at our desks wondering what the day would bring, Detective Horowitz was lowly singing "Zippity Duda." He first hummed a chorus and then he used the title "Zippity Duda" again.

Mike came storming out of his office and glared at Detective Horowitz. "Don't sing my name," he said. He turned and went back to his office.

Detective Horowitz was unnerved. He scrawled on a piece of paper, "They listen to everything we say" and held it up for me to see. I didn't respond.

We all liked Mike Duda. Most of the time he was courteous and helpful to the cops playing fed. Most of us hoped that he would become the group supervisor.

But the problem was that Mike Duda hadn't placed his name on the list for the job of task force supervisor. That meant that whoever had tossed their name in the government basket for the job had preference over him. We figured that on any given day we would have another stranger to deal with, get accustomed to and to decide if we could trust him.

After a couple of months of Mike Duda, the word filtered down to us that a new guy from Washington, D.C. (Special Agent John China) had come to the field office and was being considered for the group supervisor job.

We waited for the gossip to continue and we learned that the new federal bureaucrat was a black guy, a G/S 14, whose wife was a lawyer. We suspected that this guy wasn't a good fit for the group. At this point in the game, we were all white and racist to a fault.

We were so racist that we resented having to work on black defendants. We had streamlined our drug cases on wealthy white transit drug smugglers. We had specialized ourselves, kind of like Intelligence, and we liked it that way. Our stats of arrests and money seizures were still way up.

The gossip mill informed us that the SAC (Special Agent in Charge) advised the new guy from Washington that he should take charge of another agent group and not pursue his dream of micro managing city and county cops. The guy was pondering the SAC's advice and we would observe him milling around the Task Force trying to get a feel for us. He was a light-skinned guy, bald with a white beard.

He was a friendly guy but one hundred eighty degrees from Palance. The new black guy from Washington was a liberal, and to our chagrin, he ignored the SAC's advice and became the new supervisor of the task force.

We continued to work for him, mostly because we were in a productive mode; we were like duck dogs who dive in to freezing water to retrieve ducks.

But what the SAC knew and tried to convey to John China was the gospel: most of us were cop's kids (except for me and a few others), St. Louis cop's kids. We were raised to be untrustworthy of black people.

The community of St. Louis was and is racist. Even in the work place blacks and whites are only tolerant of one another. It's a St. Louis curse and has kept this region down for a century.

The black professionals who come to St. Louis, (government and private sector) are aware that they will only be here for a couple of years. They purchase houses in west county, white neighborhoods, where their houses will appreciate in value. They are house poor!

I had eavesdropped and heard the black special agents complaining about their racist white neighbors. The agents make attempts to be friendly and neighborly with the white folks and they are shunned.

John China knew of the problem with housing in St. Louis. I advised him that there was affordable housing in north county. Upper middle class white people were moving out and blacks were moving in. A house in north county could be half of what a house in west county would cost, and in many instances, it was the same house built by the same builder.

John China purchased a house in North County and he and his lawyer wife moved to a ritzy area of big ranch homes. He invited the Task Force guys and their wives to his home and we all reluctantly went. It was an awkward evening and after that night the stats started dwindling in the task force.

There was no chemistry there between John China, his black lawyer wife, and the racist white cop kids. Basically, we didn't trust or like him.

There were several new guys from the county and the city assigned to the task force. Every cop has his own story on how he got to where he is in the maze of politics in law enforcement, and it was interesting to me to hear these new guys tell their stories.

One of the new city cops (Detective Wayne) had the expertise to repair household items. He could rebuild anything that routinely breaks in any household. He did gratis work for the Chief of Police.

Another new arrival, Detective Kenney, was a carpenter who rebuilt the Chief's house, and as the story unfolded,

Detective Horowitz paid for the building materials.

But the new guys made a difference in the Task Force. They came with fresh informants and a new sense of enthusiasm.

Special Agent Mike Braun (the spy) was concerned about my choice of weapons. I wasn't enthusiastic about firearms (sometimes I would carry a twenty two caliber automatic) and this worried Mike. He lectured me like a big brother, even though I was ten years his senior, and he offered to loan me one of his super high velocity automatic pistols. He showed me his Sig Sauer, nine millimeter semiautomatic pistol and told me I could carry it.

I had instant thoughts as I stared at the DEA type gun. It was what the federal government stood for, kill for control (agents can kill and get away with it, cops cant), and it was big and bulky.

The basic job description for cops is to protect and serve. In actuality, it's more serve than protect. Special Agents for the United States of America have a different creed. If you violate a United States code of justice you will be arrested. If you flee, resist, or attempt to injure or maim a federal agent you will be shot, most of the time you will die.

But Braun's pistol was a beautiful weapon and I took it from Braun and weighed it in my hand. He even gave me a holster for it. It was the kind of a weapon you can stick in someone's face and gain instant respect.

I quickly thought about why feds routinely stick their pistols in people's faces. I decided it was because of fear. The law of averages determines how much fear is involved in a drug agent's life. How many doors can you kick in, how many people can you confront, buy dope from, wrestle, chase down, fist fight, or try to get onto their faces before the tables get turned on you?

Working on that hypothesis, I surmised, that fear was the reason the crazed agent in the other group stuck his impressive nine millimeter cocked pistol in my face? The crazed agent was bigger, younger and outweighed me by eighty pounds.

I continued my quick thought process. Now that I had a special agent type of a weapon, what was I going to do with it? I always hoped I would get through the cop/agent vocation without having to kill a suspect. It was part of my nonconforming personality.

In my mind the cop job was a good job for a guy like me; kind of lazy and a little bit bullheaded, sometimes confused, not a thief or a dope dealer, true to my wife, basically an honest guy. Now I had the tool of conformity. DEA was using my friend Braun as a catalyst to my conformity. I wondered if this was what the assignment to DEA was all about.

The police department referred to the transfer as a training event, so did DEA. Were they training me to conform? Can a German Shepard be trained to retrieve ducks?

John China came out of his office (he was no doubt listening to our conversation through the bug in my desk) and watched the interaction between me and Braun.

"I'll set up a qualifying session for you and you can carry the automatic legally," John China said.

"Okay," I replied.

Detective Wayne, one of the new guys, was an intelligent man. He possessed a multi engine pilot's license and he owned a twin engine airplane that he flew often.

Wayne purchased the airplane in a dilapidated condition and rebuilt it himself. I was envious of him for that God given talent. I couldn't even work on my own car.

I had attempted to gain a pilot's license. I took a course and trained on a single engine Grumman airplane. I could fly the airplane okay, but when the instructor would advise me to return to the airport, I had difficulty finding my way back. The lessons became expensive, so I gave it up.

I conveyed my flying lesson experience to Detective Wayne and he was amused.

"Wrong flight instructor," he replied. I wondered if DEA had Detective Wayne's house and telephone bugged. He fit the profile of a drug smuggler.

But Wayne was an interesting guy. He grew up on the south side and was basically his own man. His parents died early in his life and he was on his own, living in the house they left him. He was single, no children, had cash in his pocket, and flew to Florida often. St. Louis folks who can afford it go to Florida every chance they get.

The older guys in the task force shunned Wayne and I attributed it to him being a new guy. So many new guys come to the task force with grandiose ideas about being a Cracker Jack narc and when they get here they screw up deal after deal. The older guys wait until the newness wears off and then they take you into their circle.

Wayne had approached Group Supervisor, John China, about a couple of ideas he had for drug deals. John placated him and told him to work them up and he would take a look at them. Basically Wayne was spinning his wheels.

Braun was in town and we had been in Fairview Heights, Illinois meeting with AUSA Cliff Proud concerning the Robinson case. Dan Robinson was still on the lam. It had been several months since he was declared a federal fugitive and the United States Attorney's office in the Southern District of Illinois was getting anxious about his capture. It was kind of like a group of surgeons waiting to perform a complicated surgery; they don't want any hang ups. Dan was a hang up.

It was mid-January and it was pitch dark outside. Since I had befriended Detective Wayne, he figured I would help him with a case he had worked up. He came to my desk, which was right next to Braun's desk, "I've got a deal tonight," he began.

I took a toll of him to read his body language. He was sincere and longing for help. "What's to it?" I asked. Braun perked up.

"I can buy a kilo of cocaine tonight, but I need someone to come with me," Wayne said.

"What are the particulars?" Mike asked.

"Two Colombians in an apartment in south county. I got set up with them through an associate. I haven't met them but I've spoken to them on the telephone and they are ready and willing to sell the kilo," Wayne continued.

John China came out of his office and joined the conversation. "If you guys want to do the deal tonight I'll assist you," John began. "Go into the undercover telephone room and call them. Tell them you can come tonight and we'll do the deal."

Wayne prepared his Pearl recorder and walked into the sound proof room. He came back in two minutes with the taped recording. He played it for us. The Colombians were ready to sell.

"Okay," John China continued, "Mike and I will be your backup. Wayne you get wired and you and Tim go inside. Tim, you'll be the money man, "I'll get twenty thousand dollars out of the safe and you can flash it." John walked away.

Braun and I wired Wayne. I was having nervous thoughts. I always did before a deal. But with most deals there was pre-surveillance, and we knew everything we could possibly find out about the targets. We knew nothing about these guys except that they were Colombian, living in an apartment in south St. Louis County selling kilos of cocaine from their apartment.

If Palance had been the supervisor this deal would not have gone down. He would have waited until it was daylight and we would have had the whole task force on it. It was a rushed deal, which leads to surprises and every cop knows surprises in law enforcement leads to death for someone. And it was so damned dark. Dope dealer today, dope dealer tomorrow.

It was obvious that John China was desperate for stats. If this deal went down it would give him stats, a kilo of cocaine and two Colombians from an undercover buy/bust.

We tested the wire and Wayne and I climbed into his undercover "G" car pickup truck. John China and Mike Braun got on the air in about fifteen minutes and advised they were on the way.

"Wait for us to drive onto the parking lot before entering the building," Mike advised. "The code is "good as gold," got it?"

"Ten-four," I replied.

Wayne and I waited on the parking lot. John China and Braun drove up and Braun got back on the air, "Make sure the wire is turned on. When you get inside, make sure they don't lock the door. If they lock it we won't be able to get inside without kicking it. It will hinder our entry. Make sure you say "good as gold" loudly enough so that we can hear it. We'll come in at that time."

"Ten-four," I replied. I was feeling more strangely about the deal. Wayne had never worked undercover and I actually didn't know him well enough to trust him with my life. I was carrying $20,000 in a briefcase. It could be a rip. It happens all of the time in the drug game.

Wayne and I exited his pickup and trudged our way toward the apartments. It was a nice apartment complex, new and high scale. There were expensive cars parked in the parking lot and I could smell the new smell of the building materials.

The apartment was on the second floor. The stairway was open and outside, the apartment door was located on an outside walkway. Wayne rang the doorbell and the door opened.

"Come in," a dark man approximately thirty years of age said. He was checking us out and we were checking him out. We walked in and Wayne introduced himself. They shook hands. Wayne introduced me as the "money man" and I played the part of a standoff participant who wasn't in the apartment to be friendly.

The Colombian appeared to be alone and he was nervous. He kept eyeing me and referring to me as "sir." He was fixated on my briefcase. "You brought the money?" he asked.

"Yeah," I replied, "I've got the money. Do you have the dope?"

One important rule I learned from working for Palance, the dope dealer doesn't want the dope, they want the cash, and they will do anything to obtain the cash. I held my ground.

We walked further into the apartment and he motioned for us to sit in some overstuffed chairs while he sat on a couch. "Show me the money," he said.

This was the oldest game in the dope business. It was time for me to play hard to get, so I said, "Show me the dope."

I knew I was going to flash the money for the Colombian drug dealer; it's almost scripted in the annals of dope game

101. It's taught in DEA drug school, but I still had to play hard to get. "Show me the dope."

"The dope is in the bedroom," the Colombian replied. "I'll go in and get it." He walked down a hallway and into the back bedroom of the two bedroom apartment. We could hear some low conversation and we figured the other Colombian was back there. I figured he was armed and if trouble started he would come out firing.

The Colombian came back to the living room. "Show me the money first and then I will show you the dope." He had apparently been coached by the other Colombian in the bedroom.

I opened the briefcase and flashed the contents. It works every time. The drug dealers become mesmerized by the cash. They want to touch it and play with it and rub it on their faces. He tried to touch it.

"Nope," I sternly said as I quickly closed the briefcase. "If you have the kilo, then get it. I'll give you one minute and then we're leaving." It was a standoff, he went to the front door and locked it, then went back to the bedroom.

Wayne was getting nervous and glancing at me for assurance. I nodded to him and stood up and walked to the front door. I unlocked it and then stood by the kitchen counter near the front door. Wayne stood in the living room.

The Colombian came back into the living area and approached me with a package. He handed it to me and I examined it. I took a sample and tested it and it was positive for cocaine. It's as good as gold," I loudly said.

He watched me and then looked at the front door. He noticed it was unlocked; he went to it and relocked it. Wayne started nut talking him about future deals but he was intently watching me and wanting to consummate the deal. He wanted the cash.

Wayne asked him for a soda and he turned his back on us and went to the fridge. I walked over and unlocked the door. He came back with a soda for Wayne and we were standing at the counter talking. The money was still on the counter in the briefcase. The kilo was beside it.

I kept listening for Braun and John China to barge in, but they didn't. "It's as good as gold," I repeated. I thought maybe they didn't hear me or maybe they tried the door and found it locked, so I walked back to the door and checked it; it was still unlocked.

The Colombian immediately walked back to the door and locked it. I figured Wayne and me were on our own. The guy in the back bedroom was no doubt armed to the teeth and listening to our conversation.

I was leery of Colombians. I had never worked them. They were a rare breed in sleepy old St. Louis and I wasn't about to let one or two of them take my life.

I pulled Mike Braun's Sig Sauer nine millimeter and stuck it in the Colombian's face. "Get down on your knees with your hands behind your head, motherfucker," I slowly said. "Wayne, watch for the guy in the back bedroom, if he comes out with a gun, shoot him in the head."

Wayne nods in compliance. In that instant, Braun and John China came tearing through the door with sawed off shotguns and raid gear. "There's another one in the back bedroom," I shouted.

Braun and John China rushed to the bedroom and arrested the other Colombian. We searched the place. There was a sawed off shotgun under the couch where the Colombian was sitting but just the one kilo of dope. It was a successful dope deal.

After booking the Colombians and doing preliminary paperwork, I had time to reflect on the evenings deal. I had expected more from Colombian drug dealers. These guys were pussies, they went down easy.

But I had deeper emotions about the night's events. I pulled Braun's Sig Sauer. I stuck it in a drug dealer's face and I was prepared to kill him. The size of the gun stopped the aggressive behavior of the Colombian. He froze when he saw it.

I was asking myself the obvious question: would the Colombian have reacted the same way if I had stuck my little thirty eight snub-nose in his face?

On past drug deals there was always someone with a big gun and I didn't have to rely on the shock factor from my little gun. I would never know.

But I thought about that dope deal and I came to a realization, I was one of them, now. I had morphed into a full-fledged federal narc and I didn't know what to think of that revelation.

John China came out of his cubby-hole office and was looking around the big open office. It was basically deserted. The TFD's had made certain they had some excuse to be out on the street. They didn't want to deal with John China's dilemma about stats.

"I want you to come with me," John China softly said. I took a gander at him and I could tell he was distressed.

"Where are we going?" I asked.

"Down to the city," he replied. "We're going to start going on drug raids with city narcotics."

I almost laughed in John's face. City Narcotics was bare bones and bare knuckles. A liberal black man from Washington, D.C. would definitely get his feelings hurt going on drug raids with that group.

"When are we leaving?" I asked.

"Now," he replied. I gathered up my gear and we headed toward the garage. "You drive," he said as he handed me the keys to his "G" car, a brand new black Oldsmobile. It was a fine ride and I enjoyed driving it.

He gave me the address of a south side neighborhood and I drove to it. There were cars parked outside of the little bungalow house and the front door was standing open, mainly because it had been hit with a sledge hammer and would not close.

"They did the warrant without us," John muttered in disbelief. I kept watching and monitoring him. He was an upset guy.

We slowly climbed out of the Olds and walked to the house. We walked inside and a cop who I knew was standing in front of a black man without a shirt who was sitting a couch with his hands cuffed behind him. The black guy looked scared and my cop buddy (Bob Cerreotti) was jumping in the air and karate kicking the black guy in the face. Bobby was shouting, "Where's the money, motherfucker?"

Bobby karate kicked the guy several times and the guy's head was snapping back onto the wall behind the couch. He was looking poorly and about to lose consciousness.

John China looked like he was going into shock. He glanced at me and mumbled, "Is there a supervisor on this deal?"

"I don't know, John, but I'll look around for one." I checked the little house and there were several city guys roaming around tearing the place apart looking for cash and dope. They just said, "Oh, hi, Tim, what are you doing here?"

I didn't want to take the time to tell them the stat story plaguing our supervisor, so I just nodded and walked back to John China.

I shook my head in the negative and John said, "Let's get out of here." I drove back to our offices in Clayton. There wasn't much conversation. John China walked into his office and closed the door.

TFD Ronnie Been had been talking to a Mercedes dealer down in the city. One of his salesmen had a pending deal with a young "gang banger" who insisted on paying cash for a new Mercedes four door, diesel with a sun roof. We identified the young dope slinger and discovered that he was a convicted drug dealer.

We waited for the telephone call from the Mercedes dealer and it came. The guy was coming in with cash and would be at the dealership within an hour.

We headed for the downtown dealership and placed it under surveillance. The car dealer didn't want his car deal sabotaged so he asked that we wait until the deal was consummated and then take the druggie off after he drove away from the dealership. We agreed with him.

It was a bright spring day and we observed some black guys in a Chevy pull onto the dealership lot. We waited for an hour or so and the new Mercedes pulled onto the street. It was a fine looking ride, and the drug dealer was surprised when Ronnie Been and I pulled him over with a red light on our dashboard.

We told him to get out of the car. He got out and left the motor running and stood before us as if he was confused. "What did I do?" he pleaded with his arms out to his sides, his palms up.

"Whose car is this?" Ronnie Been asked.

"It's my motherfucking car. I just bought it, paid cash for it."

I slid into the driver's seat and looked around the inside of the vehicle as if I was admiring it. "Man, this is a nice ride," I said.

"Fucking right," the dope dealer replied.

I looked at the sunroof and tried to get it to open. "Hey, man," I continued. "How do you get this sunroof to open?"

The drug dealer reached inside and pointed to the control switch. I hit it and the roof opened. I closed the door and put it in gear and looked at the dope dealer, "Bye," I said as I drove away from the scene.

I looked in the rearview mirror. Ronnie Been was explaining the facts of dope dealing life to the little dope slinger. He was jumping up and down and acting like we expected him to. There were several TFD's in attendance and he knew he could act like an asshole but that's as far as he could go.

I drove the Mercedes to my wealthy friends business (St. Louis Crystal Water on S. Boyle) and showed it to them. I told them the story on how we had seized it and they laughed along with me.

Since the car had been paid for in cash, the asset forfeiture procedure was done quickly by the United States Attorney's office.

John China used the new Mercedes as his "G" car. It made him a little bit more satisfied. But in retrospect, he was living high off of the hog. He was a black professional with a new Mercedes, living in an exclusive black neighborhood in north county that he purchased for pennies on the dollar, and he had a wife who was a lawyer.

Black folks were the majority in the city of St. Louis. He could go to jazz clubs, R&B clubs, (whites couldn't safely go to these establishments) black restaurants and belong to black fraternal organizations.

John China worked for a black boss (SAC) who was certain to give him the nod for another promotion when this Task Force thing was over with. I overheard him speaking to another black agent in charge of the intelligence unit of the

St. Louis Field Office.

The intelligence unit was just a place to put errant agents, or ones who were sick or lame. The guy in charge would answer the telephone with the same old spiel: "Intelligent," he would say in a sing song tone.

"Stats?" John China said to him, "We don't need no fucking stats!" John China's future was secure and I think he finally realized it.

XVII.

TAKING DOWN DAN ROBINSON

A new toy was available to us, the cell phone. For years doctors and other important people had them installed in their cars. They were big impressive hunks of electronics installed in the trunks of Cadillacs and Lincolns.

We didn't purchase cell phones; we confiscated them from drug dealers and used them until their contracts ran out.

They weren't small and manageable phones; most were like WW II walkie talkies with big antennas. John China had one of those. I had one that looked like a typical briefcase until I opened it. There was this neat little portable telephone that I used daily to communicate with anyone I wished.

I had teamed up with a young looking St. Louis County cop detached to the task force who had taken Joe Ringer's place. This guy could buy dope from anybody.

But John China had a problem with him. The cop had shot and killed a young drug slinger in a car while a drug transaction was going down. It made John China distrustful of the young county detective. This guy, TFD Chris Wegman, was the secret weapon that John China could have used to combat sagging stats. Instead, he shunned him.

I had been contacted by an old cop from Alton, Illinois I had known as a kid. We played baseball together.

He wanted to introduce me to an informant that he had used in the past and desired to be an informant for DEA. I drove to the Riverbend and met with the guy and the cop. I didn't trust most informants but I listened to what he had to say and took note of it. There is usually some truth to informant's rants and raves; the investigator just has to sift it out.

I baited the informant with some information to see if it came back to me. It did, so I discontinued any contact with him. But I convinced TFD Chris Wegman to go to Alton with me to check out some of the places the informant mentioned to me. It was old home week for me and it was interesting to me, having been raised in the little burg, and been chased by the Alton, Illinois cops for most of my youth, that I could now investigate crooks there.

We gave up on the Alton clues and headed back to our offices in Clayton. It was after 6:00 p.m., and I figured most of the guys were in a tavern somewhere close by.

My desk phone rang and I answered it. It was the FBI agent who had been part of the federal prank on me in the Fairview Heights United States Attorney's office.

"Are you looking for Dan Robinson?" he asked.

"Yes!" I replied.

"Write this number down," he rattled a phone number to me and I copied it. "He's going to be at this number tonight at 9:00 p.m."

"Thanks," I said, and the line went dead. I thought about this clue and where it had originated. It was typical federal government. The FBI knows everything and all other law enforcement organizations, city, state, or federal, know nothing unless the FBI desires them to know.

I got a quick issue on the telephone number. It was assigned to a condo in St. Charles County, Bogey Hills, which was part of a country club and shopping area. I was familiar with it. It wasn't "hoity toity" but it wasn't low life either.

There was one small problem: this was federal Friday. Agents and cops make themselves scarce on Fridays. I was

advised at the beginning of my federal adventure that most
federal agencies have a limited staff on Fridays and not to
schedule any deals if they aren't necessary.

Federal workers are indoctrinated not to take vacations.
They retire with huge amounts of vacation time on the
books and are paid for it at the time of retirement. If a
worker takes a vacation his fellow office employees assume
he is sick, or having surgery.

I ran the Dan Robinson information down to Chris
Wegman. "It's me and you tonight, you up for it?" I asked
him.

Chris was always up for police work and we headed
toward St. Charles County, communicating via DEA closed
circuit radio.

John China heard our banter and asked me what was
going on. I told him on the air and he told us he would meet
us on the parking lot of the condo project.

We sat and waited for John. He pulled up in his newly
seized diesel Mercedes, with his walkie talky cell phone to
his ear. We exited our vehicles and walked to his. There is a
certain protocol that should be followed when dealing with
federal demigods and I didn't want to be rude to John China.
I could tell he was "put out" by our deal.

We stood and waited for John to complete his phone call.
I wondered while we waited if John China would have
intervened if I had been with Detective Sultan, or Detective
Horowitz, who had already worked his magic on John and
his wife with expensive gifts and floral arrangements. In
most cases a group supervisor lives by the mantra "Don't
get involved, just lead and direct from the office."

John ended his call and climbed out. I gave him the
particulars and we talked about where the unit was located,
but that was the extent to the conversation. I obtained a
sledge hammer from the trunk of my "G" car and John

China remarked, "What are you going to do with that?" His comment added to my opinion of his liberal background. In the Task Force we knock doors down and arrest federal fugitives when this action is needed. We walked toward the condo. Chris Wegman trailed behind us. It was obvious John China and he weren't on the best of terms.

The condo was a second floor unit and was accessible by a wooden walkway made of decking materials. The doors on both sides of the buildings faced each other and basically it was an outdoor hallway.

There was a large window facing the wood outdoor hallway, and it had a blanket covering it. We could hear a television. After perusing the condo we walked away from it to chat about what we were going to do.

"I don't want to pursue this unless we are certain Dan Robinson is in there," John China said.

"The information came from the FBI," I said. "That's good enough information for me."

"You can't always trust the FBI," John replied.

I knew that DEA and FBI hated each other. Part of the DEA indoctrination was "the FBI is our enemy."

"It came from an agent that I know," I stressed.

"Okay," John China continued. "Give me the number to the condo and I'll call it and ask for Dan." John tried to get the call to go through with his new toy phone but it wouldn't work for him.

My seized briefcase cell phone was in the trunk of my G car. It worked well, but I wasn't going to suggest anything to John China on this fine night.

"I'll go back by the cars and if it doesn't work, I'll go to another phone and call the St. Charles Sheriff Department precinct and have someone there call for us. Maybe their dispatch will call." John walked away.

Chris and I waited in the dark on the wood ramp outside of the condo in the balmy weather. I was hoping that Dan would come out to go to a liquor store or something, so we could get this done without John China mucking everything up.

John came toward us on the ramp and motioned for us to come to him. We walked toward him and he whispered that the dispatcher at the sheriff's office was going to make the call in about ten minutes.

John had been drinking. I could smell it on him when we first conversed on the condo parking lot. He looked like he was coming down from a booze high and needed another drink to get back on plane. He was drowsy!

We assumed our positions at the condo door. John China leaned his face and head against the large glass window while we waited for the telephone to ring.

The phone rang, Dan answered it and the sheriff dispatcher said, "Is Dan there?" We heard the phone hit the receiver and I was waiting for the sign from John China to hit the door with the sledge.

John was hesitating and his head and face was still resting against the window. Suddenly the blanket was snatched from the window and Dan Robinson, gangster, drug smuggler and federal fugitive was staring at the bald head, white beard and black face of John China. It startled them both.

Dan ran from the window, so did John China. I hit the door with the sledge and it swung open. I rushed inside and confronted Dan Robinson with Braun's big impressive pistol, but Dan wasn't impressed.

"Get your fucking hands up," I shouted at him, but Dan wouldn't comply.

"Don't you know who I am?" Dan shouted back at me. "I've been making arrangements with my lawyer to turn myself in, I'm Dan Robinson, you can't bust in on me like this," he screamed at me.

I stuck Braun's pistol back in my holster and grabbed Dan by the shirt. We grappled inside of the condo and I finally got control of him. I rushed him outside to the wooden outdoor hallway and placed him on the wall of the condo across from the one he was hiding in. Dan came off of the wall and I hit him in the ribs with my right fist.

During this ordeal, John China stayed outside on the hallway. Chris stayed at the door. I couldn't figure this routine out.

Dan was hurt, I could tell it. I searched him and cuffed him. I thought about what Dan Robinson really was: a drug dealer and a kidnapper and God only knows what else. He's a guy who never held a job in his life. He lived by the reputation of his gangster brother and he has gotten away with intimidation for his entire life.

We marched Dan back to the parking lot and I started to place him in the back of my "G" car for the ride to the St. Louis County jail for safekeeping.

"I'll take him," John China said. "Put him in the back seat of the Mercedes."

"Are you going to process him as well?" I asked.

"No," John replied, "Just convey him for you."

"Thanks," I meekly replied. Processing a prisoner takes time and I figured John China didn't wish to waste any more federal Friday time doing police work than he had to.

We all arrived at the Sally Port of the St. Louis County jail and walked in together. John China skedaddled, which was what I figured he'd do. Chris Wegman and I processed Dan Robinson.

He would be held for safekeeping for DEA. We would get him on Monday morning and convey him to the Federal

Courthouse in downtown St. Louis for federal processing and extradition to East St. Louis, Illinois for further confinement and arraignment.

It was a busy Friday night and Chris and I were bone tired after a long and tedious day. I drove home and crashed. The telephone rang at approximately 0300. Chris Wegman was on the phone. The county holdover called his home and told him Dan Robinson had to be taken to the hospital. It was our responsibility since we were the arresting officers.

My wife wanted to know what was going on. I told her the story and she looked concerned. She knew about the Robinson brothers from my investigation. I told her not to worry and I headed toward the jail in beautiful Clayton, Missouri.

We got Dan out and conveyed him to an area hospital. We ended up spending the entire night with him. He was x-rayed and had a couple of broken ribs. The doctor taped him up and gave him some pain pills and we conveyed him back to the jail.

Dan tried to be friendly with us, so we laughed and joked with him, just like we always did with arrested dope dealers. "You broke my ribs," he said to me.

"I'm certain you've done worse to a lot of people, Dan. You should have raised your hands and assumed the position when I ordered you to. You've been a federal fugitive for months. I wasn't going to take any chances with you."

We conveyed Dan back to the county holdover. The friendly behavior from Dan had stopped. He was as serious as a heart attack. I felt he knew his long life of crime had come to a screeching halt. His compatriots had snitched on him and his brother and there was nowhere to go but to a federal penitentiary.

The problem with Dan Robinson was the fact that he had

influential friends. His closest advisor was the famous lawyer Norm London. Dan placed too much faith in that friendship. When the DEA crock gets his jaws locked on your leg there is nothing you can do but to wait for the death roll.

Dan Robinson had been a smart/lucky dope dealer for decades. His luck had run out. He was now neither lucky nor smart. Uncle Sam wanted Paul and Dan Robinson. It was a strong case for them to win or lose. The government rarely loses such cases.

Chris Wegman and I picked Dan up on Monday morning and conveyed him to the federal courthouse. I turned him over to the United States Marshall Service and placed him in a holding cell for them to process him.

I slid the door closed as he studied me. "See ya, Dan," I said.

"When my lawyer, Norm London, gets finished with you on the stand you'll wish you never saw me," Dan loudly said to me.

"Oh, yeah?" I replied as I stopped and turned to look at him.

"Yeah, you handcuffed me and beat me. You broke my ribs."

I looked at him pathetically, "See ya Dan." I walked away from him.

The arrest of Dan Robinson was big gossip news in the DEA offices and in the United States Attorney's office in Fairview Heights, Illinois. Somebody called Braun in South America and informed him of the status of his big case. He called me and thanked me.

AUSA Cliff Proud, my beer drinking and golfing buddy, called me and told me to come to his office. I gladly drove over there to the eastside. Even though I didn't wish to admit it, the eastside was my home.

Cliff and I had a detailed meeting about the arrest of Dan Robinson. I gave him a blow by blow description of the evening.

"Dan's having a bond hearing. You will have to testify during that preceding. It's going to be this afternoon. Go get some lunch and meet me in in the courthouse and we'll talk further."

"Okay," I replied, confused about the serious tone of Cliff Proud. Dan was just another drug dealer who was going to say or do anything to try to gain freedom.

I had a quick lunch and met Cliff before the bond hearing.

"Have you ever testified during a federal bond hearing?" he asked.

"No," I replied.

"His attorney will attack you. Anything goes in a bond hearing. You will be accused of making an illegal arrest."

"Okay, I understand," I replied.

I sat in court and waited. The U.S Marshalls brought Dan into the courtroom, shackled. They sat him at the defendant table with his attorney, not Barrister Norm London. Norm was too important for bond hearings. The attorney was an old lawyer from Belleville, Illinois. He had been a defense attorney for forty years in the good old boy system of eastside politics. He and Dan spoke quietly and briefly. I was called to the bar sworn in and took the stand.

Cliff Proud asked me to describe what had transpired during the arrest of Dan Robinson. I gave my spiel. It was the old lawyer's turn to question me.

He accused me of indiscriminately sledge hammering Dan's door while he was sleeping, assaulting him in his living room, handcuffing him and beating him, breaking his ribs.

The lawyer went on and on about how brutal the arrest was and how unwarranted it was. He told the judge Dan had never been arrested before in his life and this drug charge and fugitive charge was a big mistake. He said Dan had no idea he was a wanted man. As soon as heard about it he returned to St. Louis to give himself up and to straighten this mess up.

"Why didn't you just knock on Dan Robinson's door, Detective Richards? My client would have come to the door and allowed you entry. You didn't have to hit it with a sledge hammer."

"I didn't want him to escape through a rear door," I replied. "He was a federal fugitive and had been hiding for months."

The lawyer went on about how nice of a guy Dan Robinson was and that he was an upstanding citizen and that he needed bail in order to defend himself against false accusations. "It is his right as an American citizen to have bail in these circumstances," the lawyer finally said.

"Bail denied," the judge said.

I walked out of the courtroom with Dan and his lawyer glaring at me.

George Fletcher (the first to be taken off in the case) was safely hidden in the Jersey County, Illinois jail. AUSA Cliff Proud would telephone me periodically and instruct me to go to Jerseyville and tend to George. He was one of our "aces in the hole" concerning testimony to be given against Paul and Dan Robinson.

The drive to Jerseyville took an hour but I didn't mind it. I got to have a conversation with my old friend Sheriff Frank Yocum, act important in front of the jail personnel, and take George out for a walk or a haircut.

Prisoners in county jail facilities need to be walked.

There is no period of exercise in those dungeons; the prisoners just sit and think of ways to defend themselves in court. The rectus femoris muscles degenerate and they can hardly walk when they get the chance.

AUSA Cliff Proud didn't want George Fletcher to stumble or falter when he walked to the stand to give testimony against Paul and Dan Robinson. If that were the case, it could detract from George's credibility. He wanted George to look like a normal human being who just happened to be giving testimony against a monster and his stupid brother.

When I would check George out of the jail I would have to help him to the door leading outdoors. As luck would have it, the days I walked him were mostly mild days, gorgeous and unforgettable.

He would take baby steps for about ten minutes and then the leg muscles would get fresh blood pumped into them and he would get stronger as the minutes whizzed by.

George was like a prostitute: "pay me and I'll do anything." The government wasn't paying him, but he will get a reduced sentence and be able to get on with his life after prison.

George had spent much of his life in incarceration. On one of our walks around the little town of Jerseyville he told me a story of his sister's death. They lived in Alton, Illinois, my, and George's home town.

His sister and her husband were trying to clean the paint off of a basement floor. The used a flammable liquid, maybe gasoline. The water heater ignited the flammable liquid and they both got cooked.

I remembered the incident. I had just gotten out of the Marine Corps. George was incarcerated in the Illinois State Penitentiary for armed robbery. George was incensed that the warden wouldn't allow him to attend the funeral.

I thought about George's story as we walked in the sunlight in this country town. I had grown up with guys like George. He wasn't a bad guy; he was just an Alton, Illinois guy.

I was in junior high school with guys who couldn't stay awake in class because they were out all night committing business burglaries. They would brag about them as we walked to school. I would tend to not believe them as they told their adventurous tales, but the next day there would be an article in the Alton Evening Telegraph confirming the story.

There were kids from good families, folks with means, who would do armed robberies of liquor stores and gas stations. The philosophy was, "if I want it I will get it by any means possible."

The Alton police would come to the high school and roust up the burglar or armed robber and take him away. It was with fanfare. The student being arrested would smile and laugh as he was whisked away in handcuffs. The students would applaud and cheer him on.

So taking the dope dealer George Fletcher on walks and allowing him to vent to me was not unusual. I felt I knew George Fletcher; he was a product of good old Alton, and so was I. I was lucky, he was not.

George was a talker, especially after I advised him I was from his hometown. He bragged about working for Paul Robinson. "He was the best gangster around back in the sixties and seventies," George said.

"Everybody was afraid of him. He was a ghost worker on the Poplar Street Bridge project. Never showed up one day and got paid, overtime, too. You know why," George continued.

"No," I replied.

Because he killed people for Buster Wortman, and after Buster died he killed people for Art Bernie. You didn't know that, did you?"

"I had heard those stories," I replied.

"Paul would sometimes beat people to death. His favorite move was to grab them by the Adam's apple with his left hand and beat them to death with his right fist. He was a guy not to be messed with."

"You've seen him do this?" I asked.

"Yep! I've been around Paul Robinson for twenty years. He and I went to Hollywood, Florida together. He rented that big house with the swimming pool and I had a little house nearby. We were together every day. We snorted more coke and smoked more weed than anybody alive. People came and went at the house in Hollywood, but me and Paul we stayed there and smuggled dope. It was a good life."

Rich Latchkey came and went, too, I presume," I said, trying to keep George talking.

"Oh, yeah, Rich was there a lot. Paul didn't trust him and he told me he was going to kill Rich. I told Rich he had better watch his back. Rich came back to St. Louis shortly after I informed him of Paul's intentions."

"So it all came tumbling down for you and Paul when the Hollywood Police executed a search warrant on Paul's house?"

"Yep! I knew it was coming and I told Paul that he had better clean the place up. We could have stored the dope, we had a storage locker. There wasn't that much left. What we didn't send to St.Louis for Rich and Dan to sell, we snorted and smoked. I was driving to Paul's house and I saw the Hollywood cops staging for a raid. I ran in and advised Paul. Paul never got dressed, he never put on outside clothes, he was always wearing a robe and he never wore underwear.

He was standing in the house with his robe on and I told him that the local cops were getting ready to kick the door down."

"What did he say?" I asked.

"He just looked at me. I tried to gather up the dope and drag it outside and throw it over the fence to the neighbor's yard. But Paul wouldn't help me. We had over a hundred thousand dollars in a closet and he was concerned about that, but he didn't lift a hand to help me."

"So the Hollywood cops came busting in?" I asked.

Yep! They knocked the door down and stuck guns in our faces and made us lie on the floor and they cuffed us and took us away. They seized the dope and the cash and we both went to court and then the Florida State Penitentiary."

"Paul got more time than you, right?" I asked.

"Yeah, he got sixteen years and I got about half of that. I got out and went back to St. Louis and worked for Rich Latchkey, pushing a hotdog cart around Kiener Plaza in downtown St. Louis. Then Paul got out and he came back to St. Louis and he threatened to kill Rich and his brother Dan. We had been doing real well with just smuggling a little bit of coke and weed. But Paul wanted to get big, again."

"So Paul pressured Rich to start using his contacts to get dope on consignment?" I asked.

"Yep! Before Paul came back I would get a rental car at the airport and drive to south Florida. Rich had it all set up and I would collect some kilos of cocaine and some weed, put it in the trunk of the rental and come back to St. Louis. It's what I was doing when Special Agent Mike Braun took me off in Wood River, Illinois. We never did get big in the dope game, again. Rich and Dan just had to share their profits with Paul."

There were pre-trial hearings on a weekly basis. Every lawyer and defendant would show up and the judge, The Honorable William Stiehl (hanging judge) would listen to the AUSA's and the defense lawyers going through their skits for the defendants.

Paul and Dan Robinson would glare at everyone with hatred. They, too, were just like kids I went to school with in Alton. They were big and thick and dark and hateful. Typical school yard bullies who would take your basketball and refuse to give it back. Or demand your lunch money and then laugh at you as they walked away.

I always fought back when bullied and the bullies recognized heart and wanted me to be their friend. Dan wanted me to be his friend after I broke his ribs when I arrested him. Nothing changes. The bullies always had big brothers to back them up and protect them. Dan always had Paul.

Paul demanded undying loyalty as his payment from his little brother. For that he tutored him in the art of making money without working. Pimping, stealing, hustling stolen merchandise, selling drugs; it was crime 101 with the instructor being Paul Robinson and the student being Dan, or "Dan'l" as he referred to him.

Paul had talked Dan into playing hardball with the federal system. Dan could have pled guilty to some lesser charge, gotten ten years and a reduced sentence and gone straight. He had a nice wife and family. He had support!

But instead Dan chose to trust in his lawyer, Norm London, and get into the ring with AUSA Cliff Proud and the Honorable Judge William Stiehl. It was a fight he could not win.

XVIII.

PAUL AND DAN MEET THE HANGING JUDGE

Whenever there were pretrial hearings or motions to suppress evidence or possible testimony I would have to go to Jerseyville and fetch George Fletcher. I would drive him to East St. Louis, and place him in a locked office in the United States Attorney's office. Rich Latchkey never showed up. He was the star dope dealing witness. He was free as a bird.

George wouldn't be used by the federal lawyers, but it got him out of jail and got him more prepared for testimony. I would usually wander into Judge Stiehl's court and watch the acts of the legal play.

At the beginning of the case when we arrested Paul in west county, he had the same lawyer that Little John Gipson (the Illinois heroin/cocaine dealer with the 38 Chevrolet), Frank (Tony) Fabbri, that many of the black drug dealers used.

Frank was the go to lawyer for sleazy clientele, but he was a good lawyer. He would have given Paul Robinson a fighting chance against the federal machine.

For some reason Paul changed lawyers and hired a defense lawyer from Kentucky. This guy was a good constitutional lawyer, but any lawyer going up against the testimony of two co-defendants of the Robinson brothers had a rough row to hoe.

The jury would hate the Robinsons as soon as they laid eyes on them. They were what every hard working middle

class citizen in this country disapproved of. They were the
embodiment of greed and crime. They wore it on their faces,
as if they were proud of their criminal accomplishments.

Dan Robinson had his good friend and world renowned
defense lawyer Norm London as his defense lawyer. Dan
was cock sure that Norm London could and would get him
off of this charge. But there was a problem with this
crook/lawyer scenario.

When Rich Latchkey was debriefed by DEA after he
agreed to give testimony against the Robinsons and work for
the federal government, he offered information about
Attorney Norm London.

Norm had apparently been involved with the smuggling
of marijuana. Norm gave Dan Robinson $100,000 in a major
marijuana deal with the promise of getting a return of
$200,000 in a short period of time. Dan met Norm at
Norm's safety deposit box in downtown St. Louis bank and
was given the cash by Norm.

Dan gave the cash to his brother Paul Robinson, however
Paul never paid Norm London. This made Dan Robinson
angry and he and Paul had a heated argument over it. Dan
considered Norm London his closest friend.

At a pretrial hearing Norm London identified himself as
the lawyer of record for Dan Robinson. Cliff Proud
requested to approach the bench for a sidebar meeting with
Judge Steele. The judge allowed it and AUSA Proud and
Barrister Norm London approached the bench.

Cliff Proud advised Judge Stiehl about the drug
conspiracy between Norm London and the Robinson
brothers, and that there was a possibility that Norm London
could be indicted with the Robinsons.

Norm London did not deny the accusation. He politely
recused himself from the case, packed his briefcase with
papers, and walked out of the courtroom. Dan was left

glaring and confused.

I thought about Norm London. He was part of high society in the St. Louis region. He was the St. Louis Police Officer's Association lawyer. I had been paying monthly dues to the organization for eighteen years. I was paying part of his retainer as the attorney of record of the association. I felt disgust.

I replayed in my mind the words of Group Supervisor Steve Palance: "Everybody who lives in a big house and drives a big car is a dope dealer; lawyers, doctors, professional people." It's a scary thought. It is also a DEA fabrication to make little cops work like dogs for the feds.

Dan Robinson miraculously obtained new counsel. Burton Shostak and his assistant, the lovely Debra (D.J.) Kern, somehow were retained by Dan Robinson's family.

Burton Shostak's offices were just down the street from the DEA field office in Clayton, Missouri. They visited us frequently, exercising their right to disclosure between the government and the accused, Dan Robinson.

With Braun being gone much of the time, I dealt with them. They listened to tape recordings between Dan and Rich Latchkey, viewed videos and read reports.

I always felt they were coming to our office to get a feel for us as cops and agents. They were new to the criminal defense game; they were worker's compensation lawyers.

They were no match for the federal government. If the case isn't pretty much a slam dunk, the government doesn't prosecute it.

Special Agent Mike Braun, AUSA Cliff Proud and the team of prosecutors working on this case were ultimate professionals. Burton and D.J. should have advised Dan to plead for mercy in front of the hanging judge, William Stiehl, but they didn't. They played the criminal defense lawyer game; "they put on a show for their client."

The trial started in Judge Stiehl's court in East St. Louis, Illinois. I trekked to Jerseyville, Illinois and checked George Fletcher out of jail and conveyed him to East St. Louis, Illinois every morning.

George Fletcher and I had a lot of time to talk; we became semi friends. He had a girlfriend in Wood River who he liked a lot. He talked about her. We drove through the outskirts of Wood River every time we went from Jerseyville to East St. Louis. I offered to take George by her house for a visit but he declined.

"The Robinson organization knows about her," George began. "They probably know that if I got a chance I would try to see her. She's probably got surveillance on her. If I showed up they'd kill you, me and her."

"They aren't that powerful, George,' I replied. "They've brainwashed you into thinking they are a powerful crime family, but they aren't. They're just criminal pimps in the dope business."

"Paul Robinson always gets revenge," George continued. "Me, Rich Latchkey and maybe you are dead meat. It will happen. Paul never lets things go."

"He'll be locked down for thirty years, George. Dan will probably get twenty. Their criminal enterprise is over."

"Hope you are right," George replied.

Deliberation after deliberation, sidebar after sidebar, Braun finally took the stand. Cliff Proud had Braun describe how he and his DEA counterparts arrested George Fletcher in Wood River, Illinois. Braun's testimony lasted for two days.

The lawyer from Kentucky who was hired by Paul Robinson's family tried to trick Mike into saying something stupid, but Mike was too slick for him.

Federal agents are trained in the art of testimony. In many respects they are more sophisticated than the high priced lawyers. Braun was definitely more sophisticated than the workers compensation lawyers.

Burton Shostak acted as if he was afraid of Braun and didn't want to offend him. They were trying to build a case based on the upcoming testimony of Rich Latchkey and George Fletcher.

These lawyers knew they couldn't rattle Braun; he was a pro. They wanted the jury to get the feeling that Rich Latchkey was actually the mastermind behind the drug smuggling and conspiracies, which was a feasible theory, one that I believed then and now.

Rich Latchkey was cunning like a wild animal and so was Paul Robinson. The difference between them was that Paul was like a Grizzly Bear and Rich was like a highly poisonous snake.

Rich was the only defendant who was now wealthy. He had businesses, cash, and big ideas to become wealthier. All he had to do was convince the government and the jury, that he was a pawn in the dope game and it was headed by the notorious Paul Robinson.

Braun completed his testimony and walked off of the stand a winner. The jury liked him. I could see the jurors looking at the Robinson brothers and then directing their eyes to Braun. The expressions on their faces told the story. They loved Braun and hated Paul and Dan Robinson.

A couple of more cops testified. Detective Sultan took the stand to tell about the drug deal in Fort Lauderdale. The Kentucky lawyer treated him like he was a long lost relative, even bringing up the status of Detective Sultan's attorney dad. It was sad to watch. The Kentucky lawyer was terrified of Detective Sultan.

Burton Shostak didn't waste much time on questioning Detective Sultan. I figured that he knew it was a waste of time. Debra Kern sat at the defense table and took copious notes. She would whisper to Burt Shostak when she could. It was like giving smelling salts to a fighter who had just been knocked out; ludicrous.

A St. Louis County cop, Chuck Boschert, took the stand to testify about surveillance of the Robinsons. Chuck has a tick in his face when he gets excited or pressed. He began making faces on the stand and the Kentucky lawyer thought he had something, maybe an untruthful statement, so he started drilling Chuck.

Cliff Proud intervened and asked for a sidebar with Judge Steele. The facial expressions submitted by Chuck were overlooked and the testimony was civil.

George Fletcher was called. He took the stand and told his story of a lifetime friendship of Paul Robinson. They were in business together in Hollywood, Florida smuggling weed and shipping it back to the St. Louis region.

Cliff Proud asked George who the leader of the drug conspiracies was, he said "Paul Robinson." Cliff went on and on asking about the criminal life of Paul Robinson and how he and George Fletcher went to prison in the State of Florida.

The cocaine that was seized by the DEA task force relating to the Robinson brothers case was brought out into the courtroom (by me) and placed on a table in front of the jury.

Paul and Dan's attractive wives with their children were in court for every testimony. They made faces and shook their heads when damning testimony was given against their husbands.

George Fletcher was like a relative to them, so was Rich Latchkey. George was in actuality like a servant to the

Robinsons. He feared them, especially Paul, and would do their bidding.

Anything Paul Robinson desired, George Fletcher would do, even handyman work. He would convey Paul's children to and from school if he was asked to. But when the federal government gets it's fangs in you all loyalty is lost.

The defense tried to discredit George Fletcher's testimony. They asked him about his criminal past, his trips to prison at a young age, his youth in Alton, Illinois. George told the truth, just like AUSA Cliff Proud told him to do.

The weekend was upon us. On Monday Rich Latchkey was scheduled to take the stand. I was in a meeting between Rich Latchkey, Braun and Cliff Proud.

Rich was complaining about Paul and Dan's family being in the courtroom. "They're like relatives to me," Rich began. "I'm turning on the people who have loved me for years. I'm their brother and they are my sisters. Their children are my nephews and nieces. It's going to be difficult for me if they stay in the courtroom."

"George Fletcher didn't have a problem giving testimony in front of them," Braun said.

"Well, I do," Rich replied.

"You want to scrap your testimony and let it ride, that way you can go to prison with Paul and Dan. George Fletcher can go free. Would you feel better then?" Braun said in a low voice.

"I'll take care of it," Cliff Proud said.

"And another thing," Rich Latchkey continued, "I don't want to go to an ordinary federal penitentiary. I heard there's a real nice federal prison in the Florida Pan Handle, built on an Air Force Base, for politicians and white collar criminals. I think it's called Eglin Air Base. I want to go there."

It was a standoff. Cliff and Braun stared at Rich and he stared back. It was why Rich Latchkey was a successful dope dealer and businessman. He knew when to "holdem and foldem."

Rich's testimony was crucial to the government's case, more now than ever. Rich was prepared to take center stage and build the case, insert the knife into the carotid artery of the Robinson brothers.

The stage had been set by George Fletcher, Braun, Detective Sultan, and Chuck Boschert. Rich was smug; he sat and waited.

"I'll take care of it," Cliff Proud declared. Braun pulled on his face with frustration. The DEA creed in dealing with informants was to never give them the upper hand.

Informants were to be used and abused and then thrown to the dogs. Now, this ultimate drug dealer was setting precedent and holding the hole card for his future. I had to hand it to Rich Latchkey, he was a cunning little fellow.

Rich stood and shook hands with Cliff Proud. I will see you boys Monday morning," he said as he walked out of Cliff's office.

"Dirty little dope dealing son of a bitch," Braun muttered. I thought of the time a couple months earlier when Braun asked for the recipe to Rich's steak sauce. Rich was a talented chef and he occasionally fed Braun and me. Rich gladly gave Braun the recipe. Now Rich was a dirty son of a bitch. If the feds can't use you every minute of every day friendship turns to hatred.

I gathered George Fletcher up and whisked him back to Jerseyville, Illinois. The little Chrysler Turbo "G" car was getting a lot of miles on it and they were hard miles. I drove eighty most of the time, always trying to meet a deadline, as George hung on for dear life. He never made any comments about my driving but I felt he was frightened at times.

All of those eighty miles per hour trips to and from Jerseyville, Illinois, and East St. Louis never resulted in my being stopped by a local or state cop. I used a radar detector and would slow down when alerted.

I had a scenario if I got stopped. I was transferring a federal witness in a trial in East St. Louis. Although, I never placed George Fletcher in handcuffs or leg restraints. He could have gotten out and run from me if he wanted to. Of course I would have outrun him; he had atrophy in his legs from sitting in jail. He could walk okay but he would not have been able to run.

On a trip back to Jerseyville George advised me he wanted a soda. I stopped at a gas station, gave him money and told him to go in a buy what he wanted. I waited in the car.

It was an experiment for me. I was curious as to what George would do. I waited and George came back to the car and hopped in. "You could have run," I said to him.

"Run to where," he replied. "You or someone else would have eventually caught me. If it was you I would have gotten my ass kicked. I just want this to be over. I want to fulfill my obligation to the government, do my time and get out. Hopefully I will still be alive. I hope I don't get "shanked" in prison. If I can, I'll find my little girlfriend, talk her into relocating with me and live free for a few years before I get killed by a Robinson friend or die from something stupid. I'm not running."

I picked up George Fletcher and set out for East St. Louis. Excitement was in the air. It was like the opening day of spring training, or the day your vacation starts and you can make believe that you are wealthy and living on a beach in Florida. Today was the day the star witness/drug dealer/smuggler, Rich Latchkey, was going to take the stand

and give the coup de grace to the Paul and Dan Robinson.

I marched George Fletcher into the courthouse, locked him in his office with a view of beautiful downtown East St. Louis, Illinois and headed for the courtroom.

Rich Latchkey was being sworn in and was taking the stand as I wandered in. There were some small deliberations and sidebars between the lawyers and then AUSA Cliff Proud began talking to and questioning world famous drug smuggler and entrepreneur, Rich Latchkey.

He questioned Rich about his youth in old north St. Louis and how he was addicted to marijuana at a young age. Cliff quickly directed Rich to his association with a marijuana dealer who was actively working for Paul Robinson. Rich regurgitated the information that we all knew for the jury.

It was in 1972 that the marijuana dealer (Terril Hueslman) asked Rich if he wanted to make some cash by driving to south Florida and driving marijuana back to St. Louis. Rich jumped at the offer and began his drug smuggling career with Paul and Dan Robinson.

Rich was introduced to Paul Robinson on his first trip to Hollywood, Florida. Paul sized Rich up and advised him that if he was ever arrested that he should not make a statement and should not cooperate with the police.

Paul went on to say that the organization's lawyer, Norm London, would defend him in a court of law and the organization would make his bond.

There were approximately twenty members in the Robinson organization, most of them living in Miami. Much of the time Rich Latchkey would drive his loads of marijuana to a farm outside of East St. Louis, Illinois and offload it.

Rich Latchkey told about how he had met other drug smugglers who were working for Paul Robinson smuggling marijuana from Jamaica, 10,000 pounds at a time. Much of it was moved to Carbondale, Illinois for distribution.

For nine months, in 1974, Rich attended the Culinary Institute in Hyde Park, New York and was for the most part out of contact with Paul Robinson; however he maintained contact with Huelsman.

Rich later returned to the St. Louis area and was contacted by Huelsman who wanted to know if Rich wished to continue smuggling drugs from south Florida to the St. Louis area. Rich agreed and was contacted by Paul Robinson who asked Rich to spend more time at his house in Hollywood, Florida.

"Paul Robinson controlled every move I made," Rich told the jury. "He made me go to South America and negotiate drug smuggling deals and he forced me to make arrangements for moving the drugs back to the St. Louis area."

The "Paul Robinson was the boss of the operation" story went on and on. Cliff was finished and the Kentucky lawyer drilled Rich Latchkey. He tried as well as he could to build a defense for Paul Robinson that Rich was the head of the organization.

Burt Shostak drilled Rich with the same scenario. Rich was like a bartender on Benzedrine. He would sometimes smile a bartender smile and quickly answer the questions. He played to the jury and he was a good communicator.

Rich's problem was that he was not a likeable guy. He was a drug smuggler and he smuggled drugs into the community that the jurors lived in. Not to mention he had been doing it for twenty years.

The Kentucky lawyer and Burt Shostak addressed the jury in their final arguments. "Rich Latchkey was the head of the drug organization," was their worn out theme. Paul and Dan did not take the stand. Dan may have been able to help himself if he did choose to testify in his behalf.

There was testimony from George Fletcher and Rich Latchkey that was confusing and may have had the jurors wondering if Paul was in actuality just extorting money from Rich. There was a question brought up pertaining to the presence of Paul Robinson before, during, or after the drug deals. He was never around.

AUSA Cliff Proud told the jury in his final deliberation, "The president and CEO of Chrysler is Lee Iacocca. The guys and gals on the assembly line never see him, but they know who the boss is."

Judge Stiehl gave the jury its instructions and they were led to the jury room to decide the fate of the drug smuggling gangsters Paul and Dan Robinson.

I gathered up George Fletcher and headed for Jerseyville, Illinois. There wasn't much talk between us. It was technically over with. George would be going to prison as a "snitch' and he didn't make the same kind of deal as Rich Latchkey. George wouldn't be going to country club prison.

We were on Route three in Hartford, Illinois heading north when the little Chrysler Turbo began sputtering and coughing. It wasn't long and we were dead on the side of the road. George wasn't taking this lightly.

"The fucking Robinsons," he muttered. "They fucked with your car so it would stall out and now we are dead meat."

I took a 360 degree look and there was nobody near us or coming toward us. "There's nobody around us, George," I advised him. "I figured this little car would crap out sooner or later." But I did drag Braun's big impressive Sig Sauer automatic out of my briefcase and laid it on my lap.

I got on the radio and called Braun. We are down on the side of the road on route three in Hartford, Illinois, have somebody bring me another car."

We sat there for thirty minutes when some TFD's pulled up and gave us another "G" car. We were back on our way but George was still uptight.

I walked him into the jail and tucked him into his little cell. "So long, George," I said to him. He didn't say anything to me, just watched as I walked away from him. I never saw him again.

It was the same old song and dance with the jury. Which drug smuggler do we hate the most; the bartender or the gangster bullies? They chose to hate the Robinsons more. Paul Robinson got thirty years, Dan got twenty.

XIX.

NO PARADISE FOR ST. LOUIS NARCS

Back to the Task Force! Task Force Detective Steve (Johnny) Reszler returned to St. Louis as the victorious Special Agent Steve (Johnny) Reszler. He was greeted as a war hero returning to his home town. He strolled around the St. Louis Field Office shaking hands and greeting the other agents, now his peers.

To the casual observer Special Agent Reszler was a DEA success story. He started out in the mail room and worked his way up to the marketing division of the corporation.

But, I again saw changes in Reszler that I was concerned about. He was muscular but thin, he was scowling and not the happy go lucky guy he once was. He acted like he was in fear. This was a guy who six months earlier feared nothing. Now he was reluctant in his body language and demeanor.

"Want to go to lunch?" I asked him. He nodded and we walked across the street to a burger joint. We ordered and I tried to get him talking. He wasn't buying and I could tell he was deeply upset. "Where did you get assigned?" I asked.

"Detroit," he moaned. I didn't give a response and my silence didn't do him any good.

"Fucking Detroit," he said again. "That fucking Palance told me he was going to get me a good duty assignment. Detroit isn't what I signed up for. That fucker lied to me."

"Did Doc Coopers uppers do you any good?" I asked.

"Yeah," he replied. "I used them when I needed them. I stayed up late studying for those fucking tests. I aced most of them. I aced the physical training part of the program. But a fucking ex-Marine got me by two tenths of a point. Two fucking tenths! Can you fucking believe it? Two fucking tenths kept me out of San Diego and into Detroit."

"Damn, Resz, I'm sorry to hear that," I replied. "So what are you going to do?"

"I'm going to Detroit," he replied. "I don't know how long I will be there but I'm going. If I don't like it there, which I know I won't, I have no idea what I will do."

"You still taking Doc Coopers uppers?"

"Yeah, but I'm almost done with them. I don't need to stay up all hours of the night now. They were some kick ass pills. I could lift and run and do almost anything I wanted, and with little or no sleep. Doc really knows his pills."

"What about the steroids, you still cycling?"

"No, I lost so much bulk from all of the running that we did that I quit cycling with roids. I kind of like the lean look. I don't need the extra weight."

We finished our burgers and were talking lowly at the table when Reszler started fidgeting and checking his pockets. "My creds, I lost my fucking creds," he said in panic.

We paid the tab and walked across the street to our offices. Reszler's DEA credentials were lying on the floor at my desk. He quickly seized them and stuck them in his pocket. He was unnerved by the lost creds experience. DEA had won; Reszler was a frazzled special agent just like the rest of the agent pricks we as TFD's despised. I was shocked at his transformation. The Fed can brainwash anybody at any time, it just needs your cooperation.

There were parties for the conquering hero thrown by Ronnie Been and Detective Sultan. Reszler was now the best of friends with them. They were no longer in competition for police department status.

Steve (Johnny) Reszler wandered off to Detroit and

things got back to normal in the Task Force. Reszler's pin-up-model girlfriend didn't join him in Detroit. I was told she was going to join him at a later date. Reszler was back a couple of times a month, drinking with the boys and living with his girlfriend. I saw him briefly a couple of times and he was still wearing the serious DEA agent scowl.

Detective Sultan was being treated with respect by the DEA bosses. He was St. Louis high society as far as they were concerned. He was on the way to being cop royalty, so they handed him good cases to work, cases that would give him notoriety. He was working a large marijuana smuggling case and most of the group was involved.

There was a snitch involved and the powers at DEA feared his life might be in jeopardy. The fed rented a suite of rooms at a motel at Interstate fifty five and Lindbergh Boulevard. The snitch was to have twenty four hour a day protection.

As luck would have it, the motel had a super restaurant attached to it. We could order anything we wanted from the menu and just sign for it. I had the duty there several times while the case was progressing. I ate well and watched a lot of television.

In actuality, the amount of weed involved in this case wasn't astronomical. It was an average weed smuggling caper dreamed up by some non-criminals wanting to get rich quick. Most of them are. But the case was given to Detective Sultan, and that in itself made it important.

I was nearing a rotation date to return to the city police department so DEA mostly left me alone. I quietly waited for the telephone call telling me to report to somewhere within the police department. I was ready to go. Three or four years of DEA was more than enough.

I was day dreaming at my desk when I heard the gossip

flying around the offices. Special Agent Steve (Johnny) Reszler had quit DEA and was now back at the police department trying to get his old job back. I thought about this turn of events and tried to get a handle on it. The personnel division was reluctant to immediately return Reszler to duty. Reszler telephoned Doc Cooper and the wheels quickly started turning in the right direction for him.

Reszler was placed in a retread class at the academy and was obviously having emotional problems about his decision to return.

Special agents from the St. Louis Field office went to the academy building and stared at him. He was like a rare animal in a cage at the zoo, one who had escaped captivity but had decided to return to incarceration and mediocrity.

The agents who went to view him would come back to the St. Louis Field office and report their findings. "He doesn't look good," one said.

"He just sat there and wouldn't look at me," another one reported.

I went to a St. Louis Police Department function and Reszler was there with Detective Sultan, Ronnie Been and his luscious pin-up model girlfriend. I hadn't seen Reszler since he quit DEA and returned to the police department. I felt he was avoiding me. He was now real close with Detective Sultan and Ronnie Been.

Reszler would, somewhere down the line, need someone to sponsor him for a "gravy train" job in headquarters. Doc Cooper was on his way out. Reszler's dad was a patrolman when he took an early retirement. He had no clout.

But Detective Sultan would surely gain rank and prestige because of his attorney dad and his political relatives. Reszler needed a sponsor in the worst way. If he didn't score one he would probably spend the rest of his career in uniform in a district. It was a fate we all feared.

Reszler and his friends and his mom and dad were sitting at a big table. My wife and I wandered in and I waved to them. We sat at another table near them. I walked over to Reszler and we shook hands. He didn't stand but instead looked up at me like a cowed dog would do to a passerby begging for help. Seeing him like that unnerved me.

I stayed away from the DEA guys at the function and gladly went home early. I didn't sleep that night and I wished that I had never gone to the Task Force. It was too much of everything and I realized that I was not geared for the royalty game of cops and crooks.

The next day at the office Detective Sultan and Ronnie Been were taking the expensive grips off of a seized customized 357 magnum revolver and replacing them with some cheapo grips like the ones on the issued thirty eights that the city gives its cops.

I wanted to ask about Reszler but I felt that if I did I would be obvious and not be given a straight answer. You can't start a conversation with a direct question; you have to lead up to it. The art of interviewing and interrogating never leaves the cop investigator.

I asked Detective Sultan what he was doing. "We're removing these grips and replacing them with Reszler's department issued grips. Reszler wants a customized grip on his department thirty eight," Detective Sultan replied.

"Cool," I replied. I felt like I had broken the ice, and Detective Sultan was friendly, so I asked him about Reszler.

"He's on downers, now," Detective Sultan informed me. "Doc Cooper took him off of the uppers and put him on downers. He can't get it up now and he's moved back in with his mom and dad. I told him to stop taking those fucking downers and his dick would get hard again but he said Doc Cooper told him to take them."

I had information overload, but that's the way it was on the Task Force. Everybody knew everything about everyone's personal life. I approached the group secretary who was one hundred percent DEA and in many ways the liaison between the group and the SAC. "Hey blondie," I began, "is anybody worried about Reszler? I mean does DEA have any way they could help him? I'm worried that he's going to hurt himself."

"He quit DEA," she replied. "DEA reached out to him but he wouldn't talk to them. He's not going to hurt himself, but he might hurt someone else."

I went home that evening with my head reeling. I didn't believe that DEA reached out to Reszler. The unit secretary was a DEA robot. She would regurgitate anything she was told to spit up.

I confided in my wife that Reszler was on the brink of disaster. She looked at me as if to say, "No, really? What gave you your first clue, mister investigator?"

I cooked out and worried about Steve Johnny Reszler.

My telephone rang at about eight p.m. It was the unit secretary advising me that Reszler had shot himself in the head at his parent's house and that he was dead. "Okay," I replied. "Thanks for letting me know."

I was devastated, mostly because I apparently was the only one who saw this coming. His closest friends, Detective Sultan and Ronnie Been didn't see it coming. His parents didn't see it coming and his pin up model girlfriend didn't see it coming.

I was in bewilderment. The cause and effect probabilities tortured me and they still do to this day. The phone rang again and it was Group Supervisor John China advising me of Johnny's demise. "I've already been informed," I stated to him.

"Tomorrow," John China continued, "There will be someone from Washington D.C. to talk to you when you come to work. Will you come to work tomorrow?"

"This is DEA's fault, John," I continued. "He was begging for help and nobody helped him. The fucking federal government should have intervened and given him the help he deserved. Now the fed wants to help me because I'm distraught about a friend's suicide? It's all a little late, isn't it?"

"Will you come to work tomorrow?" John asked again.

"I don't know, John," I replied. "I'm ready to go back to the department. I might just report back there."

"Come to work in Clayton tomorrow," John replied.

I walked around my house and pondered about Reszler's demise. I had the cop curse called the "what ifs". I was questioning myself and running scenarios down in my mind.

I thought back to the Christmas party thrown at Little Stevie Wonder's palatial Chesterfield, Missouri home. Little Stevie had married well and he lived like a wealthy person, because he was.

The party included the SAC and his wife, the ASAC, Group Supervisor Steve Palance and some other higher ranking DEA bureaucrats.

The TFD's were ordered to attend by Steve Palance, and we were told to bring our significant others. I didn't wish to attend but, I was still trying to be one of the boys.

The TFD's were relegated to the kitchen. I could accept being treated like a servant in the DEA offices (we were used as furniture movers when needed) but drawing my spouse into this mess was too much for me. I was pissed, and so were most of the TFD's, except Detective Horowitz. He would have had his wife serve drinks and food if asked.

The house was ultra modern with cathedral ceilings, and nice. The problem was, anything said in the house could be heard in the living room where Little Stevie, Steve Palance, the ASAC, and the SAC and spouse' were sitting and drinking and acting like high society.

Some of the TFD's, including me, were as educated as the DEA guys. The difference between them and us was that they were federal bureaucrats and we were not.

We could hear them talking and trying to act sophisticated and as a group it galled us. We were drinking and standing in the kitchen and we started getting loud. Palance came in and asked us to keep the noise down. We glared at him.

The master bedroom was situated on the main floor next to the kitchen so we wandered into it and stood around the king sized bed. The SAC and the other guest's coats were lying on the bed. The SAC and his wife were big people and the SAC's wife had a full length mink coat.

Jim Bob, the county cop hero and a country bumpkin at heart put the SAC's wife's mink coat on and started making primate sounds and jumping around the room like a gorilla. It was funny and we all cracked up. Jimmy kept it up and we got louder and louder.

The SAC came into the room to see what we were doing. He observed Jimmy mimicking his wife and wearing his wife's mink. It was racism at its finest. He walked out in a huff and complained to Palance.

Palance came into the bedroom and asked us to leave. My wife and I left in a hurry. I apologized to my wife for embarrassing her in front of a bunch of junior federal bureaucrats.

I couldn't stop thinking about the listening device in and around my desk. I had been eavesdropped on for almost four years. The SAC and the group supervisor and probably the

ASAC listened to my conversations and the conversations of the workers around me.

The SAC was a bitter black man who thought we were all KKK members and were working for him, and he hated us. He was not a worldly guy, just a big black bully with a drug job with an office and secretary.

Most of the people who worked for him were white. His secretary was white and almost all of the clerical civil servants were white. He hired his staff; he could have hired black people.

What if Reszler hadn't made a joke of him when he was walking down the street in Clayton? That hurt the SAC's feelings. I could see his body language change. He had to have wanted revenge for that racial encounter.

What if he heard Reszler telling me about the uppers Doc Cooper gave to Reszler? They were illegal drugs without a prescription. They were actually contraband in the eyes of the law. Not a federal offense, but for certain a State of Missouri violation.

What if the SAC telephoned the SAC in Detroit and advised him that Reszler was taking uppers without a prescription? He would have been ordered to take a drug screen. He would have refused and run back to the police department with his tail between his legs. The police department is our home. We, being important and with influential friends, could have skirted by on the drug screen order in the good old police department.

What if Detective Horowitz hadn't mimicked a black comedian on the DEA radio when we were going to Springfield, Missouri?

What if Doc Cooper hadn't tried to be everything to every cop he ever met? He did what he thought was right when treating cops. I do admit we are a different breed. Our medical treatment was and is peculiar. The goal was to keep us, as a group of humans, up and walking and working for the City of St. Louis. If being overprescribed is the way to achieve that goal, then so be it. It happened to Elvis Presley and scores of other working people. "Take this pill, it will help you."

What if my cop cousin in St. Clair County, Illinois hadn't decided to become a crooked cop and a drug dealer?

What if the United States Attorney's office in Fairview Heights, Illinois hadn't let my cousin go with a warning? That's where it all started. DEA and the entire St. Louis Field Office were incensed at my cop cousin being let go without even a slap on the wrist.

My cousin dropped my name and I didn't even know it. DEA was out for blood, mine. They eavesdropped and investigated me for years and couldn't find anything damaging about me. But they found out things about Reszler.

In my mind that eavesdropping cost Reszler his life. He was already on the brink but he got pushed over the side by something that happened in Detroit. I will never know for certain what happened in Detroit, neither will his dad and mom or his girlfriend.

I showed up for work in Clayton bright and early. John China was waiting for me. "You need to go into my office," John began. He was fidgety and nervous, the way black people are when it's election-day and their liberal candidate is in a tight race with the conservative.

I could tell he was super upset. I stared at him trying to figure out the scenario. I wasn't about to go behind any closed doors in the DEA offices in St. Louis.

"What's up? I asked with sarcasm.

"A counselor from D.C.," John continued. "She's a grief counselor, she wants to talk to you, just go in and close the door and listen to what she has to say."

"Okay, John," I replied as I walked into the office and closed the door behind me.

A matronly lady was sitting at John China's desk, the same desk Palance and Duda had sat at. It was the desk of power for the Task Force. It was where the decisions were made regarding the TFD's. Now some strange gal was sitting there staring at me like a shrink would do.

She introduced herself, told me she was from headquarters DEA in Washington, D.C., and advised me she wanted to talk to me about Reszler's demise.

"What are your thoughts on this matter?" she asked.

"He was a young man, not even thirty years of age," I replied. "His death could have been avoided. He was screaming for help, I saw it. Nobody did anything to help him. Not the fed, not the police department, not his friends. He was number two in his DEA academy class."

She made some notes and stared at me. "So you blame the Drug Enforcement Administration for this death? She asked.

"Yeah, I do, and I blame these used car selling motherfuckers who run this field office," I replied.

Those words were out of my mouth for approximately thirty seconds when the door burst open and the SAC came rushing in. He gave me a killer look and towered over me as I sat slumped in the chair.

"Watch what you are saying," he growled at me.

I wondered if he was listening at the door, he must have been; eavesdropping was his style of leadership. I looked up at him and stared. He was dressed expensively as he always was and had the look of a true professional.

I wanted to apologize to him for the racial bullshit he had been subjected to but, I wasn't the one who hated him for being a black man in charge of white racist cops in St.

Louis. I was what most professional black people can identify with; a guy who is at the wrong place at the wrong time.

I knew him as a person; he was a board member of N.O.B.L.E. (National order of black law enforcement executives), and he did everything in his power to retain a professional demeanor. He meant well, but he was a damned racist eavesdropper. I doubt he eavesdropped on his black buddies who were special agents.

How would he have felt about me if I was a board member of a white law enforcement group of professionals? He already hated me because I was white and from St. Louis.

He was prejudging me and he grouped me as a racist because I was forced to be one of the boys. I stood and walked out.

All eyes were on me as I walked to my desk. I plopped down and started reading DEA 6's. I listened to the banter as I pretended to read reports.

It seemed that a group of TFD's responded to Reszler's' house after he did the deed to himself. They helped his parents clean up the brain matter from the walls and floors. There is always a ton of blood when someone kills themselves with a gun.

Detective Sultan was talking about how Reszler placed the gun at the top of his head with the barrel pointing downward. That means the brain matter would come out of his ears and mouth. Most suicide victims place the gun barrel in their mouths, or at their temple, or under their chin.

"Hey Sultan," I loudly said. "What gun did he use? The one you guys placed the customized grips on for him?"

"Yep!" he replied.

One or more of them got the brainy idea to confiscate

Ollie's (Johnny's retired cop dad) pistols. Most cops have a collection of handguns. Ollie was in shock and so was Johnny's mother. Johnny was their only son. They were thankful that Johnny's friends came to help them in their time of need. No one even cared about Ollie's guns at the time.

The TFD's waltzed out with Ollie Reszler's prized collection of handguns. One of the TFD's kept them at his house. They victimized Ollie Reszler because he wasn't an important cop. He was a retired patrolman. They disrespected him, and his deceased son.

XX.

NO FAVORS, NO REGRETS

The years clicked by too quickly. I was now a district cop. My only responsibility is to show up for work. I often thought about the excitement of the Task Force. Good leaders motivate and make their subordinates feel like they are actually making a difference in their fields of endeavor.

It was what Palance did. He had convinced us that we were stopping the flow of illicit drugs into the St. Louis region.

"These drugs aren't processed here," he would say about cocaine and heroin. "You guys are putting a hurt on those Colombian drug lords." We believed him. So we worked tirelessly, beat drug dealers up, ignored our personal lives and sacrificed everything for the federal entity.

The dope dealer cash rolled in in the millions. The police department got its share, so did the fed. Most of us got nothing but unhappy spouses.

The region is awash in heroin, cocaine, marijuana, meth, and any new designer drug some weirdo chemist can invent.

My life back in mediocrity wasn't as bad as I suspected it would be. Not being important was a bitter pill for me to swallow. Not being important probably saved my life. I had stopped drinking and I didn't have the stress of cases, prosecutors, informants, and long hours away from home. I was actually a happy little cop.

In a district, the cop supervisors don't care where you've been or where you want to go. They only care about having a body in a police car and someone to answer the cop radio that never stops spitting out radio assignments.

The cop supervisors were young. They had never been involved in sensitive, big-time investigations, nor had they locked up career criminals. I had! It kept me going.

The DEA entitlement cops were destined to be rewarded, and they were. Detective Sultan made rank and had a powerful job within the police department. He took an early retirement and had several politically connected jobs. He is now a security guard. He sits in an office and watches a surveillance screen.

Ronnie Been sits in the same office with Detective Sultan. He also took early retirement to become a security guard.

Larry (Mad dog) Wheeler was promoted a couple of times by the county cops. He took an early retirement and died suddenly.

Rich Latchkey got out and made a bee line to his restaurant in the Soulard area. A grade school friend, Pat Norton, ran the place for him. It was the Irish Pub that I had eaten at and it had good food.

My wife and I frequented the place for its corned beef sandwiches. In the winter it had a large fireplace that warmed the entire restaurant.

Every time we went there I reminisced about the Robinson case. It was a big deal for me. I had worked my way up to the pinnacle of criminals. All of the players in this case were professional crooks. The crocks got them. I was lucky to have been involved with it.

A lawyer or two had gone to the United States Attorney's office in St. Clair County, Illinois and filed a motion that I had stolen items from Dan Robinson when I arrested him that could, and would, prove his innocence.

By then the scene had changed in the United States Attorney's office. I didn't know anyone there. My beer drinking and golfing buddies were long gone. I had never heard of the AUSA who had summoned me. I waltzed into his office and introduced myself. He was surly, and I quickly classified this guy as an enemy. I was now vulnerable to the dark forces of criminals and lawyers. I was on my own.

He was a short little fellow and he mostly stayed seated behind his desk after he stood for us to perform the mandatory handshake. He accused me of withholding physical evidence of Dan Robinson when I arrested him.

I couldn't believe that this jailhouse story had gotten this far. I remained calm and tried not to be surly as this little fellow berated me, stuck his finger in my face and threatened me. I was incensed and angry so I said, "Are you finished with me?"

"Yes," he replied, "but this isn't over. I've got a DEA agent from the St. Louis Field Office coming over here right now with the entire file of the arrest of Dan Robinson. I'm going to review it, and you will be getting a subpoena for a grand jury."

"Okay," I replied, and I walked out.

My wife and I were eating at Rich's restaurant. Rich always came and sat with us. He was intrigued with me since I had gone back to mediocrity and I no longer drank. Mediocrity was everything I'd remembered, but I didn't give up and quit. I took the pounding of everyday police work, just like so many other cops.

I told Rich the story about the United States Attorney's office in Illinois and the accusations from the AUSA. He laughed.

"Hey," he said, "Dan's daughter came in here and begged me to get her daddy out of prison. He has convinced his family that he is innocent. Apparently some lawyers think so, too."

I didn't get subpoenaed before a federal grand jury. Dan didn't get out of prison. Rich Latchkey went into the real estate business. He started out by purchasing several big and old houses across the street from his restaurant. He rehabbed them and turned them into office buildings. The offices rented quickly and gave him a good return on his investment. It was just the beginning.

Rich dove into the TIF method of buying city commercial real estate. He had connections in City Hall (Detective Sultan's cousin was the mayor) and Rich used every connection he could. He used the houses across the street from his restaurant as collateral for loans. Rich is a wealthy man. He owns large commercial real estate in the city. He even purchased Council Plaza on South Grand, a place that I used to go to when I interviewed Teamster gangsters. He is respected in this city. Money talks! It doesn't matter where it comes from or how it is earned.

In one of our impromptu meetings, Rich got real serious. "Hey," he began, "I will pay for you to go to school and get retrained, if you want me to. Just let me know what you want to do in life and I will pay for it."

I took a long and hard appraisal of Rich. I had allowed him to befriend me because I was still emotionally charged by my DEA experience. When I spoke with him, I was kind of back in the VIP mode of my life.

I didn't need to be retrained. I just needed to get along with my life. I figured he knew that fact and I figured he knew my answer before he presented the question. I also knew Rich Latchkey was rotten to the core and would do almost anything for money.

"No, Thanks, Rich," I replied. I stopped going to his restaurant and I never saw him again.

Detective Horowitz returned to the police department and was assigned to head the asset forfeiture section of the police department. The fox was in the henhouse.

He had a new twist in the seizure of drug assets. He would go on State of Missouri search warrants with the Narcotics Division and immediately seize any and all money, jewelry, vehicles or anything with intrinsic value, take it back to his office and document it.

He was observed removing stones from diamond rings by narcotics detectives. When questioned about his behavior he just said, "That's the way we do it here."

Horowitz took an early retirement and took over the City of St. Louis Tow lot.

He had been friendly with a crook who had become Chief of Police. City Narcotics had a couple of detectives who were bosom buddies with the crooked chief. When they seized drug dealer proceeds, instead of cataloguing the seizure, they would take the cash to the chief's office and show him their newly seized cash prize. The crooked chief would take his share then tell the detectives to take a share and to deposit the rest for forfeiture. The narcotics detectives bragged about it. There are no secrets in police headquarters.

One of these crooked narcotics detectives was investigated by the FBI for transporting strippers from the eastside to the west side (City of St. Louis) for prostitution which is a violation of the Mann Act.

This narcotic detective lived high on the hog. He drove a

$120,000 BMW seven series which Detective Horowitz had stolen from a victim who had the bad luck of having his car towed to Horowitz's tow lot. When the owner came to pay the fees and storage for the vehicle, Horowitz refused to release it. He would not return the vehicle to the owner. Horowitz refused to release many of the cars towed to the lot.

This was not a new scheme to victimize people who were already victims of the judicial system. In 1970, Tony Giordano (reputed head of the St. Louis Mafia) and one of his hoodlum friends, Jack Ballard, were awarded the towing contract from the City of St. Louis. A.J. Cervantes was the mayor. He was known to not have anything against organized criminals.

They frequently refused to return towed vehicles to their owners. A Catholic priest (dressed in soft clothing) attempted to get his vehicle out of the lot. He had the proper paperwork and was willing to pay for the tow and storage. Giordano refused his request. The priest argued with him, so Tony Giordano stuck a sawed off twelve gauge shotgun in his face and advised him he would kill him if he didn't leave.

The priest left. But unlike most victims, the priest had political connections. He contacted them. He got his vehicle out of the impound lot. A cop was placed on duty outside of the lot twenty four hours a day.

The impound lot was located at S. Vandeventer and Duncan. I was one of the cops who had the detail, eight hours a day.

I had been raised in the shadow of organized criminals and I felt I knew what they were about, so instead of sitting in a police car in front of the lot, I went inside.

I had conversations with Tony Giordano and Jack Ballard. Tony was a big talker (later I found out he was an

FBI informant).

Tony was friendly. Jack Ballard was not. I weighed their personalities, the organized criminal compared to the dirt bag car thief. Jack Ballard was scarier. Both of them had the ability to slit my throat and stuff me in one of the wrecked cars in the impound lot.

Like Giordano and Ballard, both deceased for decades by now, Horowitz would keep the cars for the legal period of time, apply for a new title and then either sell them or allow his friends to drive them.

The narcotics cop was a thief and a pimp, and he was a police detective. The strange thing about this scenario was that he didn't feel he was doing anything wrong.

Horowitz didn't feel he was doing anything wrong, either. He was supplying free cars for ranking cops, their relatives, and his friends. He made so much cash from the sales of the towed/stolen vehicles that rumor has it he buried the cash in the tow lot. It was tongue in cheek within the police department.

As a courtesy the crooked chief was notified of the Mann Act violation of one of his cops. He didn't go to bat for the narcotic's cop who made the chief wealthy; he fired him, or advised him to resign. It was okay to be a crook, on and off duty, but it was a crime to get caught. The cop is now a private investigator.

Detective Horowitz was eventually indicted, arrested and convicted of theft concerning the sales of towed vehicles and confined in a federal penitentiary. He walked out of a federal prison with a smile on his face. He owns a horse ranch in a rural part of Missouri. He raises horses and owns an equine transport company. He is a wealthy man.

The crooked chief resigned under a cloud of suspicion, but no one ever offered to testify against him for leniency.

He was now called the Teflon Chief.

He purchased a home in one of the wealthiest cities in America, so paranoid that the house is not in his name but in the maiden name of his third wife. The crooked chief is a wealthy man.

Little Stevie Wonder (Special Agent Steve Stoddard) was mysteriously transferred to San Francisco, California. He didn't want the transfer. His power base was here in St. Louis. He was all about St. Louis, from the Cardinals to the Blues. He was wealthy in St. Louis. In California he was just another government worker.

Steve's wife became terminally ill and he was not there for her, he was chasing weirdo dopers in San Francisco. He took family leave and returned to St. Louis to care for his wife. She died.

Little Stevie died a horrible death of alcoholism, alone in a large home on a golf course. He didn't get much of his lucrative government pension.

Group Supervisor, Steve Palance, didn't do well in Headquarters DEA in Washington, D.C. He got into an argument with a high ranking civilian DEA employee and was asked to resign. He did and went to work for the State Department as a security consultant.

Palance's claim to fame was that he got his evens on Little Stevie Wonder for writing the letter to his wife notifying her of Palance' extramarital affair.

Mike Braun became the Chief of Operations, Assistant Administrator for the Drug Enforcement Administration. He retired and started SGI Global LLC, a security firm with government contracts.

I had tried to purchase his big and impressive Sig Sauer semi-automatic DEA terrorizing pistol when he transferred out to Washington D.C. I was still on the Task Force and thought maybe the department had forgotten about me. We agreed on a price, but I didn't have any cash. I told him I would send him two or three payments until the gun was paid off. He declined.

AUSA Cliff Proud became a Federal Magistrate in the Southern District of Illinois. He is now retired.

Famous lawyer and St. Louis socialite, Norm London, retired from practicing law and took over the Federal Public Defender's Office for the Eastern District of Missouri. He is now deceased.

Famous lawyer to the black drug dealers, Frank (Tony) Fabbri continued to practice law, but there was a problem in his hustle. As in all hustles the hustler must make money fast and try to hang on to it. The defense attorney never knows where his next case, or hustle is going to walk through his door.

Tony had a case with a black defendant who Tony pled out for leniency in the hanging judge's court, Judge Stiehl. Part of the agreement was that the defendant forfeit a certain amount of cash to the federal government. Tony was to retrieve these funds from the defendant's relatives and convey them to the court.

Upon the delivery of said funds there was a discrepancy in the amount delivered and the amount agreed upon by the prosecution and Judge Stiehl (the stack was short). Everybody had their hand in the dope man's pocket.

Tony was charged federally for theft and some other federal charges and pled guilty, begging for leniency. He didn't get any from Judge Stiehl, but it was rumored that Judge Stiehl actually shed a tear at the sentencing of Frank (Tony) Fabbri.

Judge Stiehl, the United States Attorney, the AUSA's, they all liked Tony Fabbri. He was their adversary, much like an opponent in an athletic event. There was mutual admiration and respect. Justice hardly ever prevails, but it did this time.

Frank Tony Fabbri was sentenced to eighteen months in a federal penitentiary and a $76,000 fine and he did hard time. He lost his license to practice law, and he has never regained it.

His beloved 38 snub Chevrolet, the one he purchased for pennies on the dollar on the courthouse steps, which was once the property of heroin and cocaine dealer Little John Gipson, was sold so Tony could get cash to pay the IRS for the money he stole.

I still see the 38 snub in the Central West End of the city. It still looks good, but every time I see it I tend to think of it as a bad luck car.

Rich Latchkey continued on with his real estate business. He is connected with City Hall in St. Louis and the State of Missouri Capitol. He also owns a restaurant in west St. Louis County which is operated by a childhood friend.

Paul Robinson did twenty five years on a thirty year sentence. He lives near me in South St. Louis County. I have seen him in the local grocery. My son has seen him at the dog park while both were walking their dogs.

Dan Robinson did his full twenty year sentence. He also lived near me. At a book signing for my first book he waited in line to purchase a book from me.

Dan Robinson enjoyed his freedom for approximately seven years. He died at the age of seventy three. Prison life took its toll on him. But I didn't make the case on Dan Robinson. I was just the one who was the last cop to arrest him. Rich Latchkey implicated and testified against him.

If there is such a thing as having a distinction in death, Dan's was that he lived for seventy three years and was never gainfully employed.

I don't like being in close proximity to the Robinson

brothers, now just Paul Robinson. It's the curse of the local investigator. The feds are mostly transit. They move on, prosecutors and agents relocate to better climes. The local cop has roots, although most of us would move to Florida or California if we could afford it.

I've come face to face with Paul Robinson once since his release from the federal penal system. I know where he lives. I presume he knows where I live. My wife and children and my grand-children know what he looks like. I hope I don't have to contend with him again.

I was paid to spy on the Robinson clan and other creeps like them, and later paid to arrest them. They chose their lifestyle, I chose mine. They were career criminals. As a detective in Intelligence and DEA they were my quarry.

Judge William Stiehl (hanging judge) died....he was in his nineties.

Several years ago one of the TFD's who confiscated Ollie Reszler's collection of handguns called me and asked me to return them for him. He was apparently too embarrassed to give them back to Ollie. I met him and took possession of them.

I called Ollie (who I had never met) and advised him that I was returning his guns for another cop who had taken them from him at the time of his son's death.

He told me that he had to call the cop in question and demand his guns be returned. "I don't know why they ever took them," Ollie said to me. He asked me to place them in his garage. I did it for him, and the TFD who had taken them.

The Department of Justice recently decided that they were no longer going to share drug assets with local police departments; a financial blow for many cops and

administrators.
"INDEX"